SHUCK, HYPE OR WHATEVER YOU CALL IT,

these young writers identify it in today's society, pinpoint its evils and turn their dynamite intelligences toward its eradication. Here, for the first time, is an anthology with bite that attacks the masked and veiled outrages of a hypocritical America; here is muckraking for the 1970's.

MORE DISTINGUISHED NON-FICTION
FROM BALLANTINE BOOKS

SEEING THROUGH SHUCK

Richard Kostelanetz, *Editor*

BALLANTINE BOOKS • NEW YORK
An Intext Publisher

For Susanna Opper, R. Wasserstein
and John Brockman, terminal friends

Statements of the authors are those of the authors; not the editor or the publisher.

1. (Debunking Now-(end)). From *The Humanist* (July-August, 1972). Copyright © 1972 by *The Humanist*. By permission of the author and publisher.

2. ("Investigating Police Corruption"). Revised, from public testimony before the Knapp Commission, November, 1971. Copyright © 1971 by David Durk. By permission of the Sterling Lord Agency, Inc.

3. ("Media Freaking"). From *The Drama Review* Volume 13, Number 4 (T44), Summer, 1969. Copyright © 1969 by *The Drama Review*. By permission of the Harold Matson Company, Inc. and *The Drama Review*.

4. ("Perils of Newspaper Literacy"). From *The Humanist* (July-August, 1971). Copyright © 1971 by Richard Kostelanetz. By permission of the author and publisher.

5. ("The Poverty of Culture"). From "The Dispossession of American Museums," retitled and revised, from *Ramparts* (June, 1971). Copyright © 1971 by *Ramparts*. Copyright © 1972 by Barry Schwartz. By permission of the author and publisher.

6. ("On Cowardice"). From *Commentary* (June, 1967). Copyright © 1967 by Paul Theroux. By permission of the author and Blanche C. Gregory, Inc.

7. ("Racist Love"). Copyright © 1971, 1972 by Jeffery Paul Chan and Frank Chin. Reprinted by permission.

8. ("Catechism of d neoamerican etc."). Copyright © 1968, 1969, 1970 by Ishmael Reed. By permission of the author.

9. ("Doctor Feelgood"). From *New York Magazine* (February 8, 1971). Copyright © 1971 by the NYM Corporation. By permission of the author and *New York Magazine*.

10. ("On Training Therapists"). From THE RADICAL THERAPIST. Copyright © 1971 by Jerome Agel. By permission of Dr. Michael L. Glenn.

11. ("Radicalism in etc."). From TOWARDS A RADICAL MIDDLE, by Renata Adler. Copyright © 1967 by Renata Adler. By permission of Random House, Inc. and the author.

12. ("Das Hip Kapital"). First published in *Esquire* (December, 1970). Copyright © 1970 by Craig Karpel. By permission of the William Morris Agency, Inc.

13. ("Three Wise Men of Gotham"). Originally published as "Technological Liberalism." Revised, from *The Canadian Forum* (March, 1971). Copyright © 1971 by William Irwin Thompson. By permission of the author.

14. ("Why Users are Losers"). Originally published as "And Now a Word from the Users." Revised, from *Design & Environment* (Spring, 1971). Copyright © 1972 by Design & Environment, © 1972 by Stephen Kurtz. By permission of the author and *Design & Environment*.

15. ("Food Pollution"). From *Ramparts* (June 1971). Copyright © 1971 by Noah's Ark, Inc. By permission of *Ramparts*.

16. ("Bank of Amerika"). From *Scanlan's Monthly* (August 1970). Copyright © 1970 by *Scanlan's Monthly*. By permission of the author and publisher.

17. ("Bill Buckley etc."). From *New York Magazine* (June 14, 1971). Copyright © 1971 by the NYM Corporation. By permission of *New York Magazine*.

18. ("Kinder, Küche etc."). From THE NEW WOMEN, edited by Joanne Cooke, Charlotte Bunch-Weeks and Robin Morgan. Copyright © 1970 by The Bobbs-Merrill Company, Inc. By permission of the publisher.

19. ("Troy Donahue etc."). From *The Village Voice* (July 29, 1971). Copyright © 1971 by The Village Voice, Inc. By permission of *The Village Voice*.

20. ("The Nirvana Conference"). From *New York Magazine* (April 27, 1970). Copyright © 1970 by the NYM Corporation. By permission of *New York Magazine*.

21. ("Up Against the Wall etc."). From *Liberation News Service*. Copyright © 1970 by Claudia Dreifus. By permission of the author.

22. ("Gay News and the Times"). From *The Village Voice* (April 1, 1971). Copyright © 1971 by The Village Voice, Inc. By permission of *The Village Voice* and the author.

23. ("Mush"). From *Esquire* (June, 1971). Copyright © 1971 by Nora Ephron. By permission of Nora Ephron c/o International Famous Agency.

24. ("Beyond Words"). From *Commentary*. Copyright © 1971 by the American Jewish Committee. By permission of *Commentary* and Curtis Brown, Ltd.

25. (Cape Breton). From CAPE BRETON IS THE THOUGHT CONTROL CENTER OF CANADA. Copyright © 1969 by Ray Smith. By permission of House of Anansi.

Grateful acknowledgment is made to the contributors of selections in this book for use of copyrighted material.

SBN 345-02676-4-165

First Printing: September, 1972

Printed in the United States of America

Cover art by Elias Dominguez

BALLANTINE BOOKS, INC.
101 Fifth Avenue, New York, N.Y. 10003

Contents

Preface

> If we're going to appeal to the young,
> and to the people who are going to take
> over the reins of society, I think we have
> to avoid the bullshit factor, that is, the
> stodgy, creepy, deadly political maneuvers
> of the past.
>
> —*Ed Sanders, in a symposium, 1968*

In recent years one has become more acutely aware of disparities between fantasy and reality—between ideals and practice, between what is told and what is done, between illusory claims and the nitty-gritty—especially in understanding the institutions and pieties of American society; so that a concern with seeing through shuck, as we say, has become an increasingly passionate preoccupation of the uncorrupted young. It follows that perhaps the most pronounced current tendency in the journalism of young writers has been precisely this kind of debunking, deftly demolishing not only hypocrisies exposed by previous writers but, more typically, those falsehoods and deceptions that are either historically new or have not been so scathingly examined before.

It seems that now is both the most terribly corrupt and the most terribly moralistic of times; evils without precedent in the history of mankind are accompanied by increasingly rigorous and widespread criticism. It is true that the forces of light have always been, and continue to be, engaged in moral combat with the powers of darkness; for muckraking, to use an old-term, has had a long and distinguished tradition. Some of the following essays suggest that scrutinizing light has never penetrated so deeply before, especially into the encroaching darkness of what had once been regarded as bathed in sunshine. Most of these essays rake industries, individuals, and situations (if not "achievements")

vii

that previously went unexamined, they usually discover un-obvious sins; and perhaps the book itself contributes to one of the most remarkable developments in America today: that increasingly collective effort to make a less hypocritical society.

Seeing Through Shuck collects examples of this new high-style debunking, nearly all of it by writers still under thirty-five, many of them examining an older generation's sediments; for the young in any society are invariably less tolerant of bullshit, whether it be intellectual or political. (And old folks attacking idealistic youth usually have a privilege or hypocrisy to defend.) Perhaps this volume, in addition to epitomizing the anti-shuck art, also represents a writing generation that believes, more conclusively than its immediate predecessors, that criticism can genuinely change the world; for though nothing here deals with institutionalized religion, most of these essays exemplify the religious instinct of decrying sin.

This writing is more direct, tough-minded, and avowedly challenging than the "participatory journalism," with its novelistic techniques and subjective intrusions, which has been more typical of an older generation's writers—Gay Talese, Joan Didion, Tom Wolfe, and Dan Wakefield (all born between 1931 and 1934)—and which, as a style, may be intrinsically exhausted by now. Nonetheless, not only does this new muckraking acknowledge the previously predominant mode in both its formal liberties and its unapologetic use of the writer's personal experience, but all of those older star reporters have also published high-style muckraking, usually employing a narrative style more sober, objective, and factual than that informing their more subjective journalism. Since debunking is not identical with partisan polemic, this book eschews "radical" publicists for parties and positions that the rigorously scrutinizing mentality would regard more skeptically. Finally, it should be noted that at the publisher's request, my own critiques of literary politics and intellectual communication have been saved for two of my own forthcoming books.

Richard Kostelanetz
New York, May 14, 1972

Radicalism in Debacle:
The Palmer House

Renata Adler

The National New Politics Convention, which was held at the Palmer House in Chicago over the Labor Day weekend [1967], began as a call from the National Conference for New Politics—an organization that has given financial support to radical candidates in various elections since early in 1966—for delegates from all radical and liberal groups opposed to the American involvement in Vietnam to unite on a course of political action for 1968. The convention presented, from the first, a travesty of radical politics at work. In the quality of its radical dissent, the no longer New Left—which had seemed in its youth somewhere midway between the plain frivolity of a college prank and the struggle of a generation out of apathy into social consciousness—now seemed a vulgar joke, contributing as much to serious national concern with the problems of war, racism, and poverty as a mean drunk to the workings of a fire brigade. Throughout the convention, delegates seemed constantly to emerge, wet-lipped and trembling, from some crowded elevator, some torrent of abuse, some marathon misrepresentation of fact, some pointless totalitarian maneuver, or some terminal sophistry to pronounce themselves "radicalized." Being "radicalized" had, among alumni of earlier New Left conventions, two possible meanings: voting against one's principles with an expression of Machiavellian deviousness, or disussing one's politics as a most interesting turn in one's personal psychology. Among novices, being "radicalized" meant having been persuaded of something by radicals.

One of the reasons for the complete disintegration of the New Politics was the convention's persistent debasement of language. The word "revolution," for example, was used for every nuance of dissent. There were the electoral revolutionaries, who meant to change American foreign policy simply by voting the present administration out. And there were the moral revolutionaries, like Dr. Martin Luther King, who sought to bring about certain kinds of social change by the pressure of nonviolent civil disobedience. Closer to violence were the therapeutic-activity revolutionaries, former members of SDS (Students for a Democratic Society), FSM (the Free Speech Movement), and Vietnam Summer, who seemed to find in ceaseless local organizing—around any issue or tactic demonstrably certain of failure—a kind of personal release, which effective social action might deny them; and the aesthetic-analogy revolutionaries, who discussed riots as though they were folk songs or pieces of local theater, subject to appraisal in literary terms ("authentic," "beautiful"). There were the historical, after-them-us syllogist revolutionaries, who applauded all riots as prerevolutionary, an incitement to right-wing repression, which would, in turn, inevitably—presumably as it did in prewar Germany—bring on popular revolution and lasting peace; and the amphetamine revolutionaries, who seem to regard uncontrollable, permanent upheaval, on the model of the Red Guard, as both a prescription for restoring personal vitality and the most vigorous expression of participatory democracy at work. Finally, there were some local criminals, who, despite the determination of the "radicalized" to view them as revolutionaries, pursued their isolated acts of mugging in the elevators and vandalism in the halls, and who, as a closing touch, stole three hundred dollars from the only people present who had defied a genuinely oppressive power structure at great risk and in the name of genuine new politics—the delegation of the Mississippi Freedom Democratic Party.

It was obvious that the only way all these "revolutionaries" could find common ground—the only way Steve Newman, of the (Maoist) Progressive Labor Party, could agree in any detail with, say, Dr. Benjamin Spock, of the baby book— was by jettisoning meaning from vocabulary. Within a short time, such a phrase as "bringing down the system" was used equally for the program of a citizen who sought to speed along by legal means the natural evolution of his country— which, he would readily concede, was already the noblest social experiment, on the largest scale, in history—and for the program of an arsonist committed to the country's literal destruction. When words are used so cheaply, experience becomes surreal; acts are unhinged from consequences and all sense of personal responsibility is lost. At the Palmer House, the word "genocide" began to be tossed about as though it could apply to acts of simple rudeness, and eventually speaker after speaker—from Arthur Waskow, of Washington's Institute for Policy Studies, in plenary session, to the Reverend William Sloane Coffin, Jr., Chaplain of Yale University, at table—could argue that a list of thirteen proposals submitted, along with an ultimatum, to the convention by what was called the Black Caucus should be endorsed without modification of any kind, regardless of the substance of the individual proposals, in a spirit of interracial unity. That this implied a paternalistic white racism that would startle a South African plantation owner seemed not to enter the minds of these speakers—or of the convention at large, which endorsed the list and delegated to the Black Caucus all authority for amending the proposals in the future.

The list ranged from an accusation that blacks had been systematically excluded from "the decision-making process" of the convention (one of the convention's two chairmen, Julian Bond, the Georgia assemblyman, was a Negro, as were its keynote speaker, Dr. Martin Luther King, nine of the twenty-five members of its Steering Committee, and six of the twenty-four members of its executive board; moreover, no actual "decision-making" had taken place before the adoption of the thirteen Black Caucus proposals), through a condemnation of "the imperialistic Zionist war" (the Black Caucus itself subsequently reversed this condemnation, so the convention found itself in the position of having both endorsed a proposal and preendorsed, carte blanche, so to speak, its reversal), to demands for the formation of "white civilizing committees" to deal with "the beastlike character" of "all white communities . . . as exemplified by George Lincoln Rockwells and Lyndon Baines Johnsons," for "immediate reparation for the historic physical, sexual, mental, and economic exploitation of black people," and for support of all resolutions passed by the Black Power Conference in Newark. No white person could in good faith endorse the substance of all the proposals. Certainly many of the white people at the convention knew the statement about decision-making to be false, and many did not know what the resolutions of the Newark Black Power Conference were, since no official list was ever issued and it is not certain that any was ever drawn up.

From the moment the ultimatum was accepted, the convention became a charade. To disregard substance in favor of a spirit of unity was to justify McCarthy's empty lists of names on account of the spirit of patriotism in which he waved them about. But the real white-racist presumption lay in thinking that a specious endorsement of inane proposals was an act of support for Negroes—or, for that matter, in thinking that most Negroes could endorse the resolutions either. From the beginning of the convention, the "radicalized" whites had resolutely refused to deal with any competent or intelligent Negroes—any rational Negroes, as it turned out—as authentic blacks. Nonfailed nonwhites were simply regarded as sell-outs to the system, and ignored. The effect of this was to produce what can only be described as a new, young, guerrilla-talking Uncle Tom, to transact nitty-gritty politics with his radical white counterpart. The assembled revolutionaries (whose voting strength was determined on the basis of the number of "activists" they cared to claim at home) selected such Negroes, on the model of H. Rap Brown, to speak for the romantic, rioting, "authentic" children of the ghetto (for "the ten thousand activists in Newark," as John F. Maher, Jr., of the Cambridge Vietnam Summer, put it, in a meeting, "who were willing to die to change their way of life"), for the Black Caucus, for all the other Negroes at the convention, and for the nameless, faceless, personalityless black monolith that the American Negro has now—in the white-radical racist imagination— become.

The tragedy is, of course, that no one speaks for the young rioters, since no leader has emerged from them yet; and Rap Brown seems merely to tag along rhetorically after them. The Black Caucus, which never consisted of more than fifty delegates, sometimes spoke for the majority of the Negro delegates to the convention and sometimes did not. Its composition changed often. It occasionally broke into groups or disbanded, and entry to it was often denied to some Negroes by goons at the door. By choosing to empower the Black Caucus to speak for the entire convention, the convention simultaneously abdicated in its favor and denied it respect. A radicalism whose one worthy aim had been "to give people more of a voice in the decisions that affect their lives" relinquished its own voice at once, and celebrated the birth of the New Politics by voting itself totalitarian.

Two days of preconvention sessions—called, in the prospectus, "the preconvention"—had started off quite differently, as a gentle convocation of kooks. The main factions of plotters and counterplotters, traditional at New Left reunions, had not yet arrived to present their strategies. (The Socialist Workers Party, together with other Trotskyists, favored the establishment of a third party; in default of a permanent party, they were willing to settle for a temporary national ticket, with their own candidates for President and Vice-President. The "nonelectoral local organizers"—like the SDS and Vietnam Summer people who believe in organizing rent strikes, cooperatives, and demonstrations, rather than in the vote—came mainly for the purpose of blocking any national ticket and getting some money. The W. E. B. DuBois Clubs and the Communist Party would have liked a national ticket, but in order to preserve unity and avoid alienating the nonelectoral bloc they were willing to settle for local organizing and the option for a national ticket later on. Their position corresponded closely with the one taken by Mrs. Donna Allen, of the Women Strike for Peace. The California delegation—which was also known as the New

Politics group, because its position corresponded most closely with the original position of the National Conference—favored leaving each state free to have a national ticket if it wanted one, and possibly maintaining the conference as a nationwide hookup for the various national tickets of the states. The likely candidates for President and Vice-President in California were, respectively, Simon Casady—cochairman of the convention, and a former head of the California Democratic Council, deposed for his opposition to the war in Vietnam—and Robert Scheer, managing editor of *Ramparts* and a former candidate for Representative from California. In default of local options for local chosen candidates, the California group was willing to settle for a national ticket chosen by the convention. Democratic Councilman Theodore Weiss, of Manhattan, together with other Democrats, favored working through the regular parties for candidates opposed to the war in Vietnam. In default of that, they were willing to settle for a national King-Spock ticket. A Chicagoan named Arthur Rubin was running for President himself; his platform consisted of an explanation of "the generally misunderstood film *Blow-Up*" and a map of the universe "available in a variety of versions." A group called the Student Mobilization Committee came to recruit demonstrators to immobilize the Pentagon on October 21. And some young people came only to look for jobs with established radical organizations.)

Within hours after registration, on the Tuesday evening before Labor Day, other delegates, less firmly committed politically, were roaming the corridors of the Palmer House —a huge, ornate, labyrinthine hotel, with a basement arcade, a subbasement arcade, gusty, arctic air conditioning, and small, transient-looking rooms. The obvious intention of these delegates in coming early was to have truly sweeping reforms to offer for consideration when the convention began. Nonpolitical guests at the hotel that Tuesday seemed to view the delegates with tolerant smiles, pointing them out in the lobby as "the student convention." (On Wednesday the hotel closed the swimming pool "for repairs." By Thursday, the convention was being described bitterly as "those draft-card burners." Saturday morning, the lady clerks at the newsstand were worriedly insisting that the *New York Times* had not yet arrived: "I told you we shouldn't have opened early, Bea. Here's one of them just won't go away." But by Sunday—the day before the convention ended—things were fairly normal: players in a local bridge tournament regained their concentration, and Sandra Max and David Wasserman, two apparently apolitical Chicagoans, were married without incident in the Red Lacquer Ballroom, where a White Radical Caucus had met the night before.)

Wednesday morning, after a welcoming speech by Co-chairman Simon Casady, a kindly, bewildered-looking gray-haired man, the preconvention delegates split into committees: one for Resolutions, one for Perspectives, and one for Structures. The Black Caucus, which has been a tradition of radical conventions since the early days of SNCC (the Student Nonviolent Coordinating Committee), was already in separate session. SNCC itself (sometimes referred to as the Non-Student Violent Disintegrating Committee) is now—except as a source of publicity measured in column inches detrimental to the cause of civil rights—to all intents and purposes, defunct. Somehow, it never quite recovered from the federal government's passage of the Civil Rights Act of 1964 and the white radicals' defection to the more fashionable causes of campus free speech and Vietnam protest. The Black Caucus, however, remains, as though to preserve in memory the idealistic, soul-searching band that SNCC once was.

The Structures Committee met on the third floor, in Private Dining Room 8—a tiny, dimly lit imitation-Romanesque chapel, featuring cloudy chandeliers, a false hearth, false timbers decorating the ceiling, old branching wall lamps, folding chairs, and a medieval bestiary, with false heraldic devices, painted on its walls. The committee spent the two days before the convention discussing whether it ought to present to the conference a proposal that the New Politics disband altogether and leave its delegates to their local organizing. (Many delegates, it turned out, had come to the convention committed to its dissolution.) The Perspectives Committee, which met in the Red Lacquer Ballroom, on the fourth floor, spent the preconvention days deciding whether to propose to the convention that it endorse a permanent third party, that it choose a third-party ticket only for 1968, that it endorse no ticket or party or nationwide hookup of tickets, that it disband for nonelectoral local organizing, or that it endorse a platform set up by a Subcommittee on Perspectives, which concerned Mexican-American relations, the Dominican intervention, the Greek regime, stripmining in Appalachia, the inequities of the income tax, and a number of other issues over which there was considerable indignation.

The Committee on Resolutions, which met in the Wabash Parlor, on the third floor, was by far the most thorough and animated. Under the dual chairmanship of Steven Jonas, a bearded young man from New York's Medical Committee To End the War in Vietnam, and Bertram Garskof, a bearded psychology professor from Michigan State University (and a member of the convention's Steering Committee), the Committee on Resolutions immediately split into four subcommittees to revise the American political and social system from top to bottom. The four subcommittees all met in the same room, but each sent a courier to each of the others every fifteen minutes, to make sure there was no duplication of effort. By Wednesday noon, Resolutions had abolished the capitalist system. By evening, it had revised policy in detail, solved the problems of the cities, deplored alimony, and endorsed sexual freedom for citizens under twenty-one. ("We'll pick up votes on that when the youth reaches voting age," someone said approvingly. Jonas, normally the kindest of chairmen, looked reproachful. "I was hoping we were above winning votes," he said. "I hoped we were working on principles.") By Thursday morning, it had legalized marijuana, pronounced heroin medically harmless, established more humane old-age homes, and resolved that "if police agencies would do their jobs, organized crime can be smashed." (Garskof proposed that all white police be removed at once from black communities. "But there are understanding white cops," someone protested. "Then let them work in Scarsdale," Garskof replied.)

By Thursday afternoon, so many resolutions had been passed that the committee established a subcommittee to

improve the literary style of all its previous resolutions.
Then, perhaps dissatisfied because there was so little left to
do, Garskof deplored the lack of black representation on
the Steering Committee. Since he was on the Steering Committee himself and should have known better, it was odd
that he should make such a complaint, but his beard—even
in the context of new radicalism—was an eccentric one,
running straight, dense, and furry back along the underside
of his chin, never touching his jaws at all, and it is not
unlikely that he was just trying to liven things up a little.
Two resolutions were immediately passed: one expressing
grief over the separatism of the Balck Caucus, and the
other deploring the lack of black representation on the Steering Committee. Martin Peretz, an instructor in government
at Harvard and a member of the convention's executive
board, objected. "You are trying to railroad chaos through
this convention," he said, and he deplored the committee's
"militant ignorance." (Later, Peretz said to Todd Gitlin, of
Chicago's JOIN Community Union, that he resented the implication that the Steering Committee had been "co-opted."
"Don't let's get up tight about cooptation," Gitlin replied.)

In any case, more than half the Committee on Resolutions ultimately walked out, to form a Whites in Support
of the Black Caucus Caucus, and what turned out to be
the major preoccupation of the convention—attitudes toward
the Black Caucus—was established. From then on, there
was so much talk of caucuses of one sort or another—the
White Radical Caucus, the White Revolutionary Caucus, the
Radical Alternatives Caucus, the Poor People's Caucus, the
Women Strike for Peace Caucus, the Mobilization Caucus,
the Labor Caucus, the California Caucus, the Anti-King-
Spock Caucus—that delegates seemed to be not so much discussing a New Politics as croaking mating calls to one another from adjoining lily pads. On Thursday evening, the
Black Caucus itself consisted mainly of local Chicago teen-
agers and Black Nationalists, who ordered (and charged to
the convention) a lavish meal, and who advocated withdrawing from the New Politics Convention altogether, to
join a Black People's Convention to be held on the other
side of town. The Reverend Ralph Abernathy, of Dr. King's

Southern Christian Leadership Conference, however, briefly entered the group with what he called "some of our folk," and persuaded the others to remain—for a while, at least —with the still nominally integrated New Politics Convention.

Thursday night, in Chicago's Coliseum, a large, ugly stone fortification on the South Side, the full convention met for the first time. Julian Bond, the convention's cochairman, was introduced by the moderator, Ossie Davis, as "a black terror in tennis shoes." He spoke briefly and then left the Coliseum, and he took no further part in the convention. Dick Gregory delivered one of his less effective monologs, in an apparent attempt to unite the convention by offering an apologia for its more extreme elements ("Every Jew in America over thirty years old knows another Jew that hates niggers. Well, it's even, baby"). He remained with the convention another day and then left to march for open housing in Milwaukee. And Dr. King delivered his keynote speech, a long and, for him, rather flat peroration, in a tired voice. As he spoke, some local Negro teen-agers shouted threats and insults at him from the back of the room. Negro members of the audience tried to quiet them down, but within moments a few self-styled members of SNCC were charging through the crowd whispering, "Make way for Rap Brown." (This never failed to produce an awed "Where? Where?" from whatever white radicals were nearby.)

The Reverend Andrew Young, of the Southern Christian Leadership Conference (a member of the convention's executive board), turned to a white liberal lawyer with whom he had worked on many campaigns in the South. "These cats don't know the country has taken a swing to the right," he said. "I wish the violence and riots had political significance, but they don't."

"They just have political consequences," the lawyer said.

"Yeah. All bad," the Reverend Mr. Young said. He left the convention that evening.

Some teen-agers marked a cardboard box "Contributions for Our Black Brothers in Prison," and laughed loudly whenever whites dropped money in it. Two photographers who attempted to take pictures of these transactions were threatened ("You gonna lose that camera"), and it was only the quiet appearance of Dick Gregory, who caught two boys in a rather firm, friendly grip around the neck from behind, that dispersed the teen-agers. "Why, here's Brother Dick Gregory," they said, and they walked away, laughing and slapping each other's palms.

Dr. King left the convention the following morning.

At the convention's first official plenary session, on Friday morning, at the Palmer House, Gary Weissman, the chairman of the plenary (he had been an officer of the National Student Association but had abandoned it for the SDS), announced to the delegates, whom he addressed as "Brothers and Sisters," that "the purpose of this convention is to enable the delegates to do what they wish to do."

Arthur Waskow, of the Steering Committee, immediately introduced a motion for the democratization of the Steering Committee with "members of all regions and all caucuses, if they feel they are not represented."

Sidney Lens, of the Labor Caucus, said, "Brother Chairman, I would move that the proposal be amended to include on the Steering Committee 50 percent of the black people, to represent the thousands and millions who for four hundred years . . . ."

In one of the long speeches that ensued (there were references to "this convention, with all its beauty and power" and to "this Chicago palace, with the country looking on"), someone referred to Appalachia as being in "the South," and a delegate rose to denounce this symptom of insensitivity to the problems of Appalachia. Someone proposed an amendment to Lens's proposal, and he accepted it. The chairman pronounced this acceptance out of order. Lens disagreed. "Brother Chairman," he said, "I've been thirty years a labor bureaucrat, and if I don't know that I don't know anything."

Many delegates questioned whether the plenary should continue to meet unless the Black Caucus joined it.

Paul Booth, a former national secretary of SDS, rose and threatened, if the discussion went on much longer without a consensus, to move to table whatever motion was on the floor.

A Mrs. Warfield, a Negro woman from Rochester, rose to suggest that she lead a delegation to the Black Caucus, wherever it was currently being held, to express understanding of whatever its demands might currently be.

Someone denounced this proposal as out of order, but the chairman disagreed. "This body is free to be as parliamentary as it likes," he said.

"Perhaps we could use the old Steering Committee as adviser to the new Steering Committee," a delegate proposed, referring to the motion for more Negro representation on the Steering Committee.

"What is the criterion for being black?" someone asked. Since one of the delegates in the Black Caucus was Miss Grace Suzuki, this was not an altogether unreasonable question.

"It won't hurt the convention to send a delegation," Mrs. Warfield said, rather impatiently. "I'll be standing here, if anyone wants to approach me."

"I'll tell you who's black," another speaker began. "If you were with us in Detroit, if you were with us in Newark, and Watts, and Cincinnati . . . ."

Mrs. Warfield began to lead her delegation—ten or eleven whites and four Negroes—out of the room.

The motion was put to a vote. "What will mean an aye vote and what will mean a no vote?" someone shouted. There was no answer.

The motion passed.

Someone proposed that the plenary adjourn until the Black Caucus had given its response to Mrs. Warfield, but the Chair ruled him out of order and shut off his microphone.

A delegate from Indiana rose to deplore the enlargement of the Steering Committee.

"You are debating a motion that has already passed— is that correct?" the chairman asked.

"That is correct," the delegate replied.

Mrs. Warfield's delegation never found the Black Caucus —or, rather, Mrs. Warfield left her delegation behind while she sought out all rooms that happened to have Negroes in them. "Don't discuss among yourselves," she said as she left. "There will only be so much confusion." The members of the delegation stayed on a staircase, adjuring one another not to talk, for fear of government agencies and the press. Mrs. Warfield returned to them briefly, to announce that she would continue her search. "Go back to the convention floor," she said. "Remember who you are—the committee to bring a black structure into this convention." Barry Jones, a Negro who had actually participated in the Black Caucus, kept repeating that the caucus had disbanded earlier in the day. The whites ignored him. "Darling, not in the presence of the press," a white woman said. Mr. Jones gave up.

Friday afternoon, in what had been described in the convention program as "a panel discussion of perspectives," a number of people delivered speeches. In the middle of a discourse by Manhattan Councilman Weiss, who argued, not altogether tastefully, that the regular Democratic Party might still give dissidents "a couple of shots at Lyndon Johnson —speaking figuratively, of course," Floyd McKissick, of CORE, preceded by five Negroes in a flying wedge, walked down an empty aisle to the platform. By the time Weiss had finished speaking, all the chairs on the platform were occupied, and he unceremoniously climbed off. McKissick, standing between two impassive, bearded, gum-chewing Negroes in fezzes and khaki jackets (one of whom performed a sort of ballet with his hands while McKissick was speaking), began his speech.

In the two years since the Mississippi March and the advent of the Black Power slogan, McKissick has tried to remain in touch with radicals and liberals alike, keeping his public utterances wild and his private influence moderate. It is a strange course to take, and the effort has told on him. His rhetoric veers back and forth from center to extreme. His head bobs and his voice climbs octaves. He blinks continuously. In describing the destruction wrought by Molotov cocktails, his words to the white man were, "Hell, man. You made this problem. You clean it up." He spoke of "the twin brothers, capitalism and racism," and he referred to all Negroes who had risen to positions of national influence not as "blacks" but, contemptuously, as "Negroes." Then he remarked that no good could come to the black people from the New Politics Convention (he subsequently withdrew CORE from the conference entirely), and invited all whites to attend the Black People's Convention that night instead. (Later, apparently under pressure from members of the Black Caucus, he revoked the invitation.) Preceded by the flying wedge, he left.

Robert Scheer then made a speech urging that the convention address itself to "the vicious nightmare" (boredom, wife hatred, alienation) of life in white America. Like many radicals, he managed to refer to the unarguable proposition that material affluence has not brought complete happiness, and to make the reference itself sound like an alternative offer. He seemed to imply that a revolution of the prosperous was imminent. Regarded by many as the Bobby Kennedy of the New Left (since the New Left thinks it bitterly opposes the real Bobby Kennedy), he was given a standing ovation. Another white radical, Robert Cook, formerly of the Yale SDS, now of the New Haven AIM (American Independent Movement), argued that whites should support Negro riots by diverting police to other areas during the looting and sniping in the ghetto. He was applauded also.

That night, the White Revolutionary Caucus (which consisted mainly of pale, thin, bespectacled women and pale, torpid men, making plans for guerrilla warfare) barred Negroes from its meeting; the White Radical Caucus (which consisted mainly of members of SDS, Vietnam Summer, and other local-project organizations) plotted to sway the convention from a national ticket, in order to use the Conference mainly as a servicing facility for the local organizers; and the Black Caucus—despite a last-minute plea from McKissick, who made a brief appearance there—voted to submit its thirteen proposals, along with an ultimatum stating that if they were not passed by noon of the following day the Black Caucus would leave the convention. All through the night, in an orgy of confession about their childhood feelings toward Negroes, the whites on the Steering Committee considered the ultimatum. Ivanhoe Donaldson, a Negro member of SNCC, argued that since the blacks at the convention were the only radicals really "in motion," no real white radicals should balk at the letter of their demands.

There was a great deal of soul-searching by whites. ("I have thirty years of working for civil rights," a white liberal said. "At least, nobody can take that away from me." Where-upon, with some dime-store analysis of his motives, they took it away from him.) Martin Peretz walked out. The Steering Committee voted to submit the ultimatum to a "special plenary," to be called the following morning, and by dawn most of its members were ready to pronounce themselves "radicalized."

Casady announced to a crowded Grand Ballroom on Satur-day morning that a session's declaring itself a plenary did not make it so and that he could not participate in an extralegal plenary. Then he too walked out. (His walkout, with Peretz's of the preceding night, initiated a kind of daily ritual; the few responsible whites at the convention often found themselves walking out, only to walk right back in, and out again.) The front center section of the plenary was roped off and reserved for members of the Black Cau-cus, creating the impression that if only someone had thought to rope off the back of the buses in Birmingham and shout "Black Power!" the civil-rights movement would never have been necessary. Gary Weissman, who again presided, let the gathering "formally, duly convene itself as a plenary," and thereafter granted what he called "the indulgence of the Chair" to all deviations from parliamentary procedure that were favorable to the ultimatum. A woman who pointed out that one of the resolutions endorsed "wars of liberation," though many at the convention were pacifists, was ruled out of order. Several members of the Steering Committee, in the first of what became a series of conspiratorial jags, spoke in favor of accepting the ultimatum. The white radicals ar-gued that the thirteen proposals should be accepted, re-gardless of their content, which was pronounced "irrelevant." (White radicals were constantly consigning matters, and peo-ple, of substance to some limbo of irrelevance.) Sidney Lens, representing the Labor Caucus, favored "not propos-ing to split words or commas or periods." Everyone seemed determined to foster a black illusion that the only whites interested in political cooperation were those who would ac-cept terms of complete capitulation. Robert Scheer, who got up to make a motion to go the "Zionist imperialism" resolution one better, was inadvertently shouted down. In a heated interchange with the chairman, Charles Samson, who at that point was spokesman for the Black Caucus, denied Scheer's right to speak at all. "All of a sudden this person pops up," Samson said, pointing at Scheer in absolute outrage, "and he wants to make an amendment." Several Negroes who wished to speak against the adoption of the proposals were hustled from the room by enforcers from the Black Caucus, and threatened and silenced outside. One of the enforcers who ushered several Negroes out was an African Nationalist from California who was rumored to be the United Nations Ambassador from Tanzania. The ultimatum was accepted, three to one, and the plenary closed after the chairman proposed, and declared adopted by acclamation, a resolution to send a congratulatory telegram to Ho Chi Minh on the occasion of the twenty-second anniversary of Vietnamese independence.

That afternoon, the White Radical Caucus was troubled. It's coup against a third ticket and in favor of local organizing had never got off the ground, and, as one member after another pointed out, the Israel resolution would scare off liberal money, and the bad press that the morning's developments would receive might scare off everyone else. No one mentioned the possibility that the resolutions might be substantively wrong—only the possibility that they might alienate support. Several members of the caucus proposed that the white local organizers withdraw from the convention and form an organization of their own. Todd Gitlin pointed out that "the convention might still rise from its ash," that, in any case, most members of the White Radical Caucus had voted for the resolutions, and that it might be worthwhile staying around to "neutralize" the convention. Eric Mann, a white organizer from Newark, and one of the few radicals present who never cast a disingenuous vote, suggested that the organizers remain at the convention to paralyze it by keeping the others from endorsing a national ticket and "from doing all the screwy things they want to do."

Saturday evening, the plenary voted down the proposal

to form a permanent third party. Again, a delegate proposed that the plenary adjourn until the Black Caucus, which had again withdrawn into itself, was present, but his proposal was not accepted. The Black Caucus itself was in a state of shock. The advocates of withdrawal from the convention, who had rammed the thirteen proposals through the caucus in the first place, had been certain that the plenary would turn the proposals down, leaving the blacks with an excuse to move to the Black People's Convention on the other side of town. Now they walked out anyway, leaving the Black Caucus to the moderates. Claude Lightfoot, of the Communist Party (rated as moderate by the radical left), and several members of the Du Bois Clubs, also Communist, soon took over, to give the Black Caucus some direction.

The White Radical Caucus, meanwhile, was in session on another floor, still plotting whether to sway the convention from the idea of putting up even a temporary third ticket or to leave the convention. Theodore Steege, a white member of the Ann Arbor SDS, announced that the Black Caucus had come to a new conclusion: Since the white delegates had been willing to accept the Black Caucus ultimatum, the Black Caucus knew that it was not dealing with real radicals; it would therefore either withdraw from the convention or consider supporting a third-ticket proposal and withdrawing support from the local organizers. The only Negro present—who later turned out not to have been a participant in the convention at all—shouted from the back of the room that this information was false. His word was accepted. A delegate from the Third-Ticket Caucus appeared before the White Radical Caucus to offer what came to be known as the California Compromise. The California people, mainly the staff of *Ramparts,* wanted to be free to put up a ticket of their own, and the proposed compromise was for all states to be free to put up local and national third tickets if they liked, but for the convention to go on record as mainly supporting nonelectoral organizing. The White Radical Caucus adopted the California Compromise.

The delegates at Saturday night's plenary, however, did not understand the California Compromise. In fact, most of them had never heard of it. A little old woman got up to say that she never liked to make an important decision without "sleeping and praying," that she disapproved of all the "intrigue," and that she hoped no vote would be taken before morning. She was applauded. A hippie wearing a headband and a card reading "Free"—one of two hippies who showed up at the convention—tried to speak and was denied the microphone. Before the California Compromise could be introduced, a vote was taken and the third ticket was defeated by two votes. A Negro appeared and announced that the Black Caucus was once again being excluded from the decision-making process and that it would announce the method of its participation in the morning. A motion to postpone all decisions until then was defeated. Delegates from the White Radical Caucus and the Third-Ticket Caucus agreed privately to reintroduce the California Compromise the following day.

Sunday afternoon, Rap Brown was scheduled to speak to the plenary, but, at the insistence of James Forman, who was once the executive secretary of SNCC and is now its international-affairs director, he agreed to speak to the Black Caucus instead. Forman, however, addressed the plenary session—originally announced as a Black Liberation Panel —for several hours, in the course of which he "passed" whatever resolutions he chose (although it was not a voting plenary); denied the microphone to anyone else; declared himself "dictator" at one point and then, when Peretz and some other whites at last walked out, dismissed the whole thing, rather unconvincingly, as a joke; and made a proposal that both calumnied the genuine plight of the poor and may puzzle genuine revolutionaries in other countries for years to come. As an act of revolution, he suggested a boycott of 1968 General Motors cars. He was given several standing ovations, and by the end of his harangue most people present agreed with the amphetamine radicals that, although he might not have said anything either true or important, he had "really turned them on." (Bertram Garskof declared himself honored, at this point, to be part of "the white tail on the real movement.")

In the late afternoon, before the evening plenary, the Black Caucus made its new demands known: the plenary was to be regarded as merely another committee of the convention, and the Black Caucus was to be granted 50 percent of the total convention vote. The White Radicals, who had been thinking of nothing but their conspiratorial compromise, were bewildered. Only one of them, in their caucus, spoke against the new demands. "I know it's all irrelevant and meaningless," David Simpson, of the University of Georgia SDS, said. "I'm just not going to vote for it because it's such a sick thing. I just don't want to be part of such a sick thing."

In the California group, Simon Casady said to Warren Hinckle, executive editor of *Ramparts,* "I guess what they're asking is to let them hold our wallet, and we might as well let them."

"Especially since there's nothing in it," Hinckle said.

At the Third-Party Caucus, rhetoric had lapsed into the style of another age. "We have preserved the unity of this convention," a delegate of the Socialist Workers Party was saying, "to present an alternative to the American people." "Hear! Hear!" the delegates replied.

At that evening's plenary, where the Black Caucus demand for half the convention's vote was introduced, Communist Party and Du Bois Club members rose one after another to endorse "our black brothers'" position. What had happened, it turned out, was that while the white radicals were planning their local-organizing coup, and then settling for the California Compromise, the Communist Party and the Du Bois Clubs had temporarily, for whatever it might be worth to them, taken over the Black Caucus, and, through it, the entire convention—an achievement roughly comparable to embezzling a sieveful of smog. By inducing the Black Caucus to make the demand at all, the Communists had turned blacks against whites: if the white radicals voted for it, they lost their power over any further decisions of the New Politics (including the power to paralyze a third ticket); if against, they lost Negro cooperation. "Radicalized," they voted for. ("Masochistic fascists," the Reverend James Bevel, a Negro veteran of innumerable civil-rights campaigns, called them later on.) In the plenary, any Negro who walked up to a microphone to speak—even *for* the new demand—was approached by two tall young members of the Black Caucus and persuaded to sit down again. The demand was accepted, and a pink card representing half the convention's votes was given to Carlos Russell, a poverty worker from Brooklyn, who was now the Black Caucus chairman.

From this moment on, the Black Caucus showed itself to be more intelligent, more sensible, and more independent than any other group at the convention, and than the convention as a whole. To begin with, after a unity speech by Russell, the Black Caucus adjourned the plenary. Then, as white petitioners from the White Radical Caucus, the Third-Ticket Caucus, the newly formed Israel Caucus, and even the preconvention Resolutions Committee and the Progressive Labor Party cooled their heels in an anteroom, and delegates from SANE and Women Strike for Peace (who had either abstained or voted for) wandered about in the ranks of the "radicalized," the Black Caucus—in a surge of good feeling—let any Negro in who cared to come. As a result, the Black Caucus may have had the first genuine discussion of the entire convention. When William Higgs, a white associate of the radical National Lawyers Guild, who was out in the corridor, cast about in his mind for the name of some Negro he might know inside the caucus, and finally succeeded in summoning one—a woman delegate from the Mississippi Freedom Democratic Party—he failed to persuade her that a national third ticket would really help her much in Mississippi. ("I see what you mean, Bill," she said when she came out into the hall, "but I can't help thinking I need all the energy I got for the local issues.") And Steve Newman, of the Progressive Labor Party, who now threw in his lot with the local organizers, and against the conservative, third-ticket-strategy Communists (since Maoists believe in revolution by nonelectoral means), never got a chance to talk to anyone at all. By the time the plenary reconvened, at midnight, the Black Caucus had endorsed a proposal by the Communist Party's Claude Lightfoot: local organizing, with a third-ticket decision to be deferred. But, in another surge of fellow-feeling, the spokesman for the Black Caucus —having heard the White Radical Caucus's point of view through an intermediary, Ivanhoe Donaldson—phrased his proposal as though it were the California Compromise. No one protested. Everyone was baffled. And it passed.

Monday morning, Arthur Waskow, of the Institute for Policy Studies and of the Steering Committee, tried to dissuade a woman from the Women's Rights Caucus from introducing a proposal that women be granted 51 percent of the vote at the plenary. "You're not thinking politically," he said. "It will sound like a joke. A parody. I think you're completely insensitive to the politics of this convention." The White Radical Caucus was in session once again. Eric Mann said he thought that they would have to reckon with the possibility that most of the money except the Communist Party money would now withdraw from the conference but that there was no point in being too fussy about where money for local organizing was coming from. In the two half-black, half-white committees—one for organizing, one for the third ticket—that would be set up in that afternoon's plenary, he went on, Scheer's people could be counted on to see to it that the Communist Party did not run away with the third ticket. And the white half of the local organizers could be turned into a white SNCC.

Then the plotting began again, in the intimate, nearly inaudible voices that are part of the white-radical mystique: "people already in motion," "implement specific programs at the local level," "relate," "in that bag," "where they're at," "doing their thing," "power structure," "coalesce with," "crystal-clear," "relevant," "beautiful." It seemed that some awful rhetorical cycle was coming to a close. A radical movement born out of a corruption of the vocabulary of civil rights—preempting the terms that belonged to a truly oppressed minority and applying them to the situation of some bored children committed to choosing what intellectual morsels they liked from the buffet of life at a middle-class educational institution in California—now luxuriated in the cool political vocabulary, while the urban civil-rights movement, having nearly abandoned its access to the power structure, thrashed about in local paroxysms of self-destruction. Both had become so simplistically opposed to order of any kind that society may become simplistic and repressive in dealing with them. There just may be no romance in moving forward at the pace that keeping two ideas in one's head at the same time implies; at least, there have been no heroes of the radical center yet. But the New Politics, black and white, seems to have turned from a political or moral force into an incendiary spectacle, a sterile, mindless, violence-enamored form of play. In the final plenary, the Black Caucus, in addition to reversing its Israel resolution, managed to pass a few resolutions opposing Vietnam and the draft, and to appoint the two committees to recommend things for the New Politics—if there should be any—to do in the future.

Beyond Words

Johanna Kaplan

What can you say of a man who writes a book celebrating the deafness of his own child? Or of a culture that accepts and applauds such a book on its own terms? The reception accorded Paul West's *Words For a Deaf Daughter* (1970), assumes the kind of inversion of values we slide over from familiarity and from the fear of being thought unsophisticated: deaf is better, though it's obviously worse; we are all handicapped—most especially those, the "so-called competent," who are so graceless that they don't even know it. But the truth is we are *not* all handicapped the way Mr. West's young daughter is, and if we pretend that the distinction is irrelevant, or are seduced into believing that there is a spiritual or aesthetic superiority in imaginatively appropriating some of her misfortune, we romanticize ourselves and callowly underestimate both her integrity as a person and her suffering, which by its nature must exceed our own social malaise or various autobiographical dissatisfactions.

Mr. West's daughter, Mandy, was born deaf, brain-injured, and possibly autistic. None of this was discovered until she was already two years old—itself suspect, simply from what parents are ordinarily accustomed to observing in their children's development. Yet this kind of wishful, hopeful denial or disregard is common and understandable, because beneath it, insistent and awful, is the obligation to come to terms with a piece of life that is truly unassimilable, and

From *Commentary*. Copyright © 1971 by the American Jewish Committee. By permission of *Commentary* and Curtis Brown, Ltd.

still must daily be dealt with: what to do with the pain, and with what is never mentioned, the guilt. What Paul West has chosen to do is to push it off and view it through so many coy, overdressed, and dizzying removes that the reader (and probably the writer) can lose sight of the basic anguish and the basic fact: that this little girl is not a "juggler" or a "mystic," not an "imperious queen" or "Miss Rabelais," not "Canute, Boadicea, Mistress of Mini-Babel," as he variously, distractingly pleases to call her, but Mr. West's seven-year-old daughter who cannot hear, cannot speak, and cannot as yet make the necessary childish sense out of a world that's been known to throw even some of "the inhumanly ordinary." That West so frequently indulges in such aggrandized, poeticized name-calling not only denies the child's reality as a child and a separate person, but gives a very good clue as to what the book is really about.

Athough it purports to be an account addressed to Mandy of her early years, a letter she might read when her "years of infant Sturm and Drang" are behind her (this form itself arch), the child and the book become a playing field for Mr. West's virtuosic, self-indulgent excesses in language and in attitudes. Mandy's handicap, the author tells us, is something he has come to "welcome" as her "special gift." For whom is it a gift? Not Mandy, clearly, for so cut off is she from the ordinary and essential means of human interchange that to try to understand the function of everyday objects, to give them some kind of place in what is for her an especially confusing world, she must "smell at a pencil newly sharpened, inhaling from the beechwood its own sour-soot bouquet, or trace with addicted fingers the corrugations on the flat of a halved cabbage before eating it raw with the same naturalness with which you [Mandy] drink vinegar, steak sauce and mayonnaise, and sniff glue." It's so *interesting* to be handicapped! So interesting, in fact, that "I [West addressing his daughter] tag along on your voyages of exploration," and "steal your condition . . . like the mystic borrowing the lover's terms, the lover borrowing the mystic's." Steal? A Robin Hood of sorts, Mr. West, spiritually slumming, is willing to steal from the poor to give to the guilty rich.

West's notion of the handicapped child as having and becoming a special gift—she confers grace because she is out of the ordinary—not only suggests an eerie detachment but is profoundly misleading and simply untrue to life. It's the kind of book that can make people wish that they, too, had a "special" child: it would lift them out of the humdrum, give them a chance to prove their sensitivity, and open them up to worlds of fascinating, unique experiences and "exquisite perceptions." All very much like having your own little artist-in-residence, or as Mr. West puts it, "a small envoy to conventional minds."

For the world an envoy, for West an occasion to air some self-congratulatory, fashionable musings and newly-arrived-at ideas—new because it is through the Child that he has been led to unexpected self-discovery. Excoriating on the one hand an apparently incompetent dentist, "a Caliban of the needle," who "assumed that because you are deaf, you can be punctured like a Sunday joint, being inarticulate," Mr. West, assuming the same inarticulateness, assigns to his daughter a host of attitudes that no seven-year-old child could reasonably be expected to hold. Describing some of her rituals—rituals involving a consuming need for sameness and order, which are in fact common to, and even symptomatic of, most deeply disoriented children (here described as ventures into elegant and exotic splendors), West concludes: "You'd have understood Samuel Johnson's *having* to touch all the hitching posts as he went down Fleet Street." When Mandy does not react to physical pain, again a sad and baffling effect of her condition—this when she placed her finger in a pencil sharpener and sharpened it until it bled, West explains: "An antagonistic and often histrionic compassion is your life style, as if you think we are all hurt and although you're willing to salute the fact in a civil and sensitive way, loathe all vulnerability." Loathe vulnerability? West positively canonizes it. Mandy, because of her handicap, is related "more closely than most people to

Nature." And Nature, being capitalized, and so freed from science, reason, and other shameful blunders of civilization (when Nature goofs, it's mysterious, beautiful, and interesting, like Mandy) has got it far over people, who, except for the "spiritually awake," turn out to be mostly "good folk." You know them, "good folk": sometimes called bad guys; should you reject the scheme of this book, you might one day look into the mirror and find yourself one of them.

"Somewhere between flower power and *satori,* a place for the mentally hindered." Somewhere over the rainbow. How different is this from the old all-those-nuts-in-their-own-world-and-nothing-bothers-them? An easy and thoughtless dismissal of difficulty other than one's own, it suggests that such a condition, being preferable, should be irremediable, and implies at the same time that the "mentally hindered" are a species so apart that empathy would require mental convolutions that only a near-religious passion could bring about. If this were true, the future for children like Mandy would still be as bleak as it once was.

Somewhere, Mr. West knows this: "Not only do I want you to be the supreme Romantic . . . I want you also to be able to go and buy a pound of butter." The most telling inconsistency in this book is that now and then there is the recognition that everyday skills, however much they may interfere with "unsurpassable dreams" and spiritual awakening, are not so undesirable. " 'Words,' " West admits, quoting Samuel Beckett, " 'have their uses.' " Why, then, *mis*use them, as West does, so that meaning becomes an anachronism and language is only a toy? From the spiraling, purposeless catalogues and gaudy, luxuriant descriptions, it is impossible to know what life with Mandy is really like, or how much she can actually understand.

It seems a strange greed, this coveting of mental dislocation. Once, people recoiled from the handicapped, thinking them inferior and repulsive, but inverting an old prejudice is no less of a prejudice, and, as such, does a service for no one.

Media Freaking*

Abbie Hoffman

This sure is fun. You know, the city news bureau here in Chicago, where you can always call and get their version of what's happening, is ST2-8100. You might want to take care of a cat named Jack Lawrence from CBS who threw me out while I was fuckin' with their teletype machine last night. That was very unfair. I had some good news items. Now, let's see who else is here. The police, there's some good numbers. OK. Now this is a top secret number that like only a few of the top police have. It's the central number for the police station up here in the zoo. They're very fucked up in there. I've been up there, and you think they're organized, well you're full of shit 'cause their walkie-talkies don't work. I mean they're all stoned up there, tripping over each other, you know, they're rapping, all they want to do is fight and they don't care about all the walkie-talkie shit, they just want to fight, you know. That's their thing. All right, that number is 528-5967. Now—here's the way you use it. There's a Commander Brash of the 18th Precinct who's in charge of the general area of Lincoln Park and there's Deputy Chief Lynsky who's the cop above him. Now, the police have a system of anarchy. See, the chief might say somethin' is OK, see, then you get some low-level honky cop saying don't do it, you know. The idea is

*Lincoln Park, Chicago, August 27, 1968, talking to the Yippies. Taped by Charles Harbutt.

From *The Drama Review*, Volume 13, Number 4 (T44), Summer, 1969. Copyright © 1969 by *The Drama Review*. By permission of the Harold Matson Company, Inc. and *The Drama Review*.

to convince that honky cop on the other end that Chief Lynsky said it was OK, even if you gotta bullshit him a little. You just drop names, like Commander Brash said this was OK, you know, and if Chief Lynsky said this was OK, you know, those cops don't want to lose their jobs. They won't check it out. Cops are like Yippies—you can never find the leaders. So if you're good at guerrilla theater, you can look a pig right in the eye and say that to him, you know, and he'll do it. You know, that's the thing, to get him to do it. You just let 'em know that you're stronger psychically than they are. And you *are,* because you came here for nothin' and they're holdin' on to their fuckin' pig jobs 'cause of that little fuckin' paycheck and workin' themselves up, you know. Up to what? To a fuckin' ulcer. Sergeant. We got them by the balls. The whole thing about guerrilla threater is gettin' them to believe it. Right.

A guy just said that if you make a call and just leave your phone off the hook, then that line is tied up. That's groovy. I didn't know about that in Chicago. In New York, that doesn't work. I think we ought to be into jamming up all their lines and everythin' and really fuckin' up their communication thing. 'Cause they broke all our walkie-talk-ies. They made a definite effort to make sure that we can't communicate with each other so like we ought to start com-municatin' with them.

Theater, guerrilla theater, can be used as defense and as an offensive weapon. I mean, I think like people could sur-vive naked, see. I think you could take all your fuckin' clothes off, a cop won't hit ya. You jump in Lake Michigan, he won't go after you, but people are too chickenshit to do that. It can be used as an offensive and defensive weapon, like blood. We had a demonstration in New York. We had seven gallons of blood in little plastic bags. You know, if you convince 'em you're crazy enough, they won't hurt ya. With the blood thing, cop goes to hit you, right, you have a bag of blood in your hand. He lifts his stick up, you take your bag of blood and go whack over your own head. All this blood pours out, see. Fuckin' cop standin'. Now that says a whole lot more than a picket sign that says end the war in wherever the fuck it is you know. I mean in that demonstration, there was a fuckin' war there. People came down and looked and said, "Holy shit I don't know what it is," blood all over the fuckin' place, smokebombs goin' off, flares, you know, tape recorders with the sounds of machine guns, cops on horses tramplin' Christmas shoppers. It was a fuckin' *war*. And they say, "Right, I know what the fuck you're talkin' about. You're talkin' about *war*." What the fuck has a picket line got to do with war? But people that are into a very literal bag, like that heavy word scene, you know, don't understand the use of communication in this country and the use of media. I mean, if they give a ten-page speech against imperialism, everybody listens and understands and says, "Yeah." But you throw fuckin' money out on the Stock Exchange, and people get that right away. And they say, "Right, I understand what that's about." And if they don't know what you're doin', fuck 'em. Who cares? Take this, see, you use blank space as information. You carry a sign that says END THE. You don't need the next word, you just carry a sign that says END, you know. That's enough. I mean the Yippie symbol is Y. So you say, why, man, why, why? Join the Y, bring your sneakers, bring your helmet, right, bring your thing, whatever you got. Y, you say to the Democrats, baby, Y that's not a V it's a Y. You can do a whole lotta shit. Steal it, steal the V, it's a Y. It's up the revolution like that. Keeping your cool and having good wits is your strongest defense.

If you don't want it on TV, write the word "FUCK" on your head, see, and that won't get on TV, right? But that's where theater is at, it's TV. I mean our thing's for TV. We don't want to get on "Meet the Press." What's that shit? We want Ed Sullivan, Johnny Carson show, we want the shit where people are lookin' at it and diggin' it. They're talking about reachin' the troops in Vietnam so they write in *The Guardian*! [An independent radical newsweekly published in New York.] That's groovy. I've met a *lot* of soldiers who read *The Guardian*, you know. But *we've* had articles in *Jaguar* magazine, *Cavalier*, you know, *National Enquirer* interviews the Queen of the Yippies, someone nobody ever heard of, and she runs a whole riff about the Yippies and Vietnam or whatever her thing is and the soldiers get it and dig it and smoke a little grass and say, "Yeah I can see where she's at." That's why the long hair. I mean shit, you know, long hair is just another prop. You go on TV and you can say anything you want but the people are lookin' at you and they're lookin' at the cat next to you like David Susskind or some guy like that and they're sayin', "Hey man there's a choice, I can see it loud and clear." But when they look at a guy from the Mobilization [against the War in Vietnam] and they look at David Susskind, they say, "Well I don't know, they seem to be doing the same thing, can't understand what they're doin'." See, Madison Avenue people think like that. That's why a lot SDSs don't like what we're doin'. 'Cause they say we're like exploiting; we're usin' the tools of Madison Ave. But that's because Madison Ave. is effective in what it does. *They* know what the fuck they're doin'. "Meet the Press," "Face the Nation," "Issues and Answers"—all those bullshit shows, you know, where you get a Democrat and a Republican arguin' right back and forth, this and that, this and that, yeah yeah. But at the end of the show nobody changes their fuckin' mind, you see. But they're tryin' to push Brillo, you see, that's good, you ought to use Brillo, see, and 'bout every ten minutes on will come a three-minute thing of Brillo. Brillo is a revolution, man, Brillo is sex, Brillo is fun, Brillo is bl bl bl bl bl bl bl bl. At the end of the show people ain't fuckin' switchin' from Democrat to Republicans or Commies, you know, the right-wingers or any of that shit. They're buying Brillo! And the reason they have those boring shows is because they don't want to get out any information that'll interfere with Brillo. I mean, can you imagine if they had the Beatles goin' zing zing zing zing zing zing zing, all that jump and shout, you know, and all of a sudden they put on an ad where the guy comes on very straight: "You ought to buy Brillo because it's rationally the correct decision and it's part of the American political process and it's the right way to do things." You know, fuck, they'll buy the Beatles, they won't buy the Brillo.

We taped a thing for the David Susskind Show. As he said the word hippie, a live duck came out with "HIPPIE" painted on it. The duck flew up in the air and shat on the floor and ran all around the room. The only hippie in the room, there he is. And David went crazy. 'Cause David, see, he's *New York Times* head, he's not *Daily News* freak. And he said, "The duck is out," and blew it. We said, "We'll see you David, goodnight." He say, "Oh no no. We'll leave the duck in." And we watched the show later when it came on, and the fuckin' duck was all gone. He done never existed. And I called up Susskind and went, "Quack quack quack, you motherfucker, *that* was the best piece of information: that was a hippie." And everything we did, see, nonverbally, he cut out. Like he said, "How do you eat?" and we fed all the people, you know. But he cut that out. He wants to deal with the words. You know, let's play word games, let's analyze it. Soon as you analyze it, it's dead, it's over. You read a book and say well now I understand it, and go back to sleep.

The media distorts. But it always works to our advantage. They say there's low numbers, right? 4000, 5000 people here. That's groovy. Think of it, 4000 people causin' all this trouble. If you asked me, I'd say there are four Yippies. I'd say we're bringin' another four on Wednesday. That's good, that freaks 'em out. They're lookin' around. Only four. I mean I saw that trip with the right wing and the Communist conspiracy. You know, you'd have 5000 people out there at the HUAC demonstrations eight years ago in San Francisco and they'd say there are five Communists in the crowd, you know. And they did it all. You say, man that's pretty cool. So you just play on their paranoia like that. Yeah, there're four guys out around there doin' a thing. So distortion's gonna backfire on them, 'cause all of a sudden Wednesday by magic there are gonna be 200,000 fuckin' people marchin' on that amphitheater. That's how many we're gonna have. And they'll say, "Wow. From 4000 up to 200,000. Those extra four Yippies did a hell of a good job." I dig that, see. I'm not interested in explainin' my way of life to straight people or people that aren't interested. They never gonna understand it anyway and I couldn't explain it anyway. All I know is, in terms of images and how words are used as images to shape your environment the *New York Times* is death to us. That's the worst fuckin' paper as far as the Yippies are concerned. They say, "Members of the so-called Youth International Party held a demonstration today." That ain't nothin'. What fuckin' people read that? They fall asleep. 'Cause the *New York Times* has all the news that's fit to print, you know, so once they have all the news, what do the people have to do? They just read the *New York Times* and drink their coffee and go back to work, you know. But the *Daily News*, that's a TV set. Look at it, I mean look at the picture right up front and the way they blast those headlines. You know, "Yippies, sex-loving, dope-loving, commie, beatnik, hippie, freako, weirdos." That's groovy, man, that's a whole life style, that's a whole thing to be, man. I mean you want to get in on that.

When we stormed the Pentagon, my wife and I we leaped over this fence, see. We were really stoned, I mean I was on acid flying away, which of course is an antirevolutionary drug you know, you can't do a thing on it. I've been on acid ever since I came to Chicago. It's in the form of honey. We got a lab guy doin' his thing. I think he might have got assassinated, I ain't seen him today. Well, so we jumped this here fence, see, we were sneaking through the woods and people were out to get the Pentagon. We had this flag, it said NOW with a big wing on it, I don't know. The right-wingers said there was definitely evidence of Communist conspiracy 'cause of that flag, I don't know what the fuck it was. So we had Uncle Sam hats on, you know, and we jumped over the fence and we're surrounded by marshals, you know, just closin' us in, about thirty marshals around us. And I plant the fuckin' flag and I said, "I claim this land in the name of free America. We are Mr. and Mrs. America. Mrs. America's pregnant." And we sit down and they're goin' fucking crazy. I mean we got arrested and unarrested like six or seven times. And when we finally got arrested, it was under other names. I'm really a digger, I never was a Yippie. Was always a digger. So I said, you know, "A. Digger, Abbie Digger, Mr. and Mrs. A. Digger." They say, "Are you a boy or a girl," I say, "Girl." Right. This is where I wanna go. I don't have to prove manliness by beatin' up fourteen-year-old girls with nightsticks, you know. Fuck 'em. But ideas, you just get stoned, get the ideas in your head, and then do 'em. And don't bullshit. I mean that's the thing about doin' that guerrilla theater. You be prepared to die to prove your point. You gotta die.

You know, what's life? Life's all that fun shit. Life's doin' what you want to do. *Life's* an American magazine, and if we hook them right, they're gonna give us 10,000 flowers that are gonna be thrown out of a helicopter tomorrow afternoon. But we'll only allow them to do it if they bring a newsreel person up in the helicopter with 'em. You know, to take the pictures. So we're workin' out that negotiation with *Life* magazine. 'Cause we said, you know, "It's called Festival of Life, man, we named it after your magazine." I know that's immoral and I know that's cheatin' and that's stealin'. I wish I was a revolutionist. I wouldn't have these problems. A lot of revolutionists come here, they worry about parking the car. Where we gonna park the car, should we park it in a meter? The meter'll run out, we'll get a ticket. It's a weird revolution. Fuck it. We don't need cars; we travel in wheelbarrows. You see, just worry about your ass. Forget about your clothes, your money, you know, just worry about your ass and all the rest of us's asses. Cars don't mean shit. They grab our walkie-talkies you say, "Yeah, there you go, take it, thank you, it was too heavy to carry."

I think it's a good idea to cut your hair or get a wig or let your hair grow pretty fast or paint your face or change your clothes or get a new hat and a new name. I mean everybody ought to have a new name by Wednesday. And like you know we're all one huge happy family with all new names or no names and no faces. 'Cause when we bust out of this park and go down to Grant Park and then go out to the amphitheater, there are gonna be some mighty strange theatrical events. And you better have your theater thing down pretty pat.

Well, I've shot my load. I'm for ending the Yippie thing Thursday, killin' it all, 'cause I don't think people are Yippies anymore than they're Mobe or Motherfuckers or whatever they are. They're just people. And I think we oughta burn all our Yippie buttons and laugh at the fuckin' press and say, "Nyah nyah, we took you for a fuckin' ride." That's what we figured when we started this thing back in December—just a couple of speedfreaks hangin' around the cellar sayin', "Now how are we gonna do this Chicago trip?" We ain't got no fuckin' money, you know, we ain't got no organization, we ain't got no constituency. We went to a New Left meeting, they said, "Where's your constituency? You can't talk here, you know, you ain't against imperialism." I said, "Man, I don't want any pay toilets in this fuckin' country, I don't want to pay a dime to take a shit." SDS doesn't consider that relevant. That's the trouble with the Left you know. Did a trip on a Socialist Scholars Conference, a couple of Hell's Angels guys and I, we went up and had a capgun fight in the Hotel Hilton where the Left has their conferences, it's very interesting. So the heads of the Hilton and the heads of the socialists were gettin' together to decide how to throw us speedfreaks out of the fuckin' place, see. But they didn't, I mean, we stayed to do our thing. The problem with the Left is that there are 10,000 socialist scholars in this country and not one fuckin' socialist. I mean I talk to guys on *The Guardian* and they say, "Yeah, we're working on a serious analysis of the Yippies." I say, "That's pretty fuckin' cool, man, that's great. By that time there won't be any Yippies. I mean, what the fuck are you analyzin' for, man? Get in and do it."

The Poverty of Culture

Barry Schwartz

New York's Metropolitan Museum is the oldest, most influential art museum in the United States. That people over there seem proud of this fact is illustrated by the massive array of exhibitions and special events held in 1970 to mark their centennial celebration. For over one hundred years the country's most fruitful cherry orchard has established itself as the largest encyclopedic art museum in the Western Hemisphere. It has more than one thousand employees—guards, restorers, sales personnel, curators, and supportive staff. Covering fifty centuries in nineteen departments, the Met controls more than 365,000 art objects and has an endowment of over one hundred million dollars, which earns some four million dollars a year, or roughly half of its operating costs.

The Met is probably the last remaining major institution in New York to continue to exclude even token black and Puerto Rican members on its Board of Trustees. The Met has no community advisory committee, though Director Thomas Pearsall Field Hoving has often been heard to chastise other museums because they choose to "ignore the obvious long-range benefits to the museum of such an advisory body." That Director Hoving would urge others to do what he has not done is only one facet of the standard

From "The Dispossession of American Museums," retitled and revised, from *Ramparts* (June, 1971). Copyright © 1971 by *Ramparts*. Copyright © 1972 by Barry Schwartz. By permission of the author and publisher.

operating procedure at the Met which equates good images with the fulfillment of the institution's responsibilities.

The staff at the Met, long sequestered in less troubling centuries, looks aghast at the madding crowd that brings new sets of demands as often as notebooks. For some time now social forces have been pushing against the Met; there have been demands that it change, and change quickly. In order to create the image that the Met is changing, without actually having to change, the Board of Trustees assigned Director Hoving to the helm in 1967.

Thomas Hoving likes to refer to the museum as a "positive, relevant, and regenerative force in modern society" (a phrase, no doubt, he would have little difficulty applying to himself). The director's program is characterized by a degree of activity, politics, expansion, and publicity that has had no equal in the history of that institution. Thomas Hoving would maintain a cherry orchard while, at the same time, neutralizing those forces that have occasionally necessitated the posting of a security guard at the entrance to the executive offices.

Opposition to the Met comes from diverse elements of the community. Many feel that the Met has not significantly responded to nonwhite residents who comprise nearly 50 percent of New York's population. Some are deeply disturbed by the expansion plan. Others are equally disturbed by the methods Hoving employs when dealing with his critics. Still others are concerned with the director's Ed Sullivan–like approach to art exhibition. Almost all critics agree that Hoving's contributions thus far have been to involve the museum in politics far beyond his predecessors, introduce an unprecedented degree of arbitrariness into museum policy making, carry the idea of expansion nearly to the point of accomplished fact, and give hostesses, hosts, and particularly the caterers an importance that is to be envied. Yet it must be understood that these achievements are only the means to a very worthy end. As Education Director Harry Parker III put it, "I think that the Hoving promise, which I believe in, and which lots of people believe in, is to make the museum more responsive to people, to make the museum more a public service institution."

In fairness, all discussions of the Met must take into account its history. As Parker describes it, the museum "is a large, encyclopedic, nonspecialized institution having a general collection with a heavy emphasis on research. It has the largest curatorial staff by two hundred of any museum in the country. It's one kind of a museum, and it has accomplished certain real achievements because of the combination of scholars brought together in one place, the kind of rub off that is possible between people who are interested in different fields. For example, consider the visual possibilities that exist in comparing what was done in Islam in the sixteenth century, versus what was done in England in the sixteenth century, versus what was done in China." These fruits of the cherry orchard remind us of the wisdom of Candide, who offers as his parting remarks, *"Mais il faut cultiver notre jardin."*

However, at a time when even life-supporting systems in New York are deteriorating at an alarming rate, New Yorkers are becoming disenchanted with the cultivation of the Met's own garden. It is hard to use the telephone; hard to walk down the streets; hard to send children to school; hard to find adequate and reasonable health services; hard to travel by car, and harder still to use the subways; it is especially hard to get worked up about the sixteenth century. There is a crisis in New York and people are beginning to ask questions of the institutions that say they are there to serve. That is why some critics of the Met demand that, whatever the Met's program, it must be concerned with the positive contribution of helping to upgrade the urban environment. Like the opponents of General Gavin's once celebrated idea of "enclaves" in Vietnam, many residents take a dim view of the notion that attention should be given to preserving and upgrading structures that would function as safe zones while the rest of the environment is given up as lost.

The book *Museum* by Alvin Schwartz gives evidence of the mentality that infuriates many who have to cope with the ever-growing difficulties of living in New York City. The Met is outfitting guards with uniforms resembling the New York State Police so that "with a more military appearance the guards will command more respect. . . . The lint, dust, and grime people bring into a museum is another problem. Dirt has a bad effect on all art works. . . . To deal with conditions in New York, the Met not only has a force of one hundred sweepers and cleaners, it is installing an air door which will suck superficial dirt off visitors as they enter." I don't know if such an air door was installed but all of this seems to suggest a peculiar shift in priorities. Perhaps it was some of these factors that prompted artist Robert Rauschenberg to ask, "Is the worst thing about New York City the fact that the Metropolitan is too small?"

At this time the Met, in the name of completing its encyclopedic task, is about to expand at a cost of more than fifty million dollars for its new turf. Not only will this action deeply and permanently influence the cultural life of New York City but, because other museums tend to act less on imagination and more on precedent, the expansion will have an impact on the entire nation.

The master plan, which is apparently not one of the museum's publishable documents, calls for new structures to house the Rockefeller collection of Primitive Art, the Temple of Dendur, a European garden court, a gallery of European painting and decorative arts, an American wing, and garden court. These structures will house objects already owned but which, because of existing space limitations, were only partially exhibited, as well as the gifts of the Lehman Foundation, of Nelson Rockefeller himself, and, of the Egyptian government. Hoving explains the need for more expansion by the fact that "not one foot of gallery space has been added since 1926."

Director Hoving assures us that these expansion plans are the final plans of the Metropolitan Museum of Art; that the Met is permanently and unequivocally through with all collecting "except for newsworthy items." If this dubious criteria for the purchase of art troubles you, take comfort: "We will collect nothing unless we give something out," says the director. "We have thirty-eight Monets. We could give away twenty-five." It must be remembered that two years ago the Met paid $1,400,000 for yet another Monet, and only recently the purchase of a Velasquez for a modest six million was a newsworthy item. Disconcerting as well is Mr. Hoving's remark, made two years before the present expansion controversy, that "any work of architectural sculpture I can get my hands on I'll buy." The much discussed "New York Painting and Sculpture" exhibition was the first major effort of the newly formed Department of Contemporary Arts, which is "charged with collecting, preserving, and exhibiting the paintings, sculpture, drawings, prints, furniture, period rooms, and decorative arts of the twentieth century"—a task that would suggest that still more room will be required since few things in the twentieth century are small. If these pronouncements seem to conflict with Mr. Hoving's no-purchase policy, they are consistent with *the other policy* stated by C. Douglas Dillon, the Met's president, in the May 1970 *Museum Bulletin:* ". . . we are grateful for gifts, and bequests of contemporary art, and we will continue to purchase it on a modest scale. . . . If we are to take advantage of the steadily dwindling opportunities to upgrade and enrich our collections, our purchase funds must also be increased."

Mr. Hoving states that the present plans represent the final expansion of the museum at its present location. Yet it takes little imagination to contemplate the day when still more space will be needed. At that time only two alternatives could be offered—either move elsewhere or expand onto more park land. Since the present expansion is toward encroachment of the park, there seems little doubt that these plans will be used as a precedent for a future invasion of the park. In 2024 another director might be insisting that the proposed new use of Central Park land is necessitated by the fact that not one foot of gallery space has been added since 1975. If this is not the case—if in the future the Met would consider moving part of its collection elsewhere—why is it so absolutely unwilling to consider doing so now?

Although Mr. Hoving would have another museum reflect "the varied interests, economic levels, and ethnic patterns of the city of Oakland," he seems quite willing to accept the Met's exclusion of community participation or representation. He has ignored the conservationists and citizens who have expressed concern about the use of park land. He has failed to consult and later ignored the three planning boards of the neighborhoods bordering the museum that are opposed to expansion. He has applied for more money each year from foundations, the city, and the Arts Council knowing full well he and the trustees are far more influential than the artists, blacks, Puerto Ricans, and others who suffer from a chronic shortage of funds for community cultural activity.

To his critics Hoving answers, "This institution, like many public insitutions, is in deep, absolutely horrifying continuing trouble to stay alive and available to everybody. I just urge you not to lose sight of this overall issue. For God's sake, help the place continue to be alive and be good." If this is the case one wonders why the museum would contemplate any expansion at this time. In 1968 the museum's deficit was $407,000; this was brought down to $138,000 in 1969 as a result of postponement, cancellation, and reduction of planned projects. For construction of the Temple of Dendur alone the museum must provide about $800,000. It is estimated that in 1974 the loss of operating income due to expansion will amount to $365,000 a year. The total cost of the master plan was $250,000 of which the Met paid $150,000 and the city paid the rest. How will the museum recover these losses? Such questions generally receive the now typical museum response. As C. Douglas Dillon expresses it: "All of this means that we soon must mount a truly major effort to raise substantial funds, both for endowment and for necessary construction. Difficult as the job may be, I am confident of success. The museum is simply too important to the world for us not to succeed."

When Lincoln Center was built those who opposed the project based their objections on the prediction that the complex would come to rely on more and more monies for its continued operation, limiting the availability of funds for community cultural activities throughout the boroughs. At that time Hoving, among others, gave assurances that this would not happen. Yet the figures reveal that each year Lincoln Center has absorbed greater funds from the total city budget for the arts. Last year Lincoln Center received

$1,155,000, leaving $179,000 remaining for visual arts, community projects, and summer mobile festivals. What the additional drain on these funds because of greater city commitment to the Met will mean is anyone's guess.

The Met has a genuine distaste for answering questions. They have been particularly evasive on the matter of the Lehman collection. Although the actual arrangements with the Lehman Foundation have never been made public, impeccable sources report that the museum may receive the collection only if they: (a) keep the entire collection perpetually intact in the new wing which will be operated as a department separate from the rest of the museum; (b) employ as the first curator of the collection the person selected by the Lehman Foundation; (c) for thirty-five years after completion of the new wing accept control by the Lehman Foundation over successor curators, loans from the collection to others, publications, research projects and other artistic or scholarly activities, and rules and regulations for the organization and operation of the wing and collection. The Lehman wing is actually the Lehman Museum arbitrarily located at the Metropolitan Museum of Art. The museum is permitting private control over decisions and organization policies which in all other cases fall within the jurisdiction of the museum's staff, who are, theoretically, responsive to public opinion vis-à-vis the Hoving promise. If there is an equivalent to academic freedom in museums, then surely this arrangement is in contradiction to it. These ethical considerations seemed to have missed the attention of President Dillon who confidently states, ". . . the Metropolitan Museum is and always has been designed to serve the general public. It is truly a public museum. . . . We must do everything in our power to keep it that way. And we shall! . . . The qualities that have made the museum strong in the past must continue to make it stronger still in the future. I refer to the museum's dedication to scholarship. . . ."

The list of contradictions between museum rhetoric and museum reality could be extended indefinitely. That is precisely the dilemma and frustration of the Met's opponents; critics are impotent in the face of the muscular politics summoned by the Met in behalf of its cause. All that critics are really able to do is to *expose*. The museum counters by escalating the inaccuracy of its pronouncements. In this way Director Hoving will be able to erect a monument to the eighteenth century in the latter part of the twentieth. Although supermuseums were founded ages ago, when social needs and conditions were vastly different from our own, the expansion will be carried out in the name of serving the public and the community. The new aristocracy, which wished to create a WASP enclave in the inner city of Oakland, will be able to erect a monument to its superiority in New York.

Although the expansion of the Met, which Lewis Mumford calls "another nail in New York's coffin," is counter to the major currents of contemporary history, the Met tells the public that this action is necessary so that it may be better served. C. Douglas Dillon serves as the spokesman for the nobility of the Met's intentions: "We intend . . . to build the kind of cultural institution whose program and exhibitions are readily accessible, to be enjoyed by the broadest possible public."

We are asked to accept Dillon's word over the major tendency today, all over the world, to desanctify, democratize, socialize, and decentralize. To create *ex novo* a supermuseum at this time is to deny even the history of museums themselves. When the Louvre ceased to function as a royal palace, it became a symbol of the center of social, political, and cultural life as it had existed under the monarchy. It was a heritage of which even revolutionaries were proud. That the Louvre was turned into a museum was more a matter of emotional commitment and historical precedent than the outcome of urban planning. In 1801 the first redistribution of its works of art was carried out, at the Louvre's expense, and museums were founded in Brussels, Geneva, and Metz. Eugène de Beauharnais furthered decentralization by creating museums in Italy such as the Brera Gallery in Milan. Today one cannot envisage a new wing added to the Louvre for the installation of the collections at the Jacquemart-André or the Musée Carnavalet. The Metropolitan would wish to be modeled on the Louvre. However, it is the eighteenth century Louvre, and not the contemporary museum, that inspires the current expansion.

It is on the question of decentralization itself that the most important contradictions and the reasons for them become apparent. "I believe in decentralization," says Thomas Hoving. "We will provide whatever the communities tell us they want, when they let us know." Can it be that a museum which spends $250,000 for the development of a master plan can do nothing to develop a meaningful interpretation of community needs and wants? And if the museum is interested in community needs why has it done all that it could to discourage or monopolize public hearings on the expansion plan?

When the Met is criticized for failing to respond to the outlying boroughs, we are told that the museum serves not just the communities of New York City but the entire nation. But when the museum is asked to justify its rush to expand we hear different words. As McCandlish Phillips reported a Hoving address in the *New York Times:* "First to the speaker's rostrum came Thomas P. F. Hoving . . . and he soon raised the prospect—a fearful one in the eyes of the museum's friends—that the $100,000,000 Robert Lehman collection would go to another city should the Metropolitan fail to build a diamond-shaped wing for it. . . ."

Why shouldn't the collection go to another city? Why should residents of other cities be told that the Met belongs to them while we in New York City take the attitude that if the Lehman collection were to go to another city it would no longer belong to us? If the museum is national in its constituency, as it claims to be, why is it so local in its commitments? And why does the Met pursue massive centralization with such vigor when its very own Cloisters, which Mr. Hoving once directed, is such an outstanding example of the benefits of decentralization? Why does the Met find decentralization so *unthinkable* when other museums have found it to be an effective way of serving people. With a view toward the future, as more and more Americans move and travel, is it not common sense to disburse some of our centralized cultural resources? If, as the *New York Times* reports, the new additions to the Met "would be the equivalent of three moderate-size museums for three moderate-size cities," would it not be appropriate to place each addition in a city that presently lacks cultural resources?

There are other questions that are still more relevant. With such large sums of money committed to museum expansion, with unanswered questions about how well the expansion meets the needs of the communities and of the museum itself, with the outcrys against expansion coming from so many diverse quarters, how has it come to be that there is primarily silence in lieu of that great debate required by an undertaking of this significance and magnitude? During all the planning stages why were there no advocates of the people? When there are so many communities begging for cultural investment why has the assumption that it is best to build on Fifth Avenue gone unchallenged by city officials? Who is being served for the money spent? Are questions of this sort asked by the New York State Arts Council or the budget examiners in Albany? If art teaches us "the inherent nobility of the human being," why has Director Hoving responded to his critics with manipulative tactics designed to discredit, harass, abuse, and demonstrate that they are mere forgeries, counterfeits of the genuine community, which remains appreciative of Hoving's efforts in their behalf? Why has the Met fought for its expansion with a display of what Sophy Burnham cites as "lies, vanity, vulgarity, and arrogance of power"? These questions and others asked by critics are only temporary annoyances easily brushed aside by those who control the museum. If the great staircase in the main hall is doomed by the expansion plans, what hopes can reasonable men place on mere questions to stop the caravan of bulldozers?

Troy Donahue Was Always Just Like He Is

Ron Rosenbaum

Why interview Troy Donahue anyway?

"Believe me, you won't believe Troy when you see him," the press agent tells me. "He's a bearded hippie! And believe me, *he is fantastic in this picture*. He plays Charles Manson! Actually we can't call him Charles Manson because of the legal thing, but it's the Charles Manson story. Troy is this sex- and drug-crazed Jesus-type cult leader of a hippie commune who kills a pregnant actress and her Hollywood friends. You see the parallel? This is going to be a very big picture. I have a feeling this is going to be bigger than *Love Story*."

And if that's not enough, the press agent offers another enticement. "Listen we'll take you to lunch with Troy at the Top of the Sixes. You'll like the Top of the Sixes. They have steaks and seafood. Do you like steak?" The press agent sets a date for the Top of the Sixes and promises to send me Troy's "bio." He tells me I will recognize him, the agent, "because I wear wild shirts and wide ties. But I guarantee you won't recognize Troy."

From the "Biography of Troy Donahue" received special delivery the next day: "Troy Donahue returns to the screen as Moon, the passion-possessed leader of a vengeful hippie cult . . . in this poignant, moving drama which is inspired by

From *The Village Voice* (July 29, 1971). Copyright © 1971 by The Village Voice, Inc. By permission of *The Village Voice*.

the awesome series of events surrounding the Sharon Tate murder case and other related wanton killings of this decade."

Enclosed with the bio is a newspaper story headlined "Troy Donahue Now Bearded Hippie." The story features before and after photos of Troy, showing him as sunny angelic Sandy Winfield II of Warner Brothers' *Surfside 6* and then as sullen demonic "Moon." A note from the press agent attached to the story states: "This Associated Press story on the 'new' Troy Donahue appeared not only in the Sunday *New Jersey Bergen Record* but in countless other major Sunday newspapers in the nation."

Troy is dressed in white. White sneakers, white Levis, white t-shirt; white Levi jacket. A silver crucifix and some other trinkets hang from a chain around his neck. Troy is a large man and his white clothes look a little too small for him, as if he doesn't want to admit he has put on weight. He looks like those one-time slim and healthy California surfers who grow older, grow paunchy—and maybe a little punchy too—and turn into bikers or dopers or both. There are gray hairs scattered through Troy's blond beard, and tiny red crinkles of visible veins on his cheeks. Troy is thirty-five.

I'll never forget Troy's first words to me, when he stepped over his motorcycle helmet to greet me at his table at the Top of the Sixes. This is a literal transcription: "Hey brother. Dig the scene. Dig the scene. Wow man. Dig the scene."

If I had any doubts left that Troy was in fact a bearded hippie, he set them at rest when he twisted the conventional handshake I had offered into an interesting version of the Movement "power" grip, and concluded the greeting by saying, "Yeah. Dig the scene." Just us hippies together.

Well, there were two others waiting at Troy's table in addition to us hippies. There was the press agent, in a wild shirt and a wide tie, and Bob Roberts, the producer of *Sweet Savior*, Troy's Charles Manson movie.

"Don't sit next to them," Troy told me. "Sit over here next to me so we can really rap."

When I am seated and turn to Troy, I find we are looking into each other's eyes. The heavy gaze continues in silence until Troy breaks it off, and nods slowly. "Yeah. Right," he says with finality.

We begin to talk about Charles Manson. "I knew the dude," Troy tells me. "I used to play volleyball with him on the beach at L.A. years ago. He had short hair back then, but even then he was very big with the chicks."

"What was his secret?" I asked.

"It was his cock," says Troy.

"His cock?"

"His cock."

Before I could ask Troy for more details the press agent interrupts: "Of course the film is not completely about Charles Manson. We have Troy there at the scene to commit the murder himself while Manson didn't do it himself. We rented a whole mansion in Teaneck, New Jersey, for the murder scene. The script was written by a Pulitzer prize winner, although under a pseudonym. Troy's performance is going to shock people. I think it's an Oscar performance although the Academy would never have the guts to give it to him."

Troy talks about his role: "It was a bad scene, man," says Troy to me. "It was real. You know, but it was dirty. I felt dirty, man, evil. But it had to be done. But it's real. Death is real. Wow. Down there just a few blocks away they killed, what's his name, Joe Columbo. That's heavy. It's funny. Sitting here and talking when it's so real out there. Last night I'm with this black girl in a bar. Beautiful girl, and I'm sitting next to her just wanting to get my cock into her, and she turns to me and says, 'You know the guy who killed Columbo is black. You know what that means.' That's heavy man. That's real."

"I would make a prediction right now," producer Bob Roberts declares in the silence that follows. "I would predict there would be more murders. This Manson thing will be just the beginning. This movie is not about an isolated incident, it's about what's to come. And there *will* be more murders."

The press agent looks over at me nervously, then back at the producer: "Bob, maybe you shouldn't predict murders.

Maybe you should change that to tragedies." He turns to me. "Say that Bob feels that this is a movie about a tragedy which may not, let's see, which may not be the last of its kind."

"But I think there will be *murders* too," says Bob a little disconsolately. "I'm willing to be quoted as predicting murders."

"I just don't think it's a good idea," says the press agent.

"Shut up! You don't know anything," Troy tells the press agent.

"That's nice," the press agent says with some dignity. There is an embarrassed silence at the table.

"Oh hey man, I'm just kidding. Here." Troy reaches for the press agent's hand, takes it into a firm "power" grip, looks him in the eye. "Brothers. Right?" The press agent nods dubiously.

Troy gets back on the subject of Charles Manson and begins explaining how Manson either was or wasn't just like Hitler. "So I said to David Frost, I said, 'Did Hitler do it? I mean did he? He didn't. Man, Hitler didn't do it. You know what I mean?' And Frost looks at me and says, 'He didn't do it?' And I said, 'No man, he didn't do it, did he?' It blew Frost's mind. All he could say was, 'He *didn't* do it?' "

Troy looks at me. "But the thing is he really *did* do it. Can you dig it? He *did* do it."

"Do what?" I asked.

"I think it's more than Hitler," said the producer before Troy can respond. "It's not just Hitler. It's the beautiful people."

"Right on," says Troy softly.

"The beautiful people," repeats the producer. "I don't want people to get the idea this is an antihippie movie, because it really portrays the degeneracy and depravity of the beautiful people as well as the hippies. That whole Hollywood scene."

"That's right man," says Troy. "I know that scene. I've been there. It's these people man. It's a thrill to cruise the Strip and pick up some groovy looking hippies and take them home and play with them. Play with them. You know what I mean. Games, dig it. People playing with people.

That's what they were all into. I was there when it happened."

"You were *there?*"

"I wasn't there in person but I was *there*. You dig it. I was there. We were all there."

"I'll tell you one thing," says the press agent, breaking in on Troy's reverie. "This movie is going to polarize. I mean that. It's going to polarize this country. That's why it's going to be so big. I would not be surprised if it isn't bigger than *Love Story* and one reason will be because of this polarization."

Troy is still there. "I was there. You were there. We were all there," he tells us. "I was sitting just a few yards down in the canyon when it happened. I could feel it happen. It was like a warning."

I asked Troy if it was hard on him personally trying to play Charles Manson on screen. "No man. I'm just an actor."

"Wait till you see his performance. It's an Oscar winner," said the press agent.

But how had he been able to get into the Manson part? Had he done acid? "I took acid man. I took acid and I met the Man. I met the *Man*. And the Man said cool it."

"Cool it?"

"Cool it. That's what he said. I was with these doctors, and . . . now you know some people take 250, 350 mikes and play around and think they did acid. But I did acid. I was with these doctors in Miami and I was standing by this metal railing watching the ocean and all of a sudden there was a thunderstorm man, like the end of the world. And lightning, man. So I'm holding on and this lightning hits the railing, comes right along to me and right through me. I should have been fried, man. Then I knew. Cool it. That's what the Man was saying. Cool it."

"Troy's still big with the women though," the producer interjects. "I don't know how he does it. Have you got that set up with the girl in the hotel, Troy, this afternoon? You do, don't you? I don't know how he keeps going."

Troy points to his crotch and grins. "The day I stop going here is the day I stop going. Going to see [a black singer] tonight. Wow."

The press agent takes out some glossy pictures. There is

Troy in shoulder length hair, parted blond beard, and black leather jacket leaning familiarly on the shoulder of a stout pregnant woman.

"She plays the Sharon Tate type," the press agent explains. "And the amazing thing is she was really pregnant during the shooting. Isn't that something?"

He takes out another glossy and there's Troy in a shot from one of his Warner Brothers–Connie Stevens movies, a blond wave in his neatly parted hair, wearing a neat sweater and sportshirt. "And here's Troy before. You could use these as before and after pictures."

"Yeah, but that's bullshit," says Troy. "That 'before and after' thing is bullshit. I was always the way I am now. See that picture of me with my hands in my pockets, looking so clean-cut? You know what I've got in my pocket. You know what?"

I shake my head no.

Troy gives me a sly look, puts two fingers up to his mouth, and takes an imaginary drag on an imaginary joint. "You know what I'm talking about now? That's right," he says with satisfaction.

Our conversation is interrupted by three elderly ladies who have come over from a nearby table to ask for Troy's autograph.

"I can't believe it. The women still recognize him everywhere," the press agent says.

Troy flirts graciously with the ladies who say they want the autographs for their nieces and granddaughters. When they leave to return to their table, Troy turns to me. "Crazy. Aren't they great. Wow. Look at those heavy legs." He smacks his lips. "Wouldn't you like to mow their lawns?"

"Troy, you have a two-thirty appointment at that hotel, don't you? I don't believe this guy and his women."

Troy wants to finish explaining how there was never any before and after. "I was always like this, man. All I want in life is maybe three drinks and like half a joint"—he takes another drag from his imaginary joint—"and then I hop on my bike and I'm off. That's the real Troy Donahue you know. It's because I'm spontaneous. Spontaneous, man. I'm so spontaneous I could cry. Sometimes I go to movies and just cry. Listen, have you got any more questions? Anything else you want to know?"

"What about that crucifix you're wearing around your neck," I ask him. "How much does it mean to you?"

"Listen man, I'm not into any cults or anything. I don't believe in cults. Look, it's not just the crucifix. That's for my Man, but I've also got this Hebrew letter here, it's a Hebrew symbol. I don't know what it stands for but it's good to have. Then I've got this little Buddha figure here and, dig this, he's got one ear missing which is very heavy. You know what that means don't you? Then this thing here, this is just a piece of junk to remind me of the junk in the world."

Troy gets up to leave. He picks up his motorcycle helmet and takes out of it a shiny white package which had been stuffed inside. "You want to see junk. Look at this. Somebody up at the Warner Brothers promo office laid this on me."

He hands me a package which turns out to be a white t-shirt with three bright red roses emblazoned on the front. Superimposed over the roses in large jolly letters is the word "JUNK." Below that are the words "Dusty and Sweets McGee," the title of Warner Brothers' newly released junkie movie.

"You can have that if you want," Troy tells me.

I thank Troy but decline.

"Well, I'm off on my cycle now man. Wish I had one of these"—he takes a final drag on his imaginary joint. "Listen, are you really gonna write this up? You really are. Wow. You know if you do, you know that before and after shit—it's been done before man. It's not me. I was always just like I am man.

"Troy is a fantastic guy, isn't he?" says the press agent after Troy leaves.

"Troy is a fantastic guy to work with," says the producer. "I was amazed. He was on time for everything; he's signed for two more pictures with me. In the next one he's playing a Weatherman leader in a picture called *The Weathermen*. Then in '72 there's another big one called *The Lucifer Cell*. It's about a Chinese Communist invasion of the U.S. that succeeds. Troy is an underground resistance fighter."

"The whole thing's going to be very big. This picture. Listen," says the press agent, "one thing you might want to mention in your story is that the company that's distributing this picture is a publicly owned company. It's traded over the counter. That's kind of interesting, you know, you might want to work that into the story when you mention that Trans-World Attractions Corporation is producing and distributing Troy's movie. You know. That it's publicly owned. Something like that. I'll tell you it's only selling for maybe a buck a share now, right Bob? But when this picture is released. . . . Of course it wouldn't be ethical for me to tell you to buy. . . ."

"But I could tell him, couldn't I?" chuckles the producer.

A young sweet-faced girl wearing a black robe and a large silver crucifix stops me on the sidewalk outside 666 Fifth Avenue (see Revelations 13:18 about that). In a spacy voice the girl asks if I would like to help the work of a group called The Process, The Church of the Final Judgment. The girl hands me a slip of paper on which the address of the Church of the Final Judgment has been typed. The slip is decorated with the head of Jesus and the horned head of the devil. The girl explains: "We believe each of us has both Christ *and* Satan within us. We believe that we must acknowledge that Satan is in us. Then we can begin to love Satan the way Christ loves, and Satan will be transformed."

The girl, who says she is an acolyte of the Church of the Final Judgment, points to a passage in a booklet explaining "The Process": "Through Love Christ and Satan have destroyed their enmity and have come together for the End; Christ to Judge, Satan to Execute the Judgment." The explanation of The Process continues later with an interesting universal law: "Anything we give, whether positive or negative, will be returned to us in full measure."

I accept the pamphlet from the girl and buy a more detailed book about The Process from her. As she is digging around in her tote bag for change, I notice a familiar shiny white package sticking out. I ask her about it. "Oh some guy came along a little while ago and gave it to me. I didn't really want it, but he didn't stop to ask whether I did or not."

The girl takes it out. It is Troy's "Junk" t-shirt. She is young enough and sweet-looking enough to have been one of the girls in my junior high school who mooned over Troy a decade ago.

"Did you know that was Troy Donahue who gave it to you?" I asked.

"I don't know. It was just this tall guy with a bike helmet who looked like he was in a hurry. Who is Troy Donahue? Look, would you like it? I really have no need for it." I have the "Junk" t-shirt now.

On Cowardice

Paul Theroux

In the old days, fat young boys with nothing to do used to stand around drugstores talking excitedly of picking up girls. They now have other choices—they can pick up guns or protest signs. I tend to take the druggist's view: have an ice cream and forget the choices. I intend to give in neither to the army nor to the peace movement.

I am now certain of my reason for thinking this: I am a coward.

It has not always been this way. I used to think I was a person of high principles. The crooked thing about high principles is that they can live in thin air. I am fairly sure mine did. For the past five years my reaction to anything military was based on borrowed shock.

I still believe that war is degrading, that it gets us no place, and that one must not hurt anyone else. The pacifists say this and the government calls them cowards. The pacifists protest that they are not cowards. I feel no kinship with the government. I have some sympathy for the folk who call themselves pacifists because I believe many of them to be as cowardly as I am. But I see no reason to be defensive about it. Certainly they should not have to put up with all that humiliation on the sidewalk. As cowards they should be entitled to a little peace. They should not have to waste their time and risk arrest scrawling slogans on the sub-

From *Commentary* (June, 1967). Copyright © 1967 by Paul Theroux. By permission of the author and Blanche C. Gregory, Inc.

way or walking for hours carrying heavy signs. Guns may be heavier, but why carry either one?

A soldier shuffled nervously in front of me while I stood in line at the East Side Airlines Terminal in New York almost two years ago. He turned abruptly and told me that he was going to Oakland, California. I told him I was going to London and then to Uganda. Harmless talk—the kind that travelers make with ease. He surprised me by breaking convention and continuing what should have been an ended conversation. After Oakland he would be going to Vietnam. I clucked at his misfortune and as we both thought presumably of death he said, "Somebody's got to go."

But not me, I thought. I got my ticket confirmed and a week later I was in Africa, far from the draft board, even farther from Vietnam. Five years ago I would have hectored the soldier with some soul-swelling arguments. I was a pacifist and a very noisy one at that.

When I was told that I must take ROTC at the University of Massachusetts in 1960 I refused. Then I tried to think why I had refused. I had no friends who were pacifists but I did not need a manual to tell me that I hated violence. I dreaded the thought of marching or taking guns apart; I quietly resolved never to go into the army, the ROTC, or anything that was vaguely military. The thought of wearing a uniform appalled me and the thought of being barked at frightened me. I wanted to write a big book and be left alone. In two hours I was a pacifist, a month later I was the only healthy non-Quaker at the University exempt from ROTC. A few years later I was arrested by the campus police for leading a demonstration (that was in 1962 when demonstrations were rare and actually bothered people). I bunched together with a dozen more pacifists, organized some more protests, and, the year I graduated, ROTC was put on a voluntary basis by a faculty committee. Although the committee was composed of friends of mine it was not really a put-up job. ROTC was just not consistent with high principles.

Before I was excused from ROTC I had to meet an *ad hoc* committee: the colonels of the army and the air force

ROTC, the chaplain, and the provost. The army colonel, a man with a passion for writing patriotic letters to the student newspaper, listened to my woolly tirade against the military (quotations from Jesus, Norman Mailer, Tolstoy, and, if I am not mistaken, Eugene V. Debs). He rose, his medals jangled at me, and he thundered: "What do *you* know about war!"

It couldn't have been plainer, but for a pacifist it is an easy question to answer. "Nothing, but . . . ." And then the atrocity stories, a smattering of religion, and a few abstract nouns. I could have appealed to the governor if they had not let me out of ROTC. The governor was coming up for reelection and would not have wanted to appear a jingo by making me take ROTC or a Communist by excusing me. The committee quietly released me from my obligation.

If I had told them I was a coward they would not have wasted a minute with me. I would have been given regulation shoes and told to keep them clean; I would have been expected to know all the parts of an M-1 carbine; I would have had to stab sandbags with a bayonet every Tuesday after entomology class. So I did not tell them I was a coward, although that would have been the honest thing to do. The colonel, a man experienced in these matters, insinuated that I was one, but good taste prevented his speaking the word.

The ROTC has never done much more than bruise a man. Its contribution has been to teach college boys marching. Ironically, the people who object to ROTC end up marching many more miles than the sophomores on the parade ground. Peace movements are successful usually because they are so militaristic in organization and attitude. The language of the peace groups is always military-sounding: fighting, campaign, movement, ranks, marches—even freedom awards for valor. There is keen envy among the groups: which college has the most picketers, the bloodiest and most agonizing signs, which men have the handsome beards. Tempers are short among demonstrators; they have ridden a long way to be grim. The protester from the Amherst area gets off near the White House and begins grousing: "Jesus, we just *got here* and they expect us to start picketing!"

I was persuaded by a friend to picket in Times Square against nuclear testing one cold night in 1962. We had to report to a cigar-smoking gentleman who gave each of us a sign and instructions: "Walk clockwise, single file, around the army recruiter booth. Remember, don't talk, don't stop walking, and if you want to leave just raise your hand and I'll get someone to carry your sign. Let's practice walking without the sign first, then we'll start. Okay, everyone line up here. . . ."

The little man did not carry a sign. He was the sergeant, we were the privates. He marched beside us and used his big cigar as a swagger stick. Every so often he would tell someone to pipe down or walk straight. We got off to a rough start, but soon got the hang of it, convincing me that, if nothing else, we responded well to discipline and would all have made pretty good soldiers.

Many pacifists I have known are scared out of their wits that they will be drafted. Is this fright caused by seeing moral laws broken and all Gandhi's hunger strikes made worthless by a man's head—or let's say, a pacifist's head—blown apart? Is the fright a fear of death or a fear of failed principles? Is the refusal to join in the slaughter inspired by feelings of cowardice or moral conviction? I am thinking of pacifists who have been taught their fear after being beaten up, threatened by armed boys, and seeing brutality up close.

I lived in a crowded suburb of a large city in the United States and I had to pass through an alley—the lights at the opposite end: salvation—to get a bus when I went to the movies. The last time I passed through that alley five figures came toward me. I knew they wanted to beat me up. I stood still and hoped they would pass by, although what I imagined—being surrounded, having the youngest one push me down in the snow and punch me while I curled up and groaned, hearing them laugh, and then running away until my throat ached—actually happened, and the next ten minutes were a blur of cruelty.

There have been other occasions. Once I was walking along a street in San Juan, Puerto Rico, with a pregnant girl. An American sailor about the same size and age as myself stood in front of us and said to me, "Did you jam that broad?" His friend laughed and some people stopped to see what I would do. I slid away, glancing at his fists, and then hurried off, halfheartedly dragging the girl behind. I think if there had been a fight I would have torn myself away and left the girl to fend for herself. I brought the subject up later. I told her that I did not want to cause trouble in a large crowd, in a strange city. But she knew that I was frightened and that I would not let anger take the place of my fright.

This is really what a coward is, I believe: a person who is afraid of nearly everything and most of all afraid of anger. His own anger is a special danger to him. He accepts his solitary hardship and pays the price of withdrawing. He knows that each attempt to deal with violence may require summoning all the inhuman bravado he can contain. The bravery is a cover. Its weight intimidates the flesh beneath it. Since bravery implies a willingness to risk death, the fear to be brave becomes the fear to die. I am unable to understand what could make me risk death: neither patriotism, a desire to preserve anything, nor a hatred of anyone could rouse me to fight.

I have always wondered how people do things which require risk, whether there is not a gap in their consciousness, a suspension of judgment while the dangerous act is performed. I have never felt this release, even momentarily, from the consequences of risk. Remembered incidents intrude: street fights I could not bear to watch, threats I walked away from, vicious glares that made me sick, and some time ago being in a bar in Washington, D.C., where a woman on a stool kept calling the dishwasher a nigger. She leaned on the bar and slobbered: "You a nigger, ain't you? You know you are; you nothin' but a nigger. You ain't no Creole like you say. You a nigger. . . ." And the Negro behind the bar whistled and looked at no one. I wanted to shout at the woman. But with a fear that quickly became nausea, I left.

Leaving is a cure for nothing, though if one goes to the right spot he may have time to reflect usefully on why he left. Almost four years ago I joined the Peace Corps, was sent to Malawi, in Central Africa, and taught school. Unlike most people in their early twenties, I had personal servants, a big house, and good public relations. My relatives said I was really sacrificing and doing good work (there is a school of thought that assumes if one is in Africa he is, *ipso facto*, doing good work). I was happy in my job. I was not over-worked. And I had joined the Peace Corps for what I now see were selfish reasons: I had thought of responsibilities I did not want—marriage seemed too permanent, graduate school too hard, and the army too brutal. The Peace Corps is a sort of Howard Johnson's on the main drag into maturity. Usually life is pleasant, sometimes difficult, occasionally violent. A good time to find out whether or not you are a coward.

Violence in Malawi became common. The resignation of several high-ranking politicians and the firing of a few others threw the country into a nightmare of suspicion late in 1964. Many people suspected of collaborating with the ex-cabinet members were choked or hacked to death. One day I was walking home along the dirt road that led to my house. I saw smoke. Up ahead I saw three Youth Leaguers dashing into the bush. I knew they had just burned something, but I was not sure what it was. I was sure that it was serious and became worried. Just over the hill was a truck in flames. The cab of the truck was crackling and I could make out stiff black shapes in the holes of the flames. I detoured around the burning truck and went home. At home I had a drink, locked the door, and went to bed.

About a week later I was on a train and going north to the lakeshore. At each stop, boys, Youth Leaguers anywhere from ten to forty years old, got on the train and demanded to see the party cards of the African travelers. If a person did not have a card he was beaten. An old man next to me was dragged out of his seat, thrown to the floor, and kicked. Just before they dragged him out of the seat he looked at me (we had been talking about how terrible it was that this thing was happening and I said that it made me very angry) and his hand reached out for my sleeve. I moved—a timid reflex—against the window and he missed my sleeve. They quickly got him onto the floor. His screams were terrific and he wept as they kicked him. No one in the car moved. Several minutes later, another and another were thrown to the floor and beaten. Outside the train a man was being chased and punched as he ran through a gauntlet of people. His hands were pushed against his face for protection. He reeled across the platform and bumped into a fence. I saw him huddled against the fence—the boys hitting him with sticks—as the train pulled away. I could not tell if he was screaming. I had closed the window. By the time the train had gone about a hundred miles, the car was almost empty; most of the occupants had been dragged out and beaten. I stepped out at my station and walked to a taxi. It was hard to suppress an intense feeling of relief. The cards that the men were being asked to produce were sold by the Youth Leaguers for two shillings. Many refused to buy them because they did not believe in the present regime and would not compromise their principles.

In August of 1965 I drove a car through the northern region of Malawi. I passed through fourteen roadblocks and reached the border post at about ten in the evening. The gate—the customs barrier—was closed. I saw some men standing near it. My headlights were still on and the windows of the car were rolled up. The men appeared to be saying something but I could not hear them. Only after a few moments did I realize that my headlights were shining into their eyes. I shut off the engine and rolled down the window. As soon as the window was open a crack I heard the loud shouting of the men. They stood where they were and ordered me out of the car. They raised their rifles to my face. When the guns were pointed at me my body started to shake, my legs felt as if they had gone suddenly boneless. I was numb. I knew I was about to be shot. I was waiting to be murdered. *If they're going to shoot me let them do it quickly!* flashed through my mind. The feeling of standing there on that border—a border that had been raided four times resulting in the deaths of many more people than even the large number reported in the press—in the darkness, the bullets crashing into my shirt, bursting through my back with a fist-sized collop of flesh and clotted blood, my body dropping into the sand by the light of a fizzing lantern, the men standing over me and firing into my inert body, my head broken open ... it was unbearable. And I had done nothing. I was innocent, my papers were in order, my passport was in my hand high above my head. But the guns! The shouting! I was so afraid that I think I could have been moved to action—I felt capable of killing them, or attempting it. Yet this would have been absurd because I had done nothing wrong. The guns remained pointed into my face. The feeling persisted: I wanted to shoot them or be shot. I wanted something to happen, something violent that would settle the whole affair.

They told me I must walk toward them. This I did, all the while trying to prevent myself from lunging at them in an attempt to incite them to shoot me and get it over with. But they did not shoot me. They swore at me and took me into the police station. I pleaded with them to let me through the barrier (I felt that as long as I remained on their side of the border I was guilty of something). I convinced them and that night drove until two in the morning along the narrow bush track into Tanzania.

When my Peace Corps stretch was over I decided to stay in Africa. I realized that there was violence in Africa, but I had started to understand it. I had reached two conclusions: one, the violence was either tribal or political—I had no tribe and was not involved in politics and so the violence was not directed against me; two, life in Africa is simple, provincial, dull generally but with stirrings here and there, evidence of growth that I might help with. Day-to-day life in Africa is much like day-to-day life in New Hampshire: people strolling through a clutter of flowers or standing around the local bar spitting on the sidewalk; there is gossip about love affairs and car-buying, there is time for talking or reading or writing. Sometimes there is trouble at the castle and the gunshots echo down through the huts. Trouble happens around powerful people, politicians and chiefs. I live among neither.

On my way to work, gliding through the green in my car, I think: *you can be drafted today.* I am twenty-five; I have bad eyes, but am otherwise physically fit. I have no wife. My job as a teacher here in Uganda may exempt me from the draft, but there is no guarantee of that. My draft board knows where I am. The President has said that he will again increase the number of troops in Vietnam. The war is a jumble of figures: the number of troops and planes, the number of bombings and raids, the number of dead or wounded. The numbers appear every day in the Uganda papers as cold as football scores. I add flesh and blood to them and I am afraid.

As a coward I can expect nothing except an even stronger insistence that I go and fight. *Fight whom?* A paradox emerges: the coward recognizes no enemies. Because he wants always to think that he will not be harmed (although he is plagued by the thought that he will be), there is no evil in his world. He wills evil out of his world. Evil is something that provokes feelings of cowardice in him; this feeling is unwelcome, he wants to forget it. In order to forget it he must not risk hating it. Indeed, the coward hates nothing just as he loves nothing. These emotions are a gamble for him; he merely tolerates them in others and tries to squash or escape them in himself. He will condemn no one when he is free from threat.

The word coward is loaded with awful connotations. It does not ordinarily lend itself to inclusion in logical discourse because it quickly inspires two assumptions. The first is that cowardice does not indicate how we really feel; the second is that we have principles which are in no way related to, and always more powerful than, our feelings, our flesh. The first assumption implies that the feeling of cowardice is somehow fraudulent; a coward is discounted as authentic because of the word's associations: it is allied to "tail" (Latin: cauda); one of its synonyms is "fainthearted" or, more plainly, "womanish." To accept this definition is to reach the conclusion that the coward's head will clear, that he will cease to become woman if he thinks a bit. The second assumption is that one's principles will overcome one's feelings. I would suggest, if my flesh is any indicator, that this is not the case.

Talking a mixture of rubbish and rhetoric to get out of ROTC, picketing the Military Ball, sympathizing with those Californians who were dragged down cement stairs by the police, their spines bumping over the edges, seeing some logic in Wolfgang Borchert's simple advice to pacifists (*"Sag, 'NEIN!'"*)—these are ego-inspired feelings; the ego fights for air, rejects absorption, anonymity, and death. Since we have perhaps far less dogma cluttering our lives than any other people in history, these ego-inspired feelings which can move us to acts of protest may prove essentially good, the principle of nonviolence made out of a deep feeling of cowardice may prove the truest. It is bound to have its opposite motives: Cardinal Spellman's blessing of the war in Vietnam was one of these acts of the ego and certainly not the result of any biblical dogma *he* had been taught.

All of this goes against existing laws. It is illegal to be afraid to go into the army. If I tell the draft board to count me out because I am afraid they will answer, "That's impossible. . . ." But it is not impossible, it is only illegal, I will say; I saw a man die, I saw a man kicked to death, I held the crumbling blue body of a drowned man in my hands. . . . This is feeling; I will be asked for principles, not feelings. Fear is selfish and so no amount of fear, even if it stems from observed violence, is acceptable grounds for exemption.

Yet ours is not a military-minded nation; this is clear to everyone. The president of a Chicago draft board was quoted as saying a few months ago: "I've been threatened half a dozen times. Guys say they're gonna kill me if they see me on the street. . . ." Is it the thought that war is degrading and immoral that makes this half dozen take the trouble to threaten the life of their draft board president? Or is it something else? We know we are terrible soldiers, that we are not bold; we have placed our trust in the hardware of war. ("Thank God for the atom bomb," my brother's sergeant said when he saw the platoon marching higgledy-piggledy across the parade ground.)

I say "we"—I mean "I." If I allow myself to be drafted into the army I will be committing suicide. The army is to a coward what a desert is to an agoraphobe, an elaborate torment from which the only escape serves to torment him further. The coward marches with death; the agoraphobe stalks the rolling dunes in search of an enclosure.

I sit here in a cool dark room in the middle of Africa thousands of miles from the people in the city hall who want to draft me. I sit down in the middle of it all and try to decide why I do not want to go. And that is all anyone can do, try to be honest about what he feels, what he's seen or thinks he's seen. He can offer this disturbing vision to those who are not sure why they are unwilling. Folksongs and slogans and great heroes are no good for us now, and neither is the half truth that is in every poem or every melodious sentence that hides the barbaric notions.

When I think of people trying to convince themselves that high principles result from merely hugging answers I think of the reverse of the old fairy story: a princess in her hunger kisses a handsome prince and turns him into a toad. The answers will not come by forcing ourselves upon dogma. The issue is that we should admit once and for all that we are frightened. We will not have told ourselves a lie and, after this truth which is a simple one, maybe even ugly, we can begin to ask new questions.

Racist Love

Frank Chin and Jeffery Paul Chan

White racism enforces white supremacy. White supremacy is a system of order and a way of perceiving reality. Its purpose is to keep whites on top and set them free. Colored minorities in white reality are stereotypes. Each racial stereotype comes in two models, the acceptable model and the unacceptable model. The unacceptable, hostile black stud has his acceptable counterpart in the form of Stepin Fetchit. For the savage, kill-crazy Geronimo, there is Tonto and the Hollywood version of Cochise. For the mad dog General Santa Ana there's the Cisco Kid and Pancho. For Fu Manchu and the Yellow Peril, there is Charlie Chan and his Number One Son. The unacceptable model is unacceptable because he cannot be controlled by whites. The acceptable model is acceptable because he is tractable. There is racist hate and racist love.

If the system works, the stereotypes assigned to the various races are accepted by the races themselves as reality, as fact, and racist love reigns. The minority's reaction to racist policy is acceptance and apparent satisfaction. Order is kept, the world turns without a peep from any nonwhite. One measure of the success of white racism is the silence of that race and the amount of white energy necessary to maintain or increase that silence.

Likewise, the failure of white racism can be measured by the amount and kind of noise of resistance generated by the race. The truth is that all of the country's attention has been drawn to white racism's failures. Everything that has been done by whites in politics, government, and education in response to the failure of white racism, while supposedly antiracist, can be seen as efforts to correct the flaws, redesign the instruments, and make racism work. The object is to shut up the noise. Do it fast. Do it cheap. White racism has failed with the blacks, the chicanos, the American Indians. Night riders, soldier boys on horseback, fat sheriffs, and all them goons and clowns of racism did destroy a lot of bodies, mess up some minds, and leave among these minorities a legacy of suffering that continues to this day. But they did not stamp out the consciousness of a people, destroy their cultural integrity and literary sensibility, and produce races of people that would work to enforce white supremacy without having to be supervised or watchdogged by whites.

In terms of the utter lack of cultural distinction in America, the destruction of an organic sense of identity, the complete psychological and cultural subjugation of a race of people, the people of Chinese and Japanese ancestry stand out as white racism's only success. This is not to say that Asian-Americans are worse off than the other colored minorities. American policy has failed in Vietnam, yet no one would say that the Vietnamese are better off than the people of Puerto Rico, where American policy has succeeded. The secret of that success lies in the construction of the modern stereotype and the development of new policies of white racism.

The general function of any racial stereotype is to establish and preserve order between different elements of society, maintain the continuity and growth of Western civilization, and enforce white supremacy with a minimum of effort, attention, and expense. The ideal racial stereotype is a low maintenance engine of white supremacy whose efficiency increases with age, as it became "authenticated" and "historically verified."

The stereotype operates as a model of behavior. It conditions the mass society's perceptions and expectations. Society is conditioned to accept the given minority only within the bounds of the stereotype. The subject minority is conditioned to reciprocate by becoming the stereotype, live it, talk it, embrace it, measure group and individual worth in its terms, and believe it.

The stereotype operates most efficiently and economically when the vehicle of the stereotype, the medium of its perpetuation, and the subject race to be controlled are all one. When the operation of the stereotype has reached this point, where the subject race itself embodies and perpetuates the white supremacist vision of reality, indifference to the subject race sets in among mass society. The successful operation of the stereotype results in the neutralization of the subject race as a social, creative, and cultural force. The race poses no threat to white supremacy. It is now a guardian of white supremacy, dependent on it and grateful to it.

For the subject to operate efficiently as an instrument of white supremacy, he is conditioned to accept and live in a state of euphemized self-contempt. This self-contempt itself is nothing more than the subject's acceptance of white standards of objectivity, beauty, behavior, and achievement as being morally absolute, and his acknowledgment of the fact that, because he is not white, he can never fully measure up to white standards.

The stereotype, within the minority group itself, then, is enforced by individual and collective self-contempt. Given: that the acceptable stereotype is the minority version of whiteness and being acceptable to whites creates no friction between the races, and given: fear of white hostility and the white threat to the survival of the subject minority, it follows that embracing the acceptable stereotype is an expedient tactic of survival, as selling out and accepting humiliation almost always are. The humiliation, this gesture of self-contempt and self-destruction, in terms of the stereotype is euphemized as being successful assimilation, adaption, and acculturation.

If the source of this self-contempt is obviously generated from outside the minority, interracial hostility will inevitably result, as history has shown us in the cases of the blacks, Indians, and chicanos. The best self-contempt to condition into the minority has its sources seemingly within the minority group itself. The vehicles of this illusion are education and the publishing establishment. Only five American-born

Chinese have published what can be called serious attempts at literature: Pardee Lowe has a one-book career with *Father and Glorious Descendent* (1943), an autobiography; Jade Snow Wong, another one-book career with the most famous Chinese-American work, *Fifth Chinese Daughter* (1950), an autobiography; Diana Chang, the only serious Chinese-American writer to publish more than one book-length creative work to date, has written and published four novels and is a well-known poet; Virginia Lee has one novel, *The House Tai Ming Built* in 1963; and Betty Lee Sung, author of the semiautobiographical *Mountain of Gold* (1967). Of these five, four—Pardee Lowe, Jade Snow Wong, Virginia Lee, and Betty Lee Sung—confirm the popular stereotypes of Chinese-Americans, find Chinese-America repulsive, and don't identify with it.

The construction of the stereotype began long before Jade Snow Wong, Pardee Lowe, Virginia Lee, and Betty Lee Sung were born within it and educated to fulfill it. It began with a basic difference between it and the stereotypes of the other races. The white stereotype of the Asian is unique in that it is the only racial stereotype completely devoid of manhood. Our nobility is that of an efficient housewife. At our worst we are contemptible because we are womanly, effeminate, devoid of all the traditionally masculine qualities of originality, daring, physical courage, creativity. We're neither straight talkin' or straight shootin'. The mere fact that four of the five American-born Chinese-American writers are women reinforces this aspect of the stereotype.

The sources of Chinese-American self-contempt are white Christianity, the sojourner's state of humiliation, overt white racism, and legislative racism. Each served to exclude the Chinese-American from the realm of manliness and American culture. The Chinese were the target of the largest missionary campaign ever mounted in the history of mankind. It's now in its fifth century. The American missionary movement is now in its second century. In 1871, the Reverend John L. Nevius wrote:

> The Chinese as a race are, as compared with the European nations, of a phlegmatic and impassive tempera-

ment, and physically less active and energetic. Children are not fond of athletic and vigorous sports, but prefer marbles, kite-flying, and some quiet games of ball, spinning tops, etc. Men take an easy stroll for recreation, but never a rapid walk for exercise, and are seldom in a hurry or excited. They are characteristically timid and docile. . . . While the Chinese are deficient in active courage and daring, they are not passive in resistance. They are comparatively apathetic as regards to pain and death, and have great powers of physical endurance as well as great persistency and obstinacy. On an average a Chinese tailor will work on his bench or a literary man over books with his pen, more hours a day than our race can.

The Chinese, in the parlance of the Bible, were raw material for the "flock," pathological sheep for the shepherd. The adjectives applied to the Chinese ring with scriptural imagery. We are meek, timid, passive, docile, industrious. We have the patience of Job. We are humble. A race without sinful manhood, born to mortify our flesh. Religion has been used to subjugate the blacks, chicanos, and Indians along with guns and whips. The difference between these groups and the Chinese was that the Christians, taking Chinese hospitality for timidity and docility, weren't afraid of us as they were of other races. They loved us, protected us. Love conquered.

It's well-known that the cloying overwhelming love of a protective, coddling mother produces an emotionally stunted, dependent child. This is the Christian love, the bigoted love that has imprisoned the Chinese-American sensibility; whereas overt and prolonged expressions of hatred had the effect of liberating black, red, chicano, and, to some degree, Japanese-American sensibilities. The hatred of whites freed them to return hate with hate and develop their own brigand languages, cultures, and sensibilities, all of which have at their roots an assumed arrogance in the face of white standards, and defiant mockery of white institutions, including white religion. One of the products of these cultures born of overt racist hatred was a word in the language for white man, a name loaded with hate. A white man knows where he stands when a chicano calls him "gringo," or a black man calls him "honky," "Mr. Charlie," "ofay," "whitey," or an Indian calls him "paleface." Whites aren't aware of the names Chinese-Americans and Japanese-Americans have for them. And it's not a little embarrassing for an Asian-American to be asked by a curious white what we might call him behind his back.

The first Chinese were sojourners to America. They arrived in a state of humiliation as indentured servants, coolie laborers to California to perform the labor of slaves, which were outlawed in this free state. They never intended to settle here. The whites encouraged them with overt white racism and legislative racism to leave as soon as they could. The first Chinese so loathed this country that they regularly burned all their letters and records of their stay, journals and diaries, and tossed the ashes into the sea in the hope that at least that much of themselves would make it back to China. As a consequence of their total self-contempt, Chinese-America has no literary legacy. Of the Chinese who stayed not one complete account of one Chinese man's life in California, in diary, in journal, or in the form of correspondence, survives. Nor is there any oral history. All that survives from those old men is the humiliation of being foreign.

If life here was something to be erased from memory, death here was the ultimate humiliation. They were contemptible in life on American soil. Life they could endure. But death, no. So the practice of returning the bones to China for burial in hospitable ground, an eloquent and final expression of their loathing of America released after death, which the whites regarded as quaint and heathenish.

Legislative racism, the only form that openly survives, was invented to cope with the Chinese specifically and the first applied against them with success. Legislative racism culminated in the passage of The Chinese Exclusion Act by the US Congress, giving the Chinese the distinction of being the only race to be legislated against by name.

The racist policy applied against the blacks defined them as nonhumans, as property without legal status. This resulted in political schisms among the white majority and contributed to a costly war, thus failing as an instrument of white supremacy. It also failed to control the blacks and condition them into white supremacist self-control. The policy of extermination and incarceration applied against the American Indian was another costly failure.

For the Chinese, they invented an instrument of racist policy that was a work of pure genius, in that it was not an overtly hostile expression of anti-Chinese sentiment, yet still reinforced the stereotype and generated self-contempt and humiliation among generations of Chinese and Chinese-Americans, who, after having been conditioned into internalizing the white supremacist Gospel of Christian missionaries, looked on themselves as failures, instead of victims of racism. This wondrous instrument was *the law*. They gave the Chinese legal status, access to and protection under the law as "aliens ineligible for citizenship." We were separate but equal under the supposedly blind impartiality of the law. Legally we were masters of our own destiny, limited only by our intelligence and talent.

The game was rigged. The Chinese were forced into Chinatown and out of American culture and society by laws supposedly designed to protect fish, secure safety against fire, and protect public health. One law stated that only "aliens ineligible for citizenship" of the laboring class would be admitted into the country. A fancy way of saying only men, no women. This law was designed to control the Chinese population. It discouraged Chinese from staying by denying them access to their women, underscored the state of their (supposedly voluntary) humiliation in America, and guaranteed that even should all the Chinese stay they would not reproduce. And eventually they would die out.

This law worked. At the turn of the century the ratio of men to women was 27 to 1. Then a little after the turn of the century the Chinese population took a sudden decline. White historians like to say that suddenly a lot of us went home to China. We didn't, but our bones did, six months after we died here. This law was doubly successful in that it contributed to the myth of Chinese-American juvenile decency and thus added to the effeminization of the racial stereotype.

According to this myth, the reason juvenile delinquency stayed so low in Chinatown until the last twenty years was the maintenance of the strong Chinese family. Nothing less than Confucianist Chinese culture was making law-abiding citizens of us. The reason there was no juvenile delinquency in Chinatown has less to do with Confucian mumbo jumbo than with that law against the birth of Chinese kids. There were no juveniles to be delinquent.

What holds all this self-contempt together and makes it work is "The Concept of the Dual Personality." The so-called "blending of East and West" divides the Chinese-American into two incompatible segments: (1) the *foreigner* whose status is dependent on his ability to be accepted by the white natives; and (2) the *handicapped native* who is taught that identification with his foreignness is the only way to "justify" his difference in skin color. The argument goes, "If you ain't got Chinese culture, baby, all you got's the color of your skin," as if to say skin color were not a cultural force in this country.

The privileged foreigner is the assimilable alien. The assimilable alien is posed as an exemplary minority against the bad example of the blacks. Thus the privileged foreigner is trained to respond to the black not the white majority as the single most potent threat to his status. The handicapped native is neither black nor white in a black and white world. In his native American culture he has no recognized style of manhood, in a society where a manly style is prerequisite to respectability and notice. His pride is derived from the degree of his acceptance by the race of his choice at being consciously one thing and not the other. Black, white, chicano, or a museum of Chinese culture. In his use of language, voice inflection, accent, walk, manner of dress, and combing his hair, the handicapped native steeps himself in self-contempt for being "quick to learn . . . and imitative." At worst, he's a counterfeit begging currency. At best he's an "Americanized Chinese," someone who's been given a treatment to make him less foreign.

No stereotype is isolated or self-sufficient. In defining the role, character limitations, and cultural boundaries of a given minority, the stereotype defines relationships between that minority, the majority group, and the other minorities. The concept of the dual personality posits a disintegrated personality, a condition of constant conflict that removes the Chinese-American from the realm of white concern. The conflict between the "Chinese" part and the "American" part has been a source of white entertainment for the whole of the twentieth century. Virtually every book-length work by a Chinese-American—China- or American-born—published in America has stated the concept of the dual personality. All but one celebrates the concept, accepts it, and writes within it. That exception is the work of Diana Chang who was not educated in America and hence not taught to play the part.

Unlike Chinese-America, Japanese-America produced serious writers who came together to form a literary-intellectual community. In Chinese-America due to the reign of the concept of the dual personality that dictates that culture in this country is white, to write meant becoming white and the rejection of and by the community. Art in Chinese-America signaled contempt. In Japanese-America it encouraged community. Japanese-America through the thirties and forties produced their own literary magazines in whose pages Japanese-American English was developed and the symbols of Japanese-American experience codified. In spite of the more highly developed literary sensibility and literary skills of Japanese-America, the general belief is that Chinese-America is more literate. It's true that until very recently after a spate of Japanese-American publications, much of it commissioned by Japanese-American community organizations, more books by Chinese-Americans had been published than Japanese-American works.

As the concept disintegrates the Chinese-American's personality and keeps him busy schizophrenically playing one part of himself off the other, so, in the social sphere, the concept plays the Chinaman off against the other minorities, trains him to look on all other nonwhite races with envy, fear, and contempt, as threats to his acceptance by whites. The playing of one race off against the other is one function of all racial stereotyping. The races absorb and accept the stereotypes of each other invented and pushed by the whites, and, in doing so, authenticate these stereotypes and serve white supremacy by breeding interracial contempt. David Hilliard, Black Panther Party Chief-of-Staff, addressing a Chinatown San Francisco rally in 1969, told the Chinese-Americans they were the "Uncle Tom minority" and were contributing to holding the blacks back. If that is an extreme example, subtle and more painful ones are available. In Richard Wright's classic *Black Boy*, we meet Shorty, an elevator operator in the deep South. Shorty needs a quarter for lunch and tells the white man, "I'll do anything for a quarter." He offers the white man his ass to kick. The white man kicks, then throws a quarter on the ground. Shorty picks it up with his teeth. "You're all right, Shorty, you sonofabitch," the white man says. Shorty, by white Southern standards, is assimilated and happy.

"I'm going north one of these days," Shorty would say.

We would all laugh, knowing that Shorty would never leave, that he depended too much upon the whites for the food he ate.

"What would you do up north?" I would ask Shorty.

"I'd pass for Chinese," Shorty would say.

Wright portrays Shorty as loathsome and euphorically sick with self-contempt. More loathsome is Shorty's comparison of himself to the Chinese. Yet Shorty's vision of the Chinese is the same as white America's. Betty Lee Sung, the latest Chinese-American writer, with her *Mountain of Gold*, displaying the genius of the concept of the dual personality, manages to reassure whites that Chinese-Americans are not blacks, while patronizingly semi-identifying with them in the most general terms. She is to Chinese-Americans what Shorty is to the blacks.

The position of the Chinese in the United States is tied in not only with the international situation but with the domestic issue of race relations as well. *Although the struggle is primarily between Negroes and whites, comparisons can be made with the Chinese experiences,*

and it should be noted that the Chinese have benefited
from the Negro's struggle. (Emphasis mine.)

Having stated the cliché, the question of race relations
and blacks is never mentioned again. She makes no comparisons between black and Chinese experiences in race relations.
The closest she comes to reacting toward discrimination and
prejudice, which she does not compare to discrimination and
prejudice against the blacks, is:

The past is history. Today, the Chinese are in very favorable circumstances. The opportunities are unparalleled,
and the Chinese have much to offer.

Offer who? Need we ask? Nor does she say how the Chinese have benefited from the Negro's struggle. But it's obvious, even in the few sentences quoted, that she's working for
acceptance, indeed she defines assimilation as "letting go of
the old, taking on the new, and being fully accepted into the
dominant society." Knowing this much, it takes no great effort of mind to see that she is sensitive to what whites want
to hear. She has learned from the blacks' mistakes . . .
learned what not to do to be accepted. She subtly ac-
knowledges that our present function as a minority is to be
not black. The method of being not-black is to make a lot of
silence for all the noise the blacks make. She is meticulously
uncontroversial with potentially controversial subjects. She
practices the method of silence masterfully in the second to
the last chapter titled "The Chinese Get into the Best Places."
She notes that in the forties the Chinese suddenly enjoyed
enthusiastic acceptance. The Chinese Exclusion Act was removed from the books. A Chinese-American published a
book. She is pleased with the acceptance of the Chinese
into the dominant society, receives it like a miracle, the
answer to prayers, the reward for suffering and hard work.
She totally ignores the influence Pearl Harbor, World War II,
anti-Japanese sentiment, and the Chinese allies had on the
acceptability of Chinese in America. In the forties of her
Chinese-America there was no war, no Japanese, no obligations to Chinese allies.

The concept of the dual personality successfully deprives the Chinese-American of all authority over language and thus a means of codifying, communicating, and legitimizing his experience. Because he is a foreigner, English is not his native tongue. Because he was born in the U.S., Chinese is not his native tongue. Chinese from China, "real Chinese," make the Chinese-American aware of his lack of authority over Chinese, and the white American doesn't recognize the Chinese-American's brand of English as a language, even a minority language, but as faulty English, an "accent." The notion of an organic, whole identity, a personality not explicable in either the terms of China or white America (in the same way the black experience is not explicable in either the terms of Africa or white America), has been precluded by the concept of the dual personality. And the development of Chinese-American English has been prevented, much less recognized. The denial of language is the denial of culture.

The deprivation of language in a verbal society like this, for the Chinese-American, has contributed to (*1*) the lack of a recognized Chinese-American cultural integrity (at the most native-born Chinese-Americans are "Americanized Chinese") and (*2*) the lack of a recognized style of Chinese-American manhood. These two conditions have produced "the house of nigger mentality" under which Chinese-Americans, accepting responsibility to, rather than authority over, the state language, accept dependency—a state of dependency encouraged by the teaching of English and the publishing establishment. In 1949 a Japanese-American, Toshio Mori, published a book of short stories, *Yokohoma, California* (Caxton). Mori's friend, William Saroyan, wrote the introduction which opened with:

> Of the thousands of unpublished writers in America there are probably no more than three who cannot write better English than Toshio Mori.

Saroyan unquestioningly accepts the concept of the dual personality, otherwise he wouldn't have read his friend Mori's work as an English paper and graded his grammar without feeling he wasn't insulting the man. He assumes Mori has no command over English. He's a student, not a writer, to Saroyan. If he'd thought Mori a writer, he would have criticized a murky garbled "style," questioned the writer's skill, not his language. In the Scott Foresman anthology of "American Ethnic Writing," *Speaking for Ourselves*, the editors Lillian Faderman and Barbara Bradshaw have reprinted one of the stories from *Yokohoma, California*. They ignore the consequences of Saroyan's flunking him in English and say, "Mori never wrote another book." Mori, who has been writing since the *thirties*, now in his sixties, has the manuscripts to four novels on his shelf. Four novels written in flunkout English, English that Japanese-Americans of the thirties and forties happened to speak and make themselves known by but whites won't publish.

Language is a medium of culture and the people's sensibility, including the style of manhood. Language coheres the people into a community by organizing and codifying the symbols of their own common experience. Stunt the tongue and you've lopped off the culture and sensibility. On the simplest level, a man, in any culture, speaks for himself. Without a language of his own, he no longer is a man but a ventriloquist's dummy at worst and at best a parrot. The concept of the dual personality deprives the Chinese-American of the means to develop his own terms of self-definition. It subjugates him by forcing him to define himself in terms he knows are not his. The tyranny of language has been used by white culture to suppress Chinese-American and Japanese-American culture and exclude the Asian-American sensibility from operating in the mainstream of American consciousness.

The tyranny of language continues even in the instruments designed to inject the minority sensibility into the mainstream. Virtually every anthology of Third World writing containing Asian-American sections confuses Chinese from China with Chinese-Americans, conveniently ignoring the obvious cultural differences, and features Chinese writers from China, C. Y. Lee and Lin Yutang, who, being born and raised in China, are secure in their Chinese culture, are Chinese who have adapted to American ways. Their work inevitably authenticates the concept of the dual personality. However, their being Chinese precludes their ability to communicate the Chinese-American sensibility. The other Chinese-American writers collected in this new splash of anthologies most often include Jade Snow Wong and Pardee Lowe who also reinforce the stereotype. They were educated by the stereotype to play the role. Jade Snow Wong's father was an ordained Presbyterian minister. Lowe's book came out in 1943. The dust jacket listed among the reasons this book should be read, the need for Americans to become acquainted with and understand America's "loyal minorities." The jacket notes went on to say that Pardee Lowe, after delivering the manuscript for publication, enlisted in the army. These writers do not regard themselves as professional writers. They were putty in the hands of publishers anxious to make cartoons of real people. The new anthologies that include their work and pass it off as representing the Chinese-American sensibility in their introductory remarks—although it didn't twenty years ago when it was current much less today—are perpetuating a white monster.

In the fall of 1971, Houghton Mifflin released the first anthology of Asian-American writing ever published, edited by Kai-yu Hsu. His introduction equips the reader to read Asian-American writing intelligently. The concept of the dual personality and the stereotype of the Asian-American are discussed. Distinctions between the experiences of Asians in America and Asian-American experiences are made. He goes so far as to recognize the experiences and cultural integrity of Chinese-Americans, Japanese-Americans, and Philippine-Americans. The conscious effort by modern Asian-American writers to legitimize the languages their respective people speak is described. In spite of this, the following letter comes from Kai-yu's white editor, as stupid, culturally tone-deaf, and self-righteous as ever:

May 28, 1971

Dear Mr. Chan:

Thank you very much for so promptly sending us the telegram about the spelling of your first name. We were able to make sure that galley proofs would be correct in this respect.

We are still distressed, however, about using the word *lays* instead of *lies* in the title of your story and in a sentence near the end of the story. You see, if teachers or students using the book come upon a word usage that they think is incorrect, they write to the author or to us asking what dictionary or other source authorizes it.

Would you be willing to reconsider letting us use *lies?* We would be glad to have you call Mr. Romano or me about this and reverse the charges.

Sincerely yours,

[Name Withheld by Publisher]
School English Department

Great white bitch goddess priestess of the sacred white mouth and dumb broad ventriloquist whose lips don't move fine doesn't know us Chinamans mean to reverse the charges with our writing. The object of our writing is no different from that of any other writer. We mean to inject our sensibility into the culture and make it work there. That means we are the teachers. People should ask what dictionary or other sources authorize what we say, how we talk. That's a part of learning how to read. She is illiterate, so self-righteously illiterate I'm going to write about her. I will begin, "[Name withheld by publisher], warm in her inner stupidity, self-righteously illiterate, got a job with the White Racist Secret Service, teaching people they no good for talking trash and wondered why us wouldn't read Pearl Buck out loud at all because didn't Pearl write us nice . . . ?

catechism of d neoamerican hoodoo church

Ishmael Reed

a little red wagon for d black bureaucrat
who in d winter of 1967 when i refused to
deform d works of ellison & wright—his betters—
to accommodate a viewpoint this clerk thot irresistible,
did not hire me for d teaching job
which he invitd me to take
in d first place.

this is for u insect w/ no antennae, goofy
papers piling on yr desk—for u & others. where
do u fugitives frm d file cabinet of death get
off in yr attempt to control d artist?
keep yr programming to those computers u love so
much, for he who meddles w/ nigro-mancers
courts his demise!

i

our pens are free
do not move by decree. accept no memos
frm jackbootd demogs who wd exile our minds.
dare tell d artist his role. issue demands on

cultural revolution. 2 words frm china where an
ol woman sends bold painters to pick grasshoppers
a 3 in d a.m. w/ no tea, no cigarettes & no
beer cause ol women like landscapes or portraits
of their husbands face. done 50 yrs ago. standing
on a hill. a god, a majesty, d first chairman.
o, we who hv no dreams permit us to say yr name
all day. we are junk beneath yr feet,
mosquito noises to yr ears, we crawl on our
bellies & roll over 3 times for u. u are
definitely sho nuff d i my man.

ii

is this how artists shd greet u?
isnt yr apartment by d river enough? d
trees in d park? palisades by moonlight is
choice i hear. arent u satisfid? do u
want to be minister of culture? (minister, a
jive title frm a dead church!) dressd in a
business suit w/ medals on yr chest? hving
painters fetch yr short, writers doing yr taxes,
musicians entertaining yr mistresses, sculptors
polishing yr silverware. do u desire 4 names
instead of 2?

iii

    i do not write solicitd
    manuscripts—oswald spengler said
    to joseph goebbels when askd to make a
    lie taste like sweet milk.

because they wrote d way they saw it, said
their prayers wrong, forgot to put on their number in d
a.m., got tore dwn in d streets & cut d fool:

men changd their names to islam & hung up d phone on
  them.
meatheaded philosophers left rank tongues of ugly mouth on
their tables. only new/ark kept us warm that summer. but
now they will pick up d tab. those dear dead beats who put
our souls to d wall. tried us in absentia before
some grand karate who hd no style. plumes on garveys hat
he was.

iv

word of my mysteries is getting around, do not cm
said d dean / invite cancelld to speak in our chapel
at delaware state. we hv checkd yr background. u make
d crucifixes melt. d governor cant replace them.
stop   stop   outlandish customer.

v

i am becoming spooky & afar you all. i
stir in my humfo, taking notes. a black cat
superstars on my shoulder. a johnny root dwells
in my purse. on d one wall: bobs picture
of marie laveaus tomb in st louis #2. it is
all washd out w/ x . . . s, & dead flowers &
fuck wallace signs. on d other wall:
d pastd scarab on grandpops chest, he was
a nigro-mancer frm chattanooga. so i got it
honest. i floor them w/ my gris gris. what
more do i want ask d flatfoots who patrol d beat
of my time. d whole pie? o no u small fry
spirits. d chefs hat, d kitchen, d right
to help make a menu that will end 2 thousand yrs
of bad news.

vi

muhammed? a rewrite man for d wrong daily
news. messenger for cons of d pharaohs court.
perry mason to moses d murderer & thief. pr man
for d prophets of SET. as for poets? chapt
26 my friends—check it out. it is all there in
icewater clear.

ghandi? middleclass lawyer stuck on himself.
freed d brahmins so they cd sip tea & hate cows.
lenins pants didnt fit too good,
people couldnt smoke in front of him, on d
train to petrograd he gv them passes to go
to d head.

d new houngans are to d left of buck rogers,
ok buck up w/ yr hands. where did u stash
our galaxies?

vii

bulletin

                to d one who put our
art on a line. now odd shapes will nibble u.
its our turn to put u thru changes. to drop
dour walter winchells on u like, i predict
that tomorrow yr hands will be stiff. to d
one who gaggd a poet. hants will eat yr
cornflakes. golfballs will swell in yr jaws at noon.
horrid masks will gape thru yr window at dusk. it will
be an all day spectacular. look out now,
it is already beginning. to d one who strongarmd
a painter. hear d noise climbing yr steps? u will

be its horse. how does that grab u? how come u
pull d sheets over yr head? & last & least o cactus
for brains. u muggd a playwright, berkeley cal.
spring 68. we hv yr photos. lots of them. what
was that u just spat/up
a lizard or a spider?

viii

spelling out my business i hv gone
indoors. raking d coals over my liver,
listening to my stories w/ yng widow
brown, talking up a trash in bars (if
i feel up to it). doing all those things put down
in that odor of hog doodoo printd as
a poem in black fire. i caught d whiff of yr
stink thou sow w/ mud for thots. d next
round is on me. black halloween on d rocks.
straight no chaser.

down d hatch d spooks will fly / some
will thrive & some will die / by these
rattles in our hands / mighty spirits
will shake d land.

so excuse me while i do d sooner toomer.
jean that is. im gone schooner to a meta
physical country. behind d eyes. im gone be.
a rootarmd ravenheaded longbeard im gone be.
a zigaboo jazzer teaching mountain
lions of passion how to truck.

ix

goodhomefolks gave me ishmael. how
did they know he was d 'afflictd one'?

carrying a gag in his breast pocket. giving
d scene a scent of snowd under w/ bedevilment.
i am d mad mad scientist in love w/ d dark.
d villagers dont understand me. here they come
with their torches. there goes a rock
thru d window. i hv time for a few more hobbies:
making d cab drivers dream of wotan
cutting out pictures of paper murderers
like d ol woman w/ d yng face
or is it d yng woman w/ d ol face?
take yr pick. put it to my chest.
watch it bend. its all a big punchline
i share w/ u. to keep u in stitches.
& ull be so wise when their showstopper
comes:

> this is how yr ears shd feel
> this is what u shd eat
> this is who u shd sleep w/
> this is how u shd talk
> this is how u shd write
> this is how u shd paint
> these dances are d best
> these films are d best
> this is how u shd groom yrself
> these are d new gods we made for u

u are a bucket of feces before them.
we know what is best for u. bend down
& kiss some wood.
make love to leather. if u
dont u will be offd

x

& d cannd laughter will fade &
d dirty chickens will fly his coop
for he was just a geek u see.
o houngans of america—post this on yr
temples.

DO YR ART D WAY U WANT
ANYWAY U WANT
ANY WANGOL U WANT
ITS UP TO U / WHAT WILL WORK
FOR U.

so sez d neoamerican hoodoo
church of free spirits who
need no
monarch
no gunghoguru
no busybody ray frm d heddahopper planet
of wide black hats & stickpins. he was
just a 666* frm a late late show &
only d clucks threw pennies

*false prophet of the apocalypse.

The Perils of Newspaper Literacy

Richard Kostelanetz

A prime blight of serious political discussion in this country is newspaper literacy, which is to say that too much talk and writing reveals facts and awarenesses gleaned largely, if not exclusively, from daily newspapers. The surest sign of newspaper literacy is a sense of worldly significance reflecting a journalistic distribution of emphases, particularly with the inference that the lead stories on the front page report the most important occurrences of the moment.

Newspapers have one major deficiency as a source of information—quite simply, they function to record what happened *yesterday*. The nature of the medium's operation favors events that began after today's editions appeared and will conclude before tomorrow's go to press. Preferably an event should take no more than a few hours, so a reporter can witness its entire duration; yet it should provide sufficient information ("news") for a full-length story. A baseball game, a press conference, a theater opening, a brief military operation are all ideal newspaper stories. Even though the event may lack particular importance, the experienced journalist has usually developed a "flair" for creating the impression of significance—after all, no newspaper wants dull, or blank, columns. Television news programming also has an essentially *jour*nalistic emphasis, mediumistic (and sensory) differences, notwithstanding, for the wrap-up at eleven aims to present the "news of the day."

Fittingly, a well-staged and enthusiastically publicized polit-

From *The Humanist* (July–August, 1971). Copyright © 1971 by Richard Kostelanetz. By permission of the author and publisher.

ical demonstration which has no practical effect usually makes more news than the day-after-day activities of field workers; and, for this reason, some political groups and individuals have been known to initiate occasional displays of themselves simply to verify their public existence. Senator Joseph McCarthy, as Richard Rovere describes him, had an extraordinary talent for concocting such pseudo-events as, for instance, calling a morning press conference to announce that there would be an important disclosure in the afternoon, thereby providing the afternoon papers with an enticing headline. "Newspapers do not choose to distort," notes Leslie A. Fiedler; "they simply do not know how not to."

Reporters are habitually responsive to such organs of publicity and to voices that seemingly resound in chorus (though, of course, they also decide which ones *not* to hear); so that what appears in print as passionate public interest often turns out to be a journalistic creation built not upon outright dishonesty but upon the medium's innate capacity for fabricating interest in the course of innocently "reporting the news." Once an individual or group achieves notoriety, it develops a vested interest in preserving its life against the threatening death of public disappearance. Thus, to public figures and the like, making something reportable happen every day creates an illusion of significant activity, although the real events often consist of nothing more than fabricating, transmitting, and publishing the newspaper copy. The rule here is not *cogito ergo sum*, but *ergo sum* because my (our) name appears regularly in print.

What takes a week or longer to happen is more appropriately the stuff of magazines; yet serious periodicals in this country exemplify the deficiencies of newspaper literacy, perhaps because (as many writers have noticed) most political editors spend more time scanning newspapers than books or other sources of information. Even book publishers, one observes, feel obliged to read newspapers dutifully—"to know what's happening" is their rationalization. A reporter might be assigned to summarize important long-term developments in, say, a scientific field; but given the newspaper's limitations in space and expository style, this report is inevitably too short, superficial, and simplistic, if not trivialized and misleading as well, no matter how fine the knowledge or intentions of the reporter. With all this in mind, it is scarcely cheering to learn that Americans devote, on the average, fifty minutes each day to perusing newspapers.

Newspaper literacy is pernicious, because the events prominently featured in the daily press are not necessarily fundamental in the contemporary world; and certain events persistently emphasized are, in the ultimate analysis, part of larger, more significant political tendencies developing over longer periods of time. At their worst, newspapers emphasize yesterday's scandalous and frivolous occurrences—the murder in Brooklyn, the marriage of a luminary (his third, her second); but the better papers, even the great *New York Times,* are not immune from the limited perspective intrinsic in daily journalism itself.

Persistent reading of *The Times* in the late 1960s and early 1970s would lead one to believe that the war in Vietnam was the most significant contemporary activity; for nearly every day, the lead story, as well as at least one other on the front page, reported events relating to the war. *The Times* coverage created a hierarchy of emphasis that has informed its own Sunday magazine, other magazines of opinion, and even discussions among "radicals."

If we take a larger view of contemporary phenomena, however, what are the standards for regarding the Vietnam war as so important? It does not inflict more human damage per day than curable diseases or automobile and household accidents. As a dimension of foreign policy, U. S. engagements in Vietnam are entwined in such larger issues as the purposes and limits of our involvements abroad; it is less a cancer than a festering sore symptomatic of systemic malaise. "Winning" the war itself is patently not a primary desire of either the U. S. or the U. S. S. R. or China, as practically nothing outside the field of immediate conflict will rise or fall on tomorrow's actions. The most immediate measure of the war's historical unimportance is the sense that both sides have implicitly agreed to fight it out at less than maximal levels; hence, it is no more likely to escalate into nuclear holocaust than are several other tension points.

My point here is not that the war is acceptable—definitely

not—but that policy discussions based on newspaper literacy
obscure its larger context. Even the possibility of "pulling
out" is entwined in a larger issue—namely, in the question
of when the U. S. need no longer honor entangling alliances. Journalistic emphasis upon the small problem, needless to say, postpones necessary discussion and decision on
the larger one. Therefore, those who think that ending this
war is our greatest aim have one thing in common with
those who favor its continuance at all costs—a myopic view
of its contemporary significance. Indeed, the history of journalistic overemphasis partially explains why objections to
Vietnam serve to unify a great diversity of dissenters; poor
Spiro Agnew was not unperceptive in blaming the press for
current protests, no matter how much he misunderstood how
journalism influences, or what might be done about its mysterious power.

Why does the war get so much attention in the press?
The battles of one day are hardly different from the skir-
mishes of the next, while decisively new revelations are few
and far between; and I doubt if many people read Vietnam
stories regularly. The primary reason seems to be that wars
are the kinds of events particularly appropriate to the processing capabilities of newspapers. There also seems to be
a tradition holding that each one, no matter how distant
or inconsequential, should receive amounts of space pro-
portional to the degree of American involvement.

The dominance of newspaper literacy explains why significant developments that happen over a year's or a decade's
time take so long to penetrate political discussion, or why
many prolonged tendencies still remain invisible to the reportorial eye. Social discrimination, for instance, was not
"news" until certain publicists discovered its existence for
newspapers; the same was true of poverty or "ecology" in
America. The impression of 1969 offered by the *Britannica
Book of the Year*, say, is considerably different, especially
in its distribution of emphases, from that found in 365 issues
of the *New York Times*.

Journalistic language also corrupts wordly understanding;
for example, the phrase "Negro problem" and its variants
obscures the fact that the predicaments of colored peoples

are, as human problems, 80 per cent similar to those of noncolored Americans—the earning of a decent livelihood, preservation of the public peace, providing a better future for one's children, making ends meet, and so on. The social issue here is really discrimination, which includes more factors than race. It afflicts the very young and the very old, the lonely, the handicapped, and the culturally deprived; and racial inequalities so emphasized in the press will be most thoroughly and equitably alleviated by ecumenical social policies that transcend race or sex. "Another disadvantage of fallacious problems," perceives Jorge Luis Borges, "is that they bring about solutions that are equally fallacious."

"In our information-ridden world," notes Herbert A. Simon, "it becomes especially necessary to distinguish between fundamental and transient knowledge." Where do we learn of such long-term and continuing realities as the population explosion, new developments in agriculture, the revolutionary possibilities implicit in molecular biology, more extensive uses of the computer, the information explosion, new knowledge about man and the environment, the generation gap, the extent of pollution, the development of better methods of mechanical control, and so on? About such realities there is, and will be, unquestionably more pertinent information in books than in newspapers.

By neglecting currents that do not gush to the surface daily, newspapers encourage a superficial view of contemporary reality, providing a pathetically inadequate base upon which to build a knowledgeable and comprehensive political awareness, let alone a radical vision. Myself, I hardly read newspapers, not only because much of their information is redundant—a rehash of the background I could have (but did not) read before—but also because, as someone committed to long-term radical change, I am not particularly interested in only what happened yesterday.

Gay News & the *Times*:
an Indelicate Balance

Stuart Byron

"That's the most tortured subway poster I've ever seen!" said a straight friend of mine about the Gay Activists Alliance's catalog of sins against the *New York Times*'s coverage of gay news which is now plastered across the Manhattan subway system. And as one of the composers of that document, how could I disagree? We agonized for hours over each word.

I happen to believe that the *Times* practices discrimination against gay news, both of *de jure* and *de facto* varieties (a distinction I'll explore below). But how to explain that to a gay community so large (some 500,000 strong) and yet so long hidden and so long oppressed that it considers it a major victory every time the word "homosexual" is mentioned in print? How to explain that despite Merle Miller's Sunday *Times* magazine piece—for all its inadequacies still the most pro-gay article ever to appear in a mass medium —and Michael Kotis's Op-Ed page contribution of February 19, the *Times* has been censoring and hiding important gay news?

"Media oppression," as we know from the fact that some of gay lib's most celebrated actions have been against periodicals (San Francisco *Examiner, Village Voice, Time, Harper's*), is one of the key issues of the homophile move-

From *The Village Voice* (April 1, 1971). Copyright © 1971 by The Village Voice, Inc. By permission of *The Village Voice* and the author.

ment. I should like to divide the movement's complaints against the *Times* into three categories, and to discuss them in *ascending* order of importance: (1) the "features" about homosexuality which have run in the *Times* since last June's gay-in in Central Park, and their relationship to each other; (2) incidents of blatant anti-gay discrimination at the *Times;* and (3) a pattern of downplaying of gay news and available feature material at the *Times* which, giving the paper every benefit of every doubt, I will assume results not so much from *conscious* discrimination as from a situation which is at the very heart of homosexual oppression itself.

(1) Miller's "What It Means to Be a Homosexual" in the January 17 [1971] Sunday magazine was, for all its faults, a major breakthrough. But the effect of this article was nullified, and even overturned, by the *Times* management's allowing a reporter in its midst to "use" the Miller piece to con them into allowing her to write a couple of long-time "dream" articles. The reference, of course, is to Jane E. Brody and her two stories, "Homosexuality: Parents Aren't Always To Blame" of February 10, which presented a supposed accounting of newly found "causes" of homosexuality, and "More Homosexuals Aided To Become Heterosexual" of February 28, which detailed the "cures" for homosexuality offered by such psychiatrists as Irving Bieber and Lawrence J. Hatterer.

Despite occasional quotes from shrinks in more general stories on homosexuality, the *Times* had not printed any major story on the anti-gay "specialist" therapists ("brainwashers" might be the better word) since April 1964, when the Bieber "results" were reported. But all this time, it appears, Mrs. Brody was waiting in the wings for her opportunity. For five years, she had been asking her editors for permission to do a couple of features on the gay cure shrinks. And for five years they had turned her down.

But then Merle Miller dwelt at some length on his experiences with shrinks, declaring that they had done nothing for him during those periods when he wanted to "go straight," and implying that they never do anything for anybody on that score. He blithely stated that no one knows what "causes" homosexuality and the only shrinks he quoted were such friends of gays as George Weinberg and Martin Hoffman.

According to well-informed sources, Brody confronted her bosses with the Miller article. After eight years they had allowed one "side" to be heard from and therefore they had no right to deny her space for the "other" side. Some doctors say there are causes and some say they can cure it, etc. And so her editors at last acquiesced to her, out of "fairness."

But let us examine this "fairness" in its true light. The Miller piece was in the magazine section, reserved for non-staff opinion. It was written in a personal, confessional tone, full of first-person sentences and half sentences, and in no way pretended to reportorial professionalism. The Brody articles, on the other hand, appeared in the main news section, meaning that they gave off an air of "objective" reporting. And they were hardly that.

Parents, Mrs. Brody informed us in the first article, don't necessarily deserve the *"blame"* for homosexuality and a child can resist "even the *worst* combination of influences." And for her ending there was quoted a supposed "former homosexual" who related how "I began to *grow up.*" (Italics mine.) In her second diatribe, Hatterer and Bieber were taken completely at their word and all of the reports which question their results were unresearched or conveniently omitted. As a shirttail to her second piece, Brody did acknowledge that the "sickness" of homosexuals is under "sharp debate" in the profession but she quoted the sickness proponents *first* and the sickness opponents in "sickness terms" ("The Gay Liberation movement is the best therapy the homosexual has had in years").

So a pattern is clear. Four "features" on homosexuality in the *Times* since the gay-in (during which time the movement has made newsworthy strides); the "anti-gay" ones were granted the solemnity of the news columns, while the "pro-gay" and movement stories were co-opted into such "opinion" sections as the magazine and the Op-Ed page. And as for the last-named—Michael Kotis's February 19 piece

—it should be noted that, while no gay liberationist could take exception to most of it, Kotis confined his argument to the fact that homosexuality is "normal," "moral," and "healthy." No mention, therefore, of the militant stance which characterizes the new homosexual and which has caused the formation of such groups as Gay Liberation Front and Gay Activists Alliance. Many of my straight friends were puzzled by this first Op-Ed appearance of the movement, which the *Times* had the co-opting effrontery to entitle "Homosexual Militance" ("But we've known all that for years. I still don't know what gay liberation *means*").

(2) Turner Catledge's *My Life and the Times* reveals that "several factors" were in Punch Sulzberger's mind when he made the decision to fire Stanley Kauffmann as drama critic several years ago, but the first one Catledge mentions is that Punch's "mother was deeply disturbed by an article Kauffman had written about homosexuals in the theatre."

In the February 15 edition of *The Newsletter*, Harry Smith's underground publishing trade paper, it is revealed that the *Times* recently turned down the following ad: "For a copy of America's most respected homosexual magazine, complete with up-to-date book review, send $1 to Tangents."

Reports Smith: "After reviewing the ruling, (Advertising) Acceptability's John Furey told TN: 'It attracts people of that persuasion. . . . It was targeted at homosexuals, not the general public, whereas ads for such performances as *Boys in the Band* and *Staircase* are acceptable because they are aimed at the public, not any particular group.'" And yet, a few days after the second Brody piece, there appeared a huge book page ad for Hatterer's *Changing Homosexuality in the Male* (McGraw-Hill), which was directly pitched at: "those 2,500,000 homosexuals who want to change." Apparently it's okay to aim at a "particular group" only in a certain way; you can recruit heterosexuals, but not homosexuals.

(3) On January 12, I was part of a group of five GAA members, headed by Marty Robinson, who met for an hour

and a half with Marvin Siegel, an assistant to *Times* metropolitan editor Arthur Gelb. Our immediate complaint was
Times coverage of the gay role in the 1970 election. For
the first time ever in New York history, the position of
candidates on gay rights had been solicited, and GAA had
prepared a press release with their responses to a list of
specific questions—the favorable replies by Goldberg, Ot-
tinger, Goodell, Koch, Abzug, and others; the "no replies"
of Rockefeller, Buckley, etc.

GAA was trying to do something well within the mainstream of American politics. Previously, homosexuals had
voted pretty much as did the general population—but this
had been because candidates rarely had anything to say
about their rights and so gays were forced to decide their
votes on other bases. But certain events of the recent past
had indicated that gays, even though unorganized, did respond to certain candidates whom they identified with their
"special interest." Though it was almost never mentioned
in the press, it seemed to many that gays, voting as a bloc,
had made major contributions to Alioto's victories in San
Francisco and Lindsay's in New York, and that the identification in gay minds of Robert Wagner with antihomo-
sexual policies had perhaps been the unreported and key
"missing factor" that could explain his "upset" defeat in the
Democratic mayoral primary of 1969.

The GAA questionnaire, and distribution of its results,
was, then, the first attempt to *organize* as a bloc the votes
of New York's (and America's) "second largest minority."
The *Times* didn't run anything for several days until, finally,
there appeared a three-inch "news box" on the political jump
pages in the back. From people we trusted within GAA,
and from reliable sources at the *Times*, we had good reason
to believe that the story had originally been intended for
front-page appearance but had been metamorphosed to its
final form via orders from upstairs.

Since the election, the *Times* "brown-out"—or worse—
of gay news has continued. The introduction of the Clingan-
Burden-Scholnick-Weiss fair employment bill? Page three in
the *Post*, an amusement page filler in the *Times*. Pre-filing
of the gay civil rights bills in Albany, actual introduction of

them, and the march in Albany by gays in support of them? All given major coverage in the *Post,* and in most important upstate dailies, but as far as I know there's been not a single word of the state effort printed so far in the *Times.*

Instances of inaccurate and biased reporting abound, of which the most recent was that of Homer Bigart of the "zap" of Goldberg by three dozen gays, none of whom brought along his pet, during a campaign stop on 85 Street and Broadway last June. The incident, which I witnessed, included ten minutes of intense questioning of the candidate and the writing of "Gay Power" on his surrounded car, but was reduced by Bigart to what seemed like a minute-long harassment of Goldberg by a handful of gays, the most prominent of whom was "with a poodle."

There is, I think, a key to not only the *Times* problem but all that "media oppression" with which the gay movement is so incessantly concerned. Let me single out two facts: (*a*) every homosexual can "hide" his homosexuality, and, until and unless he is liberated, he will, and (*b*) every heterosexual can be suspected of homosexuality and wants to avoid that implication.

I've spent most of my working life in journalism and press relations, so I've seen how that operates in that field. I've seen and experienced it in myself and watched it operate in others, gay and straight. Any gay reporter or editor who takes an unusual interest in gay news or knows what it means or recognizes its importance is giving himself away. Any straight reporter or editor who does any of these or who doesn't temper his reporting with comments about poodles or suchlike sissy things is inviting suspicion. So little gets reported (and so we continue oppressed).

In view of this situation, the *Times* cannot exercise honest "news judgment" on gay matters, and thus de facto discrimination and bias result. Let me cite two instances— the one that began our movement and the most recent event in it. From the beginning the *Times* has misreported or underreported what's happened. It can hardly be doubted now that the Stonewall riots [against attempted police harassment and arrest] of June 1969 constituted the most significant event in American homosexual history—of all time. It was covered by the *Times* via half-column stories buried deep inside. At the same time—the very same time—huge front-page stories day after day related how some vigilantes in Queens had cut down some trees at a homosexual cruising area. Needless to say, the importance of the two stories was in inverse ratio to their placement. Stonewall was an extraordinary event and belonged on page one; the tree-cutting was a minor disturbance requiring minor coverage.

Siegel agreed at our January 12 meeting. It was possible to see how the *Times* had misjudged the import of Stonewall, how it had not understood at the time that a "movement" had begun. But wasn't this hindsight? And he didn't believe us when we told him that to a man we *knew* at the time that Stonewall was an ominous event, that homosexual life in America and our own lives would never be the same again. And that we knew—and could only know— because we were gay. You have to be gay to know just what "coming out" in public meant, how protesting in the streets and risking still and television camera exposure and police arrest was something entirely different and new.

More recently, 2500 gays marched in Albany, and you read about it in the *Voice* and you read about it in the *Post* and you didn't read about it in the *Times*. Why? Probably because the Albany man told them that 2500 isn't much in Albany terms, that there are sixteen to twenty Capitol demonstrations a week during the legislative season, that just a few days before that there were 4000 nurses protesting the closing of a nursing college upstate and before that 5000 welfare mothers. But unless that Albany man or his editor (Arthur Gelb) has some gay to advise him, he can't realize that 2500 is equivalent to 25,000 because "coming out" in public still involves so much risk, and so the fact that there's any demonstration or lobbying *at all* is astounding. When you march for nursing or march for peace you're just expressing a political opinion; when you march for gay rights you're taking (most of you) your life and career and family relations in your hands. And only a gay *knows* that, and only an open gay can thus contribute that "sixth sense" that goes into "news judgment." Once it is understood how the peculiarly "hidden" nature of homosexual oppression affects journalism, there are two possible solutions to the problem.

The first is to have gay news done only by reporters who are openly gay. There's some precedent on the *Times* for this, inasmuch as women do the basic reporting of women's news and there are blacks, Orientals, and Latins assigned to keep an eye on news of those minority groups in the city. Based on their familiarity with their groups and the fact that they could be trusted with tips and leads, such reporters as Thomas Johnson and Frank Ching have done some wonderful stuff in the *Times* lately on the Harlem numbers racket and on immigration agency harassment of Chinese aliens. There are fantastic stories to be told about how 10 percent of this city's population relates to the Mafia and to law enforcement officials, but there is no one on the *Times* to whom gay people could feed information on such stories without fearing Bigartry and Brodyism. It would be nice for someone at the *Times* to come out of the closet to his editors, at the very least so that they could have some fair method of judging the importance of any given piece of homosexual news; this is unlikely, however, since, as far as I can tell, the *Times* is so uptight about gayness that most of the gays there don't even know *who each other* are.

That being the case, the *Times*, as a second solution, could assign some (courageous) straights to the beat, as has the *Post*. To prove my point, I might add that one of these, Barry Cunningham, was so astounded to discover how unreported and misreported was not only a "movement" but also a whole *life* and subculture of an oppressed minority that he has been able to get a whole book out of his assignment.

Postscript: After the above was written, there appeared in last Sunday's *Times* magazine an article by staffer Judy Klemesrud on the lesbian organization Daughters of Bilitis. According to DOB president Ruth Simpson, "Judy's article was completed and then her editors insisted she interview some psychologists in order to include the 'other side.'"

Thus the *Times'* "fairness" policy: nobody apparently asked Jane Brody to immerse herself in gay life or talk to homosexuals in order to "balance" the views of the doctors. In such a psychological context did some important political events in the gay movement first reach *Times* readers; presumably three months from now those readers will learn about the Albany march in some magazine piece questioning the sanity of gays. It's as if you couldn't do a story on black life or civil rights in the *Times* without interviewing those few antiblack zoologists on the genetic differences between Negroes and Caucasians.

Doctor Feelgood

Susan Wood

The first Dr. Feelgoods practiced in Europe in the 1930s
and left their imprint in the annals of dubious medical practice by injecting amphetamines into the veins of the leaders
of the Third Reich. Their disciples have since spread throughout the world.

Nobody can say exactly how many Dr. Feelgoods now
practice in New York City. Fashionable people—that is,
those who get their names in the papers from time to time—
seem to go to just four or five of them, including one who
is said by his admiring patients to have attended President
Kennedy and some of the nation's best-known politicians,
businessmen, and entertainers.

Regardless of which Dr. Feelgood has the most promi-
nence at the moment—fashions change—each patient, aglow
with the incredible zap of his latest shot, is sure his doctor
alone is the real Dr. Feelgood. But each Dr. Feelgood has
at least two things in common with the next—a persuasive
personality and a lucrative practice.

Their offices tend to be located conveniently close to where
the bulk of their patients live—near, if not on, Park and
Fifth Avenues from the Fifties to the Nineties. One Dr.
Feelgood, not unlike Elizabeth Arden and Saks, ran a summer
branch in the Hamptons for a while. Another currently in
vogue also fixes teeth.

With injections in veins or buttocks, Dr. Feelgood can

From *New York* Magazine (February 8, 1971). Copyright ©
1971 by the NYM Corporation. By permission of the author and
New York Magazine.

cure everything: the common cold, pimples, infectious hepatitis, impotence, alcoholism, heroin addiction . . . his followers swear. They firmly believe their doctor can delay aging. One Dr. Feelgood claims dramatic results in cases of arthritis and multiple sclerosis.

Unfortunately, Dr. Feelgood doesn't publish the kind of research papers that enable scientists to verify his work. Ordinary doctors and scientists working to find cures on grants from, say, the Multiple Sclerosis Foundation or the Arthritis Foundation are not impressed with Dr. Feelgood's approach and continue their research along other lines.

The majority of his practice flock to him not for the sake of research but to find relief from what one observer calls "environmental and executive diseases." The symptoms range from low-grade malaise to intense anxiety. The patient goes to him in response to an inner call. Some go daily. Most go three times a week. Appointments are not necessary; the patient need only show up during office hours, which tend to be long. One Dr. Feelgood has a 6 a.m. to 10 a.m. session for the early birds. Another, who caters to a show-biz crowd, has been known to be in his office after midnight.

His patients are for the most part intelligent, educated, talented, affluent achievers. But their very intelligence and income seem to deny them the protection less fortunate souls get from our medical watchdogs. Many public health officials think Dr. Feelgood's practice is questionable, even dangerous, but they don't appear to regard it as an urgent problem. As one public health doctor put it: "It only affects a small segment of our population—the very rich. We can only do so much. Our priorities start with protecting those who don't know better, like slum kids eating paint peelings."

But Dr. Feelgood's patients regard him as an altruist . . . a Dr. Schweitzer of the urban jungle.

I began to look into the Dr. Feelgood phenomenon several years ago because I thought he and his patients added up to a good story about a special New York scene. To get into that scene I would become a patient—for a few visits anyway. I realized that this would involve letting a doctor and chemicals play with my psyche and my health. A few years earlier I might have regarded this as a violation. A few years later I would surely regard it as a risk. But at the time, I had no special concern about making myself a guinea pig. I saw taking Dr. Feelgood's shots as not only essential to the story but as a chance to get a better notion of the drug generation, an opportunity at last, laggard that I was, to have a drug experience safely—with a doctor in charge. Also, I had a lot of time to try new things; my marriage had just come apart.

New York Magazine underwrote the expense of several visits to three practitioners I had heard about through friends and gossip. Not long after I began the story, arrangements were made with the then brand-new narcotics laboratory of the New York County Medical Examiner's office to run tests on me after I received the shots.

My first encounter was with a doctor whom I shall call Doctor A. I was taken by a friend, a regular patient, who assured me that Doctor A's shots were harmless and would merely initiate me into the modern world and good life of the hip, the rich, and the beautiful. The only reason other doctors don't mete out similar shots, my friend told me, is that conventional medical men are too puritanical to dispense drugs that simply make you feel good.

Doctor A's office occupies about half of the ground floor of an old mansion. On the street near his door, when I arrived, were a pair of double-parked Cadillacs. One had M.D. plates and was, I later learned, the doctor's. The other had a stack of parking tickets piled visibly on the dashboard inside the car. A policeman was placing yet another ticket between the wiper and the windshield. The scofflaw Cadillac, it turned out, belonged to one of Doctor A's patients, a 22-year-old oil heir who was then in the doctor's waiting room. He looked like a nervous little frog decked out in a superbly tailored suit. He and a half-dozen sartorially splendid young men formed a golden circle of rich kids around a low table. In that group, too, were two girls, one a former fashion editor, the other the youthful star of a then-current Broadway musical. They were the other halves of couples who "took together."

Beyond the fringes of that golden circle were a half-dozen other patients scattered on various chairs who looked quite different. Huddled into herself was an utterly blank-faced girl, the picture of alienation, who, my friend told me, was a Playboy Club bunny. In a corner two aging women wearing identical black leather jackets out of a 42nd Street rough-trade store, chino slacks, and Keds sat on a bench holding hands. There was also a freaky mulatto man of indeterminable age who upon entering pranced about the waiting room striking dueling poses with a cane until a nurse appeared and shouted at him. He responded by instantly sitting down, like a dog who had just heard his master's command. For beautiful people, Doctor A's patients seemed a mixed bag.

Perhaps four other patients were being treated in the examining rooms, I learned, while about a dozen of us waited. After almost an hour's wait, a crisp nurse in starchy white, who directed the flow from room to room, finally waved the oil heir, my friend, and me into one of the treatment rooms. We perched on a long examining table, our legs dangling, like three kids on a country fence. That seemed the proper spirit.

"Well, well, my children . . . ." I heard Doctor A before I saw him. My eyes had been fixed on the other of two doors at opposite ends of the examining room and, when I turned around, there before me was a Slenderella Santa Claus, a cheerful, well-proportioned man with white hair, merry eyes, and an avuncular manner. "Are you about to go off for a nice weekend?" he said. And for me, after being introduced, there was a gentle hug.

I followed him into a large office carefully done in Airport Modern. There he registered no surprise when, although I wasn't fat in the least, I said that I had come because I wanted to lose some weight. (My friend had suggested I say this.) He waved me to a scale and noted my weight.

He then had me take a chair next to his desk. He drew up another chair to take my pulse, blood pressure, listen to my heart, and ask about my racial origins. Doctor A had some interesting notions about blood. To have European blood is good, he said. Eastern European blood may be all right, but not so good as German and French. A Celtic strain is fraught with physiological peril—a weakness for alcohol, the real killer. Did I drink, and how much?

Doctor A then filled a large syringe with a liquid mixture assembled from bottles clearly labeled as various vitamins and minerals. We sat very close, my knees between his. He gripped my arm below the elbow with one hand and with the other found a vein instantly. I saw my own blood float into the pink fluid in the syringe. Ever so slowly, he pushed the whole mixture into my bloodstream.

His large warm eyes looked deep into mine. His voice was gentle. I remember him saying what a nice fellow the guy who brought me was. The rest was lost to me in the incredible warmth that suffused me, glowed within me, and billowed against the limits of my skin and beyond. Click! Muscles bunched at the top of my neck loosened, and now I was dropping thirty floors in the Pan Am elevator and spinning on in an undulating thrill marked not by fear but by a kind of orgasm. By all physical signs I was, as Masters and Johnson describe it, "on the final plateau of arousal."

The syringe was empty, Doctor A slowly withdrew it, and I almost dropped in a slow-moving heap in his arms. Gently, gently, he applied a small Band-Aid to the puncture in my arm and retreated behind his desk.

"Losing weight is mostly a matter of diet," he purred, "but this does help a bit." He looked at me knowingly, as if waiting for me to say something. It all seemed—the whole meaning of the shot—brilliantly clear. My heart raced.

"Reward principle," I said, feeling sure he knew what I meant, "very clever. But my heart! Are you sure it's all right?"

"Yes, yes," he replied. "You're just a little excited."

As I got ready to leave, I blurted out something that had been gathering in my mind: "Are you sure you are doing the right thing for all those neurotic kids out there?" Never had I felt so sure of an insight, so intelligent. I felt like Superman, as if I were ripping off my timid-girl disguise to reveal the real, powerful me. "Shouldn't they be getting analyzed instead of a shot in the arm?" Hardly stopping for breath, I went on about how great it feels and began mumbling something about in the long run, and . . . and . . . I was, in fact, running off at the mouth.

Doctor A cut me off, saying, "Trust. Trust Papa. He knows what he's doing. If there's a physical symptom, there's a physical condition—and a medicine to deal with it." He gave me a paternal kiss on the cheek and a final word. "Don't worry about all this," he said. "Have fun and I'll see you when you get back."

Time remained elusive throughout the rest of the day. Floating sensations alternated with moments of unprecedented decisiveness and confidence. Relaxed, happy, I went on a buying spree at Gucci. Money meant practically nothing. I was absolutely sure I could pick up extra free-lance jobs to pay for anything I wanted to buy.

The sensual kick of the shot lasted only about six hours. But my euphoria extended through the weekend. I went to Fire Island. Late Sunday night the only adverse reactions I was aware of were neck glands a bit tender and a slight feeling of fatigue. But that could have been the late hours I had kept and the rigors of a Sunday night drive from Long Island to Manhattan in summer traffic.

On Monday, I found myself seated once more on a chair facing Doctor A. He looked into my eyes and asked how I felt.

"Terrific," I said.

"Well, then, you don't need anything," he replied evenly. I had the uneasy feeling that he could read my mind. He seemed to sense that I was ambivalent about continuing. He seemed to want me to express more eagerness before he would suggest doing anything more. I wanted more, but I also liked the idea of just dropping the whole thing. I suppose I just looked slightly dumbfounded.

"I see people who drink a lot and exhaust themselves," he said, without any further prompting. "Some are alcoholics, some have been drug addicts, some overeat. Most overindulge in many ways and all abuse their bodies.

"All this," he went on, with a casual wave, almost a salute, to his office, "helps them, but I do more than simply help medically. I'm like a conscience for my patients. I scold them. I make them adhere to at least one discipline—coming here within the prescribed hours. I talk to them and listen to their troubles. One patient was punishing himself for being a homosexual and I encouraged him to admit to it and value himself anyway. I'm not like Doctor ———— [another Feelgood], who is evil. He addicts his patients to things. I don't."

I was puzzled. I said, "Are you saying you don't use. . . ."

"I give amphetamines when I think it necessary," he interjected smoothly, "but not all the time." He seemed suddenly to remember all the patients in his waiting room. With the impatience one might show with naughty children pestering for ice cream, he blurted: "Oh, it's always one thing or another. First it was pot they wanted, and now it's meth. This fuss over it is a lot of nonsense. All it does is make them feel a little stimulated."

As he talked, he was ushering me out of his office. He clearly had no intention of giving me another shot. He had sensed my wariness. A good patient, I began to think, wouldn't have felt terrific by Monday.

I began speaking to friends about the shots. I was astonished to learn how many not only had heard about them but had actually experienced them.

There seemed to be two groups. One was composed of middle-aged, old-guard intellectuals who said they had gone to a Dr. Feelgood for their work, to get more work out of their brains. Few of them seemed aware, or would admit, that the shots were a turn-on.

But the second group, an under-thirty crowd, thought of their doctors mainly as a legal source for zappo highs— the top of a mountain where establishment and hip meet. Their elders talked mainly of the vitamin ingredients of the shots that promoted health, work, and other virtues. The younger speedsters talked mainly, excitedly, about the amphetamine content of each syringe. The vitamin or other content mattered, if it mattered at all, only as they speculated on its ability to provide new kicks. Regardless of age, they all saw the shots as tomorrow's medicine here today and a mind-expanding extravaganza that had to be good, for it *was* medicine.

I decided to go on with the reporting. This wasn't just a story about some rich-kid speed freaks getting legal jolts. It was about some of New York's most attractive and accomplished people developing a habit. If I was to return to Doctor A and get to others, however, my editors and I decided that for my own protection, for reasons of both health and law, some tests should be run to determine what I was getting in my shots. If I were to report that there was amphetamine in a shot I had received, I had better be able to prove it. The drug had only recently been placed on the Food and Drug Administration's dangerous drug list. Tests for vitamin and hormone levels, it turned out, were staggeringly expensive and not especially reliable. However, reliable tests to determine the presence of narcotics, barbiturates, and amphetamines were available. Therefore, urine specimens were analyzed from time to time at the Medical Examiner's toxicology lab on First Avenue and 31 Street, considered one of the best in the country.

"Of course I'll take care of you," Doctor A said with fatherly warmth when I saw him again. "I thought you didn't want me." This time when the needle pierced my flesh I momentarily feared that I was starting something I might never want to stop but. . . . Oh! there was that fantastic warmth spreading through me again.

I had planned to stop in two weeks. But I had a sudden bout of intestinal trouble that could be cured, Doctor A told me, by daily shots during a two-week period. There were other odds and ends of medical problems that I ordinarily might have brought to my own doctor, but I would think, "What the hell, for the same price I can feel great immmediately."

There were days, including one gloomy Sunday, when I felt down. A few drinks might have been the conventional recourse, but it was just as easy to hop into a cab and visit Doctor A and have him take care of it. All told, through a ninety-day period, I had twenty-two injections.

During those three months, I never knew exactly what went into each injection cocktail. But the injectables were clearly labeled and stacked in large supply in each of Doctor A's examining and treatment rooms. Massed and ready for use on all the work tables were hormones, vitamin B complexes, vitamin C, iron, calcium gluconate, procaine hydrochloride, the antidepressant Tofrānil, Benadryl, and methamphetamine. A toxicologist I later consulted told me that methamphetamine, calcium gluconate, and procaine hydrochloride are valued in some quarters for their ability to create sensations of euphoria.

Of six shots I had tested in the three months, two proved positive for amphetamine, another showed an indication of it, and three showed none present. (The tests on barbiturate and narcotic content were negative.) The fact that no meth showed up in a test did not preclude the possibility that there *was* some in that shot. Toxicologists say there is a 15 percent chance of error in such tests. Moreover, the body can metabolize enough of the drug to prevent detection of small amounts.

Doctor A was not a cold clinician. We would exchange confidences all the time, the doctor and me. He would tell me of small burdens and minor irritations, or of petty betrayals and his transient losses of faith in people. I had the same kind of problems and found him utterly sympathetic.

When I was sloppy, he would suggest tenderly that I tidy up—such a pity for a pretty girl not to look her best. He would tell stories and jokes whose moral was that life should be enjoyed. The perfect, permissive father.

And I came to sample the ebb and flow of patients—the early morning people in the 6 to 10 a.m. session, the lunch-time crowd between 11 a.m. and 2, and the sunset ones from 6 to 8 p.m.

The early crowd was older, more dour. Except for the occasional jet-set type getting an eye-opener, it could be any doctor's waiting room. The early faces were tense, middle-aged, New York-gray. Lunch-time patients were a mixed bag, dominated by those rich kids I met on my first visit—

though I began to note an occasional mink-coated middle-aged weight-loser and an occasional fat kid.

But, ah, the sunset people! Here was the velvet underground swathed in mind-blowing pajama suits, thrift-shop wonderments, big-knife ties, antique shoes, the hairdo of the moment. "If this creep doesn't hurry," one impatient velvet undergrounder once muttered to another, "we're going to misss the next one." On with it, on with it, the undergrounders would wish mightily, apparently rushing from one office to the next to double and triple the ante, rushing, rushing.

Providing a sympathetic ear, some encouraging words, a place to go at just the right time, Dr. Feelgood has probably saved some lonely soul from suicide or at least the painful thoughts of it, I began to think. I would not be surprised if Doctor A in particular had saved some foolish patients from inadvertent suicide—an accidental overdose of a self-administered drug.

If Doctor A finds in his work any special reward, apart from money, it may well be the knowledge that he does help where, perhaps, no one else will. Most conventional doctors, I think, would regard his kind of patient as a nuisance. As a further reward, there may be pleasure in having an interesting group of patients, even some with social cachet. Toward these latter Doctor A seemed to feel a special closeness. Even if he didn't know them personally, Doctor A seemed to regard any old-line rich family as part of his flock. Their black sheep were his special care. He often referred to the *Times* society page. "If only they had sent him to me I could have saved him," Doctor A said one day, commenting on one wealthy young man who got involved in a messy death caused by a drug overdose.

My only problem—which I certainly didn't notice at the time—was that I was happily floating along doing nothing about some real problems. There was a divorce I had meant to get months ago. I was keyed up with energy, full of smiles and laughter, which would give way to feelings of depression. But my happiness, sadness, and even my occasional periods of intense activity were unfocused states of being. I could swing a broom or focus my camera with the same zeal. I seemed to drift. A rude awakening came with the bill. I had already spent far more at his office than I had expected to spend to research all three doctors. And that line at the top—"period of treatment covered"— that was the first time I realized I had been going to Doctor A for three months.

I got the divorce. I became grimly determined to get on to the other two doctors on my list with a maximum of three visits each. I really wanted to chuck the whole thing, but finishing this story became a matter of honor, a test of professionalism.

Picture a gallery of modern art in some fashionable quarter. Bamboo benches elegantly upholstered in bright orange. Beatles and Bach and Beach Boys and Scarlatti on tapes. And, oh yes, a half-dozen paintings. Enormous canvases, they were—Pilgrim fathers among riotous nudes, splashes of black and white colliding with flesh pink, authority enmeshed in sensuality. The people in the waiting room of the physician I shall call Doctor B might debate the meaning of these paintings with as much ease and interest as they might an Allen Ginsberg poem, the politics of Carter Burden, the value of smoking pot, or their identities. Doctor B told me his offices had evolved into a forum for the exchange of ideas. These paintings were one of many changing exhibits. Often, Doctor B would invite a guitarist to play in the waiting room. The doctor was creating "a new medical environment," a sort of pilot model for what he hoped to develop into a preventive medicine center.

But when I entered that office there were only a couple of thin young men in shooting goggles, an obviously rich (Hermès and Gucci everything) but very fat young girl, and an undistinguished photographer's model—to be expected, as I knew one leading model agency sent some skinny girls here to get skinnier still.

My appointment was for 2 p.m., and I was on time. After a mere half hour, zip service compared to the usual wait at Doctor A's, I was ushered into Doctor B's office, a cool gray, white, and glass room, supermod, a *Playboy* version of a bachelor study. The doctor, a short puckish ash-blond with blue eyes, bade me take a chair facing him across the Parsons table that served as his desk. Leaning back in his chair, lighting a cigarette, he bluntly asked who had sent me. I named a fashion model, a friend of mine.

"Ah yes," he said, "then you know about the shots."

"Well, not fully," I said. Would they make me smarter, sexier, more dynamic?

"You'll feel your body more, of course, but the rest depends on where your head is."

He spoke in that plain undramatic way a personnel director of a large corporation might in explaining a routine job to a trainee. "One patient," he continued smoothly, "tells me he sees people with greater clarity. He says he sees right through their heads. Shots won't make you particularly happier or sadder but just intensify whatever mood you're in. They will help you organize your thinking. The treatment for you would run for three weeks, three times a week. ["Treatment for *what?*" I almost blurted out.] There's also a weight-losing program, but that's a little different."

Leaning over the waist-high bookshelves along one wall, my bottom exposed, I accepted a fast intramuscular injection. It was a small needleful, injected matter-of-factly. He had not taken a blood sample, had not taken my blood pressure, had not listened to my heartbeat, or anything else. He was hip. We both knew I was not there for my yearly checkup. Because the shot was intramuscular, I had no immediate reaction. Just a quick heart beat in anticipation of wonders to come.

His receptionist told me I had to pay before leaving: ninety dollars for the three-week program. Couldn't I be billed? No. Then could I pay in installments? Sure. Ten dollars, please.

As I wrote a check, a lanky young man was walking out. I caught up to him at the door and asked chummily: "How do you like the shots?"

"I don't take them anymore," he said. "I'm here because of an allergy."

"Oh? Is he good on that?"

"Do you think I'd come here if there was something

wrong?" he said. "I just came to get the name of a specialist."

For stimulating intellectual productivity, Doctor B's shots hadn't worked any better, or worse, than Doctor A's. But the crashdown was definitely worse than anything I had known before. Tense, irritable, I crashed into a fit of melancholia and found myself crying over inconsequential problems. But within a day or so I was back to my old self and, in fact, feeling quite relaxed and cheerful.

I had pretty much forgotten about the crash period when I went back about a week later. This time the nurse, not the doctor, wielded the needle. I wondered whether I could influence the dosage. "The first shot didn't energize me enough," I said. Could she alter the formula?

She warned that it wasn't a good idea to put too much of the "adrenal stimulant" in the cocktail, but she said she would add a bit more. I paid the ten dollars.

It was now about 11:30 a.m. and I had a lunch appointment with an attractive man. As lunch progressed, I felt a new wave of onrushing sensuality. But was it the shot or was it the man? Would the sensation be the same in the company of this man even without the shot? In the confusion, I felt my research experiment toppling. I didn't return for my third shot. Tests on the two shots I had taken showed: Barbiturates—negative; narcotics—negative; methamphetamine—positive.

That small taste of Doctor B's medicine seemed to be all the research I could stand at his hands.* I was now ready

---

*Some months later, the story not yet finished, I thought I would check some points with another visit to Doctor B. But he was nowhere to be found. His New York number was, as the girls at the phone company say, temporarily disconnected and there was no longer a listing for his office in the Hamptons. Some people said he was dead. I recently learned, however, that he is alive and well. I called on him, not as a patient, but as a journalist. He told me he had given up his practice and his hope of creating a "new medical environment." He discovered, he said, that he couldn't trust his patients. "They had no responsibility." But he still believes in his injections. He said the next thing he'd like to work on is a "biochemical approach to sex" with "carefully selected, responsible patients."

to visit the most celebrated—indeed, fabled—Dr. Feelgood of them all, the one reputed to have treated Presidents, a princess, a congressman, and even Eddie Fisher.

Doctor C, as I shall call him, doesn't see just anybody. To be accepted as a patient, those in the know said, I would have to offer credentials and prove my sincerity. I sent him letters of recommendation, tear sheets of my best work as a photographer, and a fawning letter expressing my admiration for the great work I had heard he had done. I pursued him for three months. Finally, I was granted an appointment.

Doctor C's small waiting room: A pay phone on the wall, a desk cluttered with papers and a tray of gummy brown injectables in sealed bottles, a badly groomed receptionist who turned out to be an unemployed actress. No Eddie Fisher, no international royalty in sight. Just a kid in a wheelchair who really looked sick, some menopausal ladies, and several pot-bellied intellectual-looking men in their middle years. The atmosphere was homey, one big, aging family offering to get sandwiches for one another, drop dimes in parking meters, or comfort one poor lady retching into her handkerchief.

After a two-hour wait, I was led by a nurse to a small examining room where she took a blood sample and my blood pressure. (Several weeks earlier I had forwarded, at Doctor C's request, a rather full medical history.) She then brought me into the doctor's office-examining room-laboratory. A beam of ultraviolet light shot through a chunk of quartz formed strange wavy patterns on the ceiling. Tall piles of dog-eared papers everywhere. Odd bits of what appeared to be magnetic sculptures, with pieces of dark metal clinging together. Thick objects wrapped in velvet, tied with string. Bottles and vials rising to the ceiling on long shelves.

In the midst of the clutter sat a man in a rumpled white shirt, hunched over something, his back toward me. "Sit!" he said, without turning around, and he pointed to a small stool. Then he wheeled his chair around. His shoes were cracked. His worn blue trousers, with faded patches from knees to pockets, looked as if he habitually wiped them with hands smeared with chemicals. His shirt was open at the neck, the sleeves casually rolled to the elbows. One rolled sleeve had a large fresh blot of what appeared to be blood on it where it touched his skin. From wrists to elbows, where his sleeves cut off the view, the skin of both inner forearms was marked by what appeared to be needle tracks —tiny scabs, very close together.

"Look!" he said, peering at me as he gathered up a pile of snapshots from a work table. "Look!" he repeated, reaching for a velvet-wrapped club of some sort. A twisted piece of rusted metal dangled from the velvet head, apparently held by magnetism. When he tried to pull the bit off, it fell out of his grasp and clanged to the floor. I picked it up for him and he shoved it on the table. "Look!" he said again, and he began rubbing an ordinary color snapshot.

The photograph showed Doctor C and a middle-aged lady sitting on a terrace in what appeared to be a vacation spot. In front of them were some half-eaten papayas. Behind them was a clutter of palm trees and, in the far background, an overexposed body of pale green water. Rub, rub, rub, rub, rub.

"Look now!" he said excitedly. "Three dimensions!" He looked expectantly at me as I stared at the photograph. The color might have become a bit richer, if one wanted to be friendly about it, but it didn't seem three-dimensional at all.

"My," I said, "the colors certainly do seem a bit richer." I wasn't ready to lie, but I wasn't ready to fail any sincerity test either.

"Yes, I can bring the color out," he said. "You bring your bad photos to me. I can fix." He rubbed now over a pinkish flower and it certainly appeared to get redder. He began rubbing another snapshot.

"Now do you see three dimensions?" he demanded. Well, frankly, no, I said. Helpfully, I told him that I had often rubbed color Polaroids just after they were developed and the heat did bring out the more slowly developing tones.

"Look again," he demanded impatiently. This time he took a picture of an atomic explosion out of a magazine and he began rub-rubbing again. He *can't* get anything out of a magazine photo, I thought. "Look!" he said, holding it up. "Well? Well?" he demanded.

"Well," I said, "it does bring things out a bit."

His heavy, lined face relaxed a bit.

"All right," he said. "Why are you here?"

"Well, I heard a lot about you and I'm, well, interested in your approach to medicine."

"Yes, yes. You wanted to see the great man. What else?"

"Well, I'm tired a lot and feel depressed, and since my divorce I don't have much interest in things."

"Your 'wells' tell me more than everything else you've said. Do you have a boy friend?"

"Not really."

"Why not? You should. Do you drink?"

"Well, yes."

"You're a drunk, aren't you?"

"No, I drink, but . . . ."

"I think you drink too much. No, you can't drink and come to me. You must stop. Have you ever been to a psychoanalyst?"

"Yes."

"No, it doesn't work. Have you ever been to a doctor who gave you shots?"

"Yes."

"Why didn't you continue?"

"It was in Europe," I lied.

"Who?"

I named someone in England I'd heard about.

"Yes, I've heard about him. Did you like it?"

"Yes."

"You look sneaky. You keep things back. You're not telling me everything. You don't tell *yourself* everything."

There was a long pause. His eyes seemed to be penetrating my mind. Should I leave quietly?

"All right," he said at last. "If you come to me, you stop drinking. If not, I don't see you. You cannot drink with these shots. You come to me for a while, then I teach you to give them to yourself."

I was soon lying on the examining table watching him, still sitting in his office chair, wheel himself to the racks of injectables in small vials. He would rub his jowls, hold a vial up to the light. I would see a brilliant flash of green or purple light reflecting off precious stones that were in the vials. He seized one vial, then another, extracting some liquid each time into a small disposable syringe. In the process, he knocked a bottle to the floor and simply left it there.

"Why do you wear glasses?" he demanded. "Take them off and you'll be able to see." He was standing over me with a small syringe. "Take off your glasses and roll on your side." He gave my bottom an intramuscular shot.

"Don't you do it i.v.?" I asked, surprised he didn't use a vein.

"That's the other—I'm not so sure I believe in them anymore. Give me your arm." He found a vein easily and gave me another shot. It was like that first time with Doctor A.

"What do you feel?"

"Like I've just made love."

"Some people say they feel that," he said, smiling. Then he abruptly pushed an eye chart up close to my nose, much too close for me to read it. "Take it," he ordered. "Read! Read!" He seemed to speak mainly in the imperative mood.

"Read!" he said, guiding the chart by pulling my hands about two feet away from my eyes.

"I can't. It's upside down." We turned it right and, yes, I could read it without glasses. A slight improvement, maybe.

"Your vision will improve," he said. Then he stared at at me, quietly, and it seemed a most relaxing way to pass the time. "You're embarrassed about something," he said after a long pause. "You're hiding something." Another long pause. Then he picked up some bars that had bits of metal clinging to them. "Stand and hold," he said, indicating the eye chart. He passed the bars back and forth over my head, and he asked me to say when my vision was clearest. But I perceived no visual changes.

He rang his nurse and she brought in a bottle of thick yellow liquid. I was instructed to rub the liquid between my palms, cup my hands over my nose, and inhale the fumes. It made me feel dizzy, but I was to use the stuff twice a day for three weeks. "Call tomorrow," he said and, turning his back, dismissed me.

"That's twenty-five dollars for the visit, ten dollars for the blood test, and five for the medication," the receptionist said.

"Please bill me."

"You pay now. We don't bill."

I wrote out a check and headed for the lab to get an analysis done. (The test indicated the presence of methamphetamine.) The trees, the kids, the sun, the dogs—New York looked loving, loved, lovable. "Life *is* like a fountain." What a great first line for a magazine article, I thought, after I had settled into a taxicab. "The time of the apocalypse is *now*." Another great article was writing itself in my all-encompassing mind.

Doctor C looked much more together on my next visit, one month later. Trousers clean and pressed, hair combed, shoes gleaming, freshly tanned, the sleeves of his natty turtleneck pullover rolled down to his wrists—he looked positively with it. Once we got past another demonstration of his 3-D photo process, and after the magnets, the conversation went well, too.

I told him I liked the shot, all right, but the ointment didn't do much for me. Didn't do much for him either, he confided. As he turned to the syringes, he asked how I wanted to feel: "Relaxed? Conversational? Brilliant?"

"Relaxed and brilliant will do," I said. "I don't feel like talking at all."

My mood changed as he withdrew the needle with a cool smile. "Can this harm me in any way? Can it addict me?" I asked.

The doctor apparently didn't feel like talking much either. He offered some perfunctory assurances—"After all, what's wrong with continuing something good?" The main ingredient, he said, is the enzymes, highly cell-building. "How old is your father?" he asked as I was leaving. "You should send him to me."

I couldn't find the receptionist and simply walked out. The bill arrived within three days: twenty-five dollars. The doctor's rates apparently varied for, earlier that evening, as I waited for the shot, I met a fortyish lady artist, a prototype for Raphael Soyer's downtrodden beauties used and abused by the capitalist system, who told me she paid only five dollars.

It had been a long wait that night, but not so long as the wait in store for me on my next visit, one afternoon a week later: three hours. At the end of the third hour, I walked out without the shot. Twice more I came for shots and twice more I walked out because of the endless wait—and because of the time it gave me to question the wisdom of pursuing this story another minute.

In time, word got around that I was writing an article about these doctors. I began to get calls from friends and friends of friends to inform me of assorted disasters or cures that they or their friends attributed to one Dr. Feelgood or another, or to tell me incredible tales involving an unbelievable list of celebrities. There was an *Iliad* and *Odyssey* of Doctor C stories.

Among the calls was one from a distinguished artist. He offered to help. He knew more about the subject and about Doctor C, he said, than anyone else. I knew of him by reputation, of course, but I had never met him. I thought he'd make a good interview.

The interview was arranged the very day I first spoke with him. He picked me up at my studio and took me to his studio where, he said, we could talk freely and where he had at hand various documents on the doctor's work.

There was a catch: he wanted to edit my manuscript. If I let him do that, he would tell me about the doctor's most arcane work, about secret government experiments, about the doctor's contribution to space medicine, about supersecret reports that would astonish me. I refused the deal, basing my position on journalistic ethics.

"What a dumb and old-fashioned idea," he said. Then his manner changed. He turned tough. "Doctor C is connected with some very powerful and influential people," the artist said, "so powerful they can see you never work for a magazine again. Influences in government, like the CIA, can see that what you write is never printed. There are ways."

Then he produced some documents and said they would reveal to me the importance of Doctor C's work. They were mine to see if I would let him edit this article.

The drama was getting me and I made a little statement: I don't have any knowledge of secret government work and don't want to know about it. If you're afraid about my talking about the "speed" content of the shots, don't. Doctors have the right to prescribe it.

Electrical connection!

Through an unbearably long pause, he stared coldly at me. Then, slowly, firmly, he said, "There is no amphetamine in his shots!"

For the first time I was really afraid to be alone with him. But he soon broke off staring. "If there was amphetamine as an ingredient in the formula," he said more softly, "mixed with other ingredients it becomes something else, something that is essentially what they put in high-energy breakfast cereals."

"So why not just eat Wheaties?" The bad joke broke the tension. He wasn't scary anymore. He became a friendly guy showing me his latest injection site—the fleshy part of his thumb. He proposed lunch with an "important man from Wall Street" and a lawyer who, he said, was connected with the CIA. The idea was to "talk more about the article" and "straighten things out."

At lunch, it turned out that the Wall Street man was a patient of Doctor C and the lawyer was Doctor C's lawyer. They were all very sweet. The lawyer cautioned that I might be open to libel actions while the artist and the Wall Street man tried to persuade me of the value of the doctor's work. At last, they hit on an idea: why not let an associate of Doctor C be spokesman for their position? Why not, indeed?

A few weeks and many phone calls later, some literature—essentially fund-raising brochures, it seemed to me—came to me by mail. I recognized them as the "secret reports" that the artist had dangled before me in his studio.

I finally had an interview with Doctor C's associate—at 7 a.m. at his office. He starts working at 6 a.m., he explained, and he considers 7 a.m. a perfectly normal hour for an appointment. Yes, he takes Doctor C's shots and thus, being in the pink of health, needs little sleep. The doctor is misunderstood, he said. Doctor C is totally devoted to his work, is a real humanitarian, isn't concerned at all with money, and is, in fact, poor. Of the doctor's patients, 65 percent pay partial fees and 25 percent pay none at all. A famous Hollywood director, I was told, had tried to set up a fund for the doctor's research, but, ironically, he died before this dream was realized—and before paying up $38,000 to the doctor for his own medical bills. All Doctor C is interested in, his associate said, is curing people and carrying on his research.

I asked him to explain the point of Doctor C's research. The brochures, I confessed, didn't make much sense to me. The doctor's experimentation is far-reaching, I was told. He is seeking the key to all illnesses—the universal cure—something you can take that rebuilds damaged cells and defends healthy cells against invaders.

I asked what, exactly, Doctor C's shots did for patients suffering from multiple sclerosis, one of the diseases he was working on.

The doctor's medications give organisms more vitality, more alertness, more ability to fight diseases and meet stresses of modern life, his associate said. And since every organism derives its energy from cosmic rays and transforms them into life, physical changes are but changes in energy levels and therefore a mechanism that increased an organism's ability to do that would be highly beneficial.

Maybe if the doctor himself could see me, I suggested, I could understand all this better.

The doctor is a genius, I was told, and so involved in his work that he doesn't link up with the minds of persons he talks to. Ordinary people who don't have the scientific background cannot follow him. But if I should see him as a patient, his associate suggested, perhaps I could discover the value of his work for myself. He would be happy to arrange that. Apparently no one connected with Doctor C—neither the artist, nor the lawyer, nor the Wall Street man—knew that I *had* been a patient. I declined with thanks and quietly said that I had already seen the doctor several times.

This was a big step for me. I find it hard to close doors on things, and I assumed that this would terminate all contact with the doctor. It did. I called Doctor C directly a number of times thereafter. I was repeatedly told the doctor was out of town indefinitely.

I had a hard time finishing this story. I personally liked many of the people who took Dr. Feelgood's shots, I liked their style, charm, talent. And I disliked the idea of presuming to judge them. I stalled and avoided the story. I accepted an offer of a staff job from a British magazine. I'll finish the story there, I promised myself. But I let it slide. Yet I continued to stay in touch with the Dr. Feelgood scene. In London, as in New York, it's almost unavoidable in some circles. Like a defrocked member of a secret society, I'd recognize the rhetoric of anyone who was in it. "Got a vitamin shot today," a Londoner connected with the theater would say, adding an elated "Whoooeee!" Within days of my arrival I had the names of London's most fashionable Dr. Feelgoods. From my New York experience, I could tell most of the time whether a person's charm belonged to him or to his latest shot.

About a year later I returned to New York. Motivated by doggedness and shame, I picked up the Dr. Feelgood story again. More interviews, library work, a refresher visit to Doctor A. Bad trip. My jaw muscles ached. I felt as if my teeth were loose. I couldn't chew for a week. I had felt again the physical symptoms of arousal, but where the turn-on really counts—in the head—I merely felt drugged and tense at the same time. Whatever appeal the shots once held was gone. Totally gone.

A postscript: Not long after my return I learned of the death of the artist who had offered to "help" with Doctor C. He was only forty-seven. The obituary I read gave the cause of death as heart attack. But the official death certificate told a different story.

He had died suddenly, on a Sunday. As in all sudden deaths in New York unattended by a physician, the coroners' office was informed. His body was brought to the morgue.

An autopsy was put off until Monday. By then, a report arrived from the office of his physician, Doctor C, stating that the dead man had a history of rheumatic heart disease. Medical examiners found, however, that both arms, from his thumbs to his elbows, were tracked with pinpoint lesions and recent injection marks.

After a thorough autopsy, heart attack was ruled out as a possible cause of death. There was no swelling of the larynx, which might have indicated an anaphylactic drug reaction. The only unusual finding was the presence of methamphetamine in the liver and other organs. Noted in the autopsy report was a "history of self-administered intravenous injections of vitamin B complexes and sometimes amphetamines for twenty years. . . ."

The death certificate concluded: "Cause of death: acute and chronic intravenous amphetamine poisoning."

Investigating "Police Corruption"

David Durk

At the very beginning, the most important fact to understand is that, though a policeman for several years, I had and have *no special knowledge* of police corruption. We knew nothing about the PEP Squad that Waverly Logan didn't know. We knew nothing about the Divisions that wasn't known and testified to by officer Philips, that wasn't known to every man and officer in those Divisions. We knew nothing about the police traffic in narcotics that wasn't known and testified to here by Paul Curran of the State Investigations Commission. Patrolman Frank Serpico, Paul Delise, and I knew these things and brought our charges because we were involved in law enforcement in New York City. And anyone else who says he didn't know had to be blind either by choice or by incompetence. The facts have been there waiting to be exposed. The Knapp Commission, to its enormous credit, has exposed them in a period of six months. We simply could not believe, as we do not believe today, that those with authority and responsibility in the area—whether the district attorneys, the police commanders, or those in power in City Hall—couldn't also have exposed them in six months, or at least in six years, if they wanted to do it.

To be explicit, I am not saying that all those who ignored the corruption were themselves corrupt. Whether or not they were is almost immaterial, in any case. The fact is that the corruption was known and yet ignored. The fact is that when

Revised, from public testimony before the Knapp Commission, November, 1971. Copyright © 1971 by David Durk. By permission of the Sterling Lord Agency, Inc.

we reported the corruption to the "Investigations Commissioner," he refused to act upon his responsibility. The fact is that almost wherever we turned in the Police Department, wherever we turned in the city administration, and almost wherever we went in the rest of the city, we were met not with cooperation, not with appreciation, not with an eagerness to seek out the truth, but with suspicion and hostility, and laziness and inattention, and we feared that any moment our efforts might be betrayed.

These are very tough things to believe if you're a cop, because to me being a cop means believing in the rule of law. It means believing in a system of government that makes fair and just rules and then enforces them. Being a cop also means serving, helping others. If it's not too corny, to be a cop is to help an old lady walk the streets safely. To help a twelve-year-old girl reach her next birthday without being gang-raped. To help a storekeeper make a living without keeping a shotgun under his cash register. To help a boy grow up without needles in his arm.

Therefore, to me being a cop is not a job but a way to live a life. Some people say that cops live with the worst side of humanity—in the middle of all the lying and cheating, the violence and hate; and I suppose that in some sense is true. But being a cop also means being engaged with life. It means that our concern for others is not abstract, that we don't just write a letter to the *New York Times* or give ten dollars to the United Fund once a year. It means that we put something on the line from the moment we hit the street every morning of every day of our lives. In this sense police corruption is not about money at all, because there is no amount of money that you can pay a cop to risk his life 365 days a year. Being a cop is a vocation, or it is nothing at all.

And that is what I saw being destroyed by the corruption of the New York City Police Department—destroyed for me and for thousands of others like me. We wanted to believe in the rule of law; we wanted to believe in a system of responsibility; but those in high places everywhere—in the Department, in the DA's offices, and in City Hall—were determined not to enforce the law but to turn their heads away when law and justice were being sold on every street corner. We wanted to serve others; but the Department was a home for the drug dealers and thieves. The force that was supposed to be protecting people was selling poison to their children.

And there could be no life, no real life, for me or anyone else on that force, when every day we had to face the facts of our own terrible corruption. I saw that happening to men all around me—men who could have been good officers, men of decent impulse and even of ideals, but men who were without decent leadership, men who were told in a hundred ways every day: Go along. Forget about the law. Don't make waves. Shut up. So they did shut up, they did go along, they did learn the unwritten code of the Department. But in going along, they lost something very precious. They weren't cops anymore. They were a long way toward not being men anymore. And all the time I saw the other victims too—especially the children. Children of fourteen and fifteen and sixteen, wasted by heroin, turned into street-corner thugs and whores, ready to mug their own mother for the price of a fix. That was the price of going along, the real price of police corruption; not free meals or broken regulations, but broken dreams and dying neighborhoods and a whole generation of children being lost. That was what I had joined the Department to stop.

So that was why I went to the *New York Times*. With my evidence and my case, in a last desperate hope that if the facts were known someone must respond. Attention had to be paid. And now it is up to you of the Knapp Commission. I speak to you now as nothing more and nothing less than a cop: a cop who's lived on this force, and who is staying on this force, and therefore as a cop who needs your help. I and my fellow policemen didn't appoint you; you don't report to us; but all the same, there are some things that we, as policemen, must have from you.

First, we need you to fix responsibility for the rottenness that was allowed to fester. It must be fixed both inside and outside the Department. Inside the Department, responsibility has to be fixed against those top commanders who allowed or helped the situation to develop. Responsibility has to be fixed because no patrolman will believe that he should care about corruption if his superiors can get away with not caring. Responsibility also has to be fixed because commanders themselves have to be told, again and again, and not only by the Police Commissioner, that the entire state of the Department is up to them. And most of all, responsibility has to be fixed because it is the first step toward recovering our simple but necessary conviction that right will be rewarded and wrongdoing punished.

Responsibility must also be fixed outside the Department— on all the men and agencies that have helped bring us to our present pass, against all those who could have exposed this corruption but never did. Like it or not, the policeman is convinced that he lives and works in the middle of a corrupt society—that everyone else is getting theirs, and why shouldn't he; and that if anyone really cared about corruption, something would have been done about it a long time ago. We are not animals. We are not stupid, and we know very well, we policemen, that corruption does not begin with a few patrolmen, and that responsibility for corruption does not end with one aide to the mayor or one Investigations Commissioner. We know that there are many people beyond the Police Department who share in the corruption and its rewards. So the report of your Commission has to tell us about the district attorneys and the courts and the bar, and the mayor and the governor—about what they have done, and what they have failed to do, and how great a measure of responsibility they also bear. Otherwise, if you suggest, or allow others to suggest, that the responsibility belongs only to the police—then for the patrolman on the beat and in the radio car this Commission will be just another part of the swindle.

Second, you have to speak as the conscience of this city— speak for all those without a voice, all those who are not here to be heard today, although they know the price of police corruption more intimately than anyone here: the people of the ghetto, and all the other victims, those broken in mind and spirit and hope. Perhaps more than any other people in this city, they depend on the police and the law to protect not just their pocketbooks but their very lives and the lives and welfare of their children. Tow-truck operators can write off bribes on their income tax, the expense account executive can afford a prostitute, but no one can pay a mother for the pain of seeing her children hooked on heroin. This Commission, for what I am sure are good reasons, has not invited testimony from the communities of suffering in New York City. But this Commission must remind the force, as it must tell the rest of the city, that there are human lives at stake—that when police protect the narcotics traffic we are participating in the destruction of a generation of children.

Third, as a corollary, you must help to give us a sense of priorities, to remind us that corruption, like sin, has its graduations and classifications. Of course, all corruption is bad. But we cannot fall into the trap of pretending that all corruption is *equally* bad. There is a difference between accepting free meals and selling narcotics. If we are unable to make that distinction, then we are saying to the police that the life of a child in the South Bronx is of the same moral value as a cup of coffee. That cannot be true, for this society or for its police force. Finally, in your deliberations you must speak for the policemen of this city—for the best that is in them, for what most of them wanted to be, for what most of them will be if we try.

Once I arrested a landlord's agent who offered to pay me if I would lock up a tenant who was organizing other tenants, and as I put the cuffs on the agent and led him away a crowd of people assembled and started yelling, *"Viva la policía!"* Of course, it was not just me, or even the police, that they were cheering. They were cheering because they had glimpsed, in that one arrest, the possibility of a system of justice that could work to protect them too. They were cheering because if that agent could get arrested then that meant they had rights, they were citizens, and maybe one day life would really be different for their children. For me, that moment was what police work is all about. But there have been far too few moments like it, and far too many times when I looked into the faces of the city and saw not hope and trust but resentment and hate and fear. Far too many of my fellow officers have seen only hate; far too many of them have seen their dreams of service and justice frustrated and abandoned by a corrupt system and superiors and politicians who just didn't care enough.

Cape Breton Is the Thought-Control Center of Canada: A Centennial Project

Ray Smith

Why don't we go away?
Why?
Why not?
Because.
If we went away things would be different.
No. Things would be the same. Change starts inside.
No. Change can start outside.
Possibly.
Then, can we go away?
No. Perhaps. All right. It doesn't matter.

So you believe in Canada and you're worried about American economic domination? But you can't understand international finance? What you do know is that a landlord can give a tenant thirty days to get out, eh? And the tenant can stay longer if he has a lease, but you don't recall having signed a lease with the Americans?

So you're saying to yourself: 'What can I do? What can I

do? I can't influence Bay Street . . . what can I do? . . .'
Well . . . uhhh . . . thought of blowing the Peace Bridge?

The Americans are loathe to fight without a divine cause.
Assume we provide this by electing an N.D.P. Government,
stirring ourselves up with Anti-American slogans like: 'Give
me liberty or give me death!' or (the most divine of all)
passing legislation that is prejudicial to American money.

With their divine cause, the Americans would destroy our
Armed Forces in one week. (This makes a fine game; you
can play it out on a map.) Canada will have ceased to exist
as a free nation. Now: *Think of the fun you'd have in the
Resistance!* It's a great subject for daydreaming: Be the first
kid on your block to gun down a Yankee Imperialist.

A virgin named, say, Judy, an attractive girl in her early
twenties, is so curious about sexual intercourse that, despite
certain misgivings, she goes to a party determined to find a
man willing to do the deed. She wears an alluring but taste-
ful dress, has her hair done, and bescents herself with a
flattering perfume.

At the party are certain men of her own age whom Judy
knows and finds attractive; and certain men of her own age
whom she doesn't know and finds attractive. All realize that
Judy is a virgin and that she wishes to experience intercourse.
Each feels he would like to help her. At the party are other
girls, but they do not figure in the story, being all the same as
Judy.

The party progresses pleasantly enough. The guests dance
and sing and drink enough alcohol to feel light-headed, but
not enough to become maudlin, violent, or unconscious. A
good time is had by all.

The end of the party nears, and Judy has not yet been
offered help. Desperate, she decides to make the proposal
herself. In no time at all, the men are seated about her dis-

cussing the problem with her. This goes on for several hours until the men pass out and Judy walks home alone. On a dark and lonely street, she is pulled into an alleyway and raped by a stranger who leaves her with her clothes torn, her body sore and bleeding, and her eyes streaming tears.

A week later, her virginity restored in a Venus-wise bath, she goes through the same events. Judy is a happy girl, for she leads a sane, healthy, and well-balanced life.

Consider the Poles. They have built a nation which, if not great and powerful, is at least distinct.

Of course, the Poles have their own language, and they have been around for a thousand years. But they have survived despite the attentions paid them by their neighbours, the Russians and the Germans.

Analogies are never perfect, but the Poles do have what we want. Consider the Poles; consider the price they have paid and paid and paid.

Wit: Did you hear about the Canadian Pacifist who became a Canadian Nationalist?

Self: No; why did he do that?

Wit: Because he wanted to take advantage of the economical Red, White, and Blue fares.

Recently a friend conned me into explaining my interest in compiled fiction, an example of which you are now reading.

'Hey, that's great,' he said. 'That really sounds interesting.'

'I'm interested in it,' I replied, razoring out the distinction.

'But I hope you aren't expecting to sell any of these compilations. The publishers won't touch anything as new as that.'

'Well, that's their business, isn't it? I mean, if they figure t's not for their magazine or it's lousy or something, they reject it. It's a basic condition. If you want to demand they publish your stuff, the best and fastest way is to buy the magazine, fire the editor, and hire a yes-man.'

'I didn't mean . . . .'

'I know what you meant; but, in fact, the technique isn't new at all. I got it from Ezra Pound and he got it from some French poets. Other precedents might be Francis Bacon's essays, the Book of Proverbs . . . the whole *Bible* . . . .'

'But . . . .'

My friend babbled on. He talks a lot about writing but, so far as I know, doesn't do any.

You can't see up through the mist (up through the high timber where the air is clean and good) but you know the dawn is already gleaming on the snow peaks; soon it will reach down here and burn away the mist and then it will be too late. Where the hell is that bloody supply column? You hunch forward between the rock and the tree and peer into the gloom. The armoured-car escort will appear . . . there: when it gets . . . there Mackie and Joe will heave the cocktails and when the flame breaks Campbell will open up with the Bren . . . Christ, you hope you get some arms out of this because if you don't you'll have to pack it up soon . . . Christ, it's cold, your joints can't take much more of . . . a growl from down around the bend . . . a diesel growl . . . .

Do you love me?

Yes. I love you. You're my wife.

Why did you say, You're my wife?

Uhh . . . .

You said it because you think just because I'm your wife you have to love me when really it has nothing to do with it.

Perhaps. It's more complicated than that.

It's always more complicated. Why can't it be simple? You

always say things are too complicated when what you really mean is you don't want to talk to me. Why can't things be simple?

They are. I love you. As simple as that. So simple there's no point talking about it.

Complicated, too, I suppose.

So complicated that to talk about it would always over-simplify it. It's the same with everything.

Then what . . . . Oh! You're impossible to talk to.

You know that isn't true.

Yes.

So . . . .

Then what is important?

Doing.

Doing what?

Mmmmm . . . .

Ohhhh . . . .

Toronto is a truly despicable city.

'. . . like a horse's arse!' Einar finishes. You all laugh be-cause Einar tells a good joke and because you're all damned scared as the car flees through the prairie night. 'And what about the girl from . . . .' Suddenly the night is day . . . si-lence . . . then the roar . . . someone gasps, 'Did we do that?' You stop the car and stare back down the road at the towering flames . . . another flash . . . its roar . . . and again . . . thousands of gallons of oil . . . . 'Well,' says Einar, 'Now I seen the sun risin' in the west. I guess I can die happy.' Your laughter shakes some sense back into you: you'd better get the hell out of here or you'll maybe die quick . . . .

Two men sit on a park bench. They are just men; perhaps office workers enjoying the sunshine during their noon break.

For the sake of convenience, let us call them Bill and George. They are acquainted.

   Bill: Nice day.
   George: Yes it is. Though the weatherman said we might get rain later.
   Bill: Yeah, it looks like it.
   George: It's in the air.
   This chatter goes on for a while. Presently Bill remembers a bottle of whisky in his pocket.
   Bill: Like a sip of rye?
   George: Ummerrahhohhehh . . . .
   This mumbling goes on until George, quivering through his entire frame, dies.
   Bill: What a crazy guy.

Bill opens the bottle and takes a drink. He sighs with satisfaction, replaces the bottle in his pocket, takes from another pocket a revolver, and blows his brains out.

A distant whirr and three more flights of geese knife south through the big Manitoba sky. There was a day when you might have shot at the geese. Now you're waiting for something else to come down the wind through the sedge; there it is, the peculiar aroma of Lucky Strike tobacco and a Texas accent quietly cursing the mud . . . .

Well, I suppose we could move to England.
I hate England, you know I hate England. It rained and rained . . . .
Oh hell, it didn't rain that much; that was just overcast and occasional drizzle. Besides we were there in March and April.
Well, it was so dirty, God. I don't mean filth, you know, just . . . grime . . . centuries of grime on everything . . . .
But the pubs, don't forget the pubs.

Sure, I know, but who wants to spend every evening drinking beer?

Yeah, I suppose.

Perhaps we could move to the States.

Be serious.

I was only joking.

The Americans believe they answered all first questions in 1776; since then they've just been hammering out the practical details.

'Then *boom!*' cries Johnny. 'Boom and the plant got no roof anymore, eh? Ha-ha-ha!' The smoky room fills with laughter. Johnny knows no fear . . . but no nothing else either. When will they ever learn? You'll try again; your fist hits the table. 'A big boom? Fine. Great. So the papers photograph it for the front page, and it's producing again the next day. But two pounds of plastic at the right place on a few essential machines and this joint won't put out a pound of steel for two years . . . .'

Well, then, consider one Pole. Consider Count Z. Count Z. is a Pole: *ergo,* a Polish patriot. He has his fingers into both the Defence and Foreign Affairs pies. Perhaps he is Prime Minister, perhaps an *éminence grise*. At forty he is vigorous, experienced, and intelligent.

From the window of his office, Count Z. gazes down into the bustling streets of Warsaw. Fifteen years of peace have prompted a cultural revival. In the near distance, several lines of new smokestacks puff their evidence of Poland's stable and bullish economy. Count Z. shades his eyes; in the far distance, the wind washes over the wheat fields which, in two months time, should become the third bumper crop in three years.

Yet Count Z. is not happy. Of course he is proud to be leading Poland to a new prosperity. But the peasants on his estate have been whispering an old saying: The Pole only buys new clothes so he'll look respectable when he commits suicide. Count Z. sighs and sits down to his work: how can I commit suicide today? (Count Z. has a subtle and self-deprecating sense of humour.)

An aide enters with the Foreign Office reports. Count Z.'s ambassadors in the Balkans say the Germans and the Russians are supplying arms and money to opposing factions in Bulgaria, Hungary, and Rumania (or whatever they were called in Count Z.'s time). The tension is moderate but unstable. Count Z. frowns.

Next the Count looks through an economic estimate sheet. Trade with Germany will increase by 12.5 per cent over the next year. This is because of a Polish-German trade agreement of two years ago. Count Z. smiles.

But next is the latest note from St. Petersburg. A deadlock has been reached in talks over the disputed ten square miles of Pripet marshland. Resumption of talks is put off indefinitely. Count Z. frowns.

Another aide enters and hands Count Z. a report on Polish defences. He reads it with great interest, although he already knows what it will say: both the eastern and western defence lines are out of date and out of repair. To construct new ones would require half the capital in the country. Financially, given five years, one could be constructed. Diplomatically, however, both must be built at once so as not to risk provoking (or tempting) either the Germans or the Russians. Count Z. sighs. If he were English, he would jerry-build something. But in the holy name of St. Stanislaus, how can he insult his Poland with jerry-building?

A visitor is announced: the paunchy, guffawing, monocled Baron Otto von und zu something-dorf, who was instrumental, from the German end, in working out the trade agreement. After four of his own utterly unfunny and incomprehensible jokes, the German says:

'But my dear Count Z., Poland a Defence Line in the East against the Depredations of the savage Cossack Hordes wishes to build, I understand, ja? Your friendly German

Cousins in the spirit which the Trade Agreement possible was made the Cost of this Defence Line to share would be willing. We Germans, as you well know, *Kultur*love, and we to Civilization a Duty it consider Mankind from the Ravenings of the Bear to protect . . . .'

'Sharing only the cost?'

'Well . . . ho-ho-ho . . . of course, we a few Divisions to garrison . . . Transportation Arrangements . . . Security Measures would want . . . ho-ho-ho, and to a Slice of Liverwurst yourself help . . . .'

A few minutes after Baron Otto has gone, Prince Igor is announced. Prince Igor is lean and foppish. Only the most delicate efforts prevented his being recalled last year when a prostitute was found beaten to death. He speaks elaborately epigrammatic French, using the occasional Russian phrase to illustrate the quaint wisdom of the peasants.

'*Mon cher* Count Z., I have heard from Petersburg of the unfortunate breakdown in talks. Of course, love shall always exist between the Tzar and his beloved Slavic cousins . . . . The fat Prussian loves war . . . . As a token of his esteem, the magnanimous Tzar wishes his gallant Polish brothers to take immediate and indisputable possession into perpetuity of the invaluable ten square miles of Mother Russia. In addition, our mutual father wishes to build for his valiant Polish children a defence line along the Polish-German (ah, that term, it disgusts me: *c'est une mésalliance,* the union of an eagle and a pig) border . . . . But will you have a sip of vodka? . . . .'

Prince Igor returns to his villa where he finds his aides taking practice shots at the neighbour's cattle. He tells them of his subtle joke: both the pig and the eagle are interchangeable symbols of Germany and Poland.

This subtlety has not been lost on Count Z. He takes a last look at the bustling streets, the puffing smokestacks, and the waving wheat which may or may not get harvested . . . .

In the following weeks, Count Z. more and more frequently plays host to Baron Otto and Prince Igor. As politely as possible, he explains that he prefers Polish sausage to liverwurst; that vodka upsets his digestion. Baron Otto tells jokes which turn like millstones; Prince Igor weaves his *chinoiseries*. They smile till their jaws crack; they drop threatening innuendoes.

Count Z. broods. His wife and his mistress both comment on the pallor of his complexion. He will not be consoled. When he looks into the streets below his office, his eyes imagine a scene filled with arrogant, swaggering Prussians or cruel, drunken Cossacks. Tension is mounting in the Balkans: a Russian uhlan and a German dragoon have fought a duel in Sofia. The salons are hissing with rumour.

Baron Otto and Prince Igor deliver their ultimata on the same day. Accept the liverwurst and not the vodka, accept the vodka and not the liverwurst, or else. Count Z. takes a last glance out the window and sighs. At least they got the harvest in. He rejects the offers. Three weeks later he is cut down while leading a hopeless cavalry charge.

Some time later, Baron Otto and Prince Igor sit down together in what used to be Count Z.'s office. They agree that the treacherous Poles are a blot on humanity, else why did they start a war they were sure to lose (as has been proven)? Baron Otto and Prince Igor agree to divide Poland, using the line where their armies met as a basis for discussions. There will be no arguments over a few square miles here and there, for Poland is a ravaged wasteland. Of course the harvest will be seized to feed the occupying troops: the Poles are pigs, let them root in the ground for acorns if they are hungry. Prince Igor accepts some liverwurst; Baron Otto praises the vodka.

The Balkan situation is smoothed out. The Germans begin building a defence line along the eastern border of their Polish provinces; the Russians begin building a defence line along the western border of their Polish provinces. These lines will take ten years to build (the Polish slave labourers are so lazy). At that time, both the Germans and the Russians will want to test the other's line. They will go to war. The war will rage back and forth across Poland until . . . .

But let the reader construct the rest. Polish history is very simple in this way. The Poles also are simple: they love Poland.

Would you rather be smothered under a pillow of American greenbacks or cut open on a U.S. Marine's bayonet?

Curfew for civilians is long past. You sit hunched by the window listening to the laughing soldiers staggering back to their billets. *Tabarnac!* they cannot take a *grosse Mol;* it is too strong for them. If you were allowed in the *tavernes* you would show them . . . . *'Venez-vous-en les gars,'* whispers Jean-Paul. Silently, silently you slide the window up and wait as the others slip onto the roof. You follow, letting the window slide down behind you. You must hurry; already the others are on the next roof, creeping toward the fourth house along where the CIA is holding Marc prisoner . . . .

Visit/ez EXPO 67

Uhh . . . I guess I'd better tell you I don't like eggs fried in butter.

But . . . but . . . .

I'm sorry, but it's true.

But . . . ohh, why the hell didn't you tell me before? God, all this time I've been frying your eggs in butter and . . . .

I didn't want to hurt you.

Well, why did you tell me now? Do you want to hurt me now?

No. Of course, you might have decided all by yourself, but if I have any more eggs fried in butter, the cumulative hurt to me (and of course to you) will have been more than the single sharp hurt of telling you. Do you see?

Ohh . . . .

It took a long time to decide when was the right moment . . . .

Yes . . . yes, I see. Yes. It was the right thing to do.

I love you.
Oh! I love you.

During the winter, he was twenty-five; George found his work tending more and more to figure drawing. He was interested and getting good results. So, as artists will do, he set out to explore the subject more fully, spending most of his time drawing and perhaps three days a month painting this and that in a variety of styles just to keep his hand in. During the next three winters, he got together three shows of the figure drawings and each year he got better press and sales. *Canadian Art,* as it was then called, gave the third show a very good review indeed.

On the basis of these successes, George applied for and got a Canada Council grant. He used it to visit the Arctic. When he returned to Toronto, he started twelve paintings, forty-three drawings, and twenty-two prints in silkscreen, lino, and wood. He destroyed each upon completion. At last he gave up trying.

For five months he drank, slept with a variety of women, and read detective novels. A newspaper reviewer came to interview him, and George told him to go to hell.

Finally George prepared a canvas, rectangular with proportions of 2:1. On this canvas he painted the Maple Leaf flag. He hung this painting on the wall of his studio and went back to drawing nudes. Because he had already satisfied himself, at least temporarily, about figures, the drawings were quite bad. But they got him working again, which is the only way to start. After a few weeks, George found a few curiosities and set about exploring these. They led him back to painting, and since that time his work has gotten steadily better, despite the fact that his recent show received confused and confusing reviews, and one critic was angry about something.

'Are you sure it's the right cove?' whispers the man in the trenchcoat.

'Keep shut,' mutters Willard. Willard is being tough, but it's for the stranger's own good; he wouldn't like going ashore to the wrong reception party. Still, he's got a right to be nervous: it's an hour since you cut the Rachel B's engine and no light yet. You peer through the gathering fog. If they don't show in five minutes, you'll have to take the man in the trenchcoat back to the mainland, and that'll mean coming back again and again until you see . . . the light: one long, three short . . . one long, three short. You answer: two long, two short. 'Take her in, Willard,' and the man in the trenchcoat fumbles with his suitcase while Willard dips the muffled oars into the slick black water . . . .

I have had stories rejected by a number of magazines in Canada and the U.S. No American magazine has ever kept a story longer than three weeks, and no Canadian magazine has kept one less than three months.

These stories have averaged ten pages each. That means the Canadian editors were reading just over one page a week; about two words an hour.

Do you realize that most people with the appropriate dictionary can read any language (even limiting it to our own alphabet) faster than two words an hour?

North America is a large island to the west of the continent of Cape Breton. (Pronounced: Caybrittn)

So what if you have to stay at home with the children? Lots of women in France fought in the Resistance; you can do your part too. Take the church supper tonight, for instance. All those National Guardsmen from New Jersey just got homesick; they wanted a home-cooked meal. So Mrs. Parsons said to their commandant, 'Why, Colonel, we've always been friendly with your people, living so close to the border. I'm sure the Ladies Auxiliary would love to give your boys a meal . . . .' The commandant didn't object when you were chosen to make the soup, and he still doesn't know you've planned a very special soup in memory of your Bill who was shot down in front of his customs shed the day it all began . . . .

If the Americans would just read their own Constitutional documents instead of memorizing them . . . .

Do you love me?

Yes, I love you.

Ohhh!

What now, hmmm? Come here.

Oh.

What? Eh? What is it?

The . . . the way you said it . . . .

Said what?

You know, the way you said I love you.

What about it?

You know very well—you didn't mean it.

I did so . . . really.

No you didn't. You hardly looked at me and you went right back to reading your book.

I did mean it. You see . . . hell, I hate explaining . . . .

(He explains for half an hour. The burden of his thesis is that married love is different from single-people love. Thus, he loves her twenty-four hours a day, loves her in such a way that it affects his whole life, including the way he pours himself a glass of orange juice in the morning. 'It is a love beyond saying,' he explains, 'I state it in my every action, my every word, my every thought. It is like "presence" or something.' He explains that saying "I love you" is for single people and that he prefers not to say it except at certain times when he feels for her that simple, heart-throbbing love of single people that comes to him when he watches her hip as she bends over or as she sweeps her hair from her eyes. 'At times like that I say, "I love you."' She says she sees and he says, 'Do you see?' and she repeats, 'Yes, I see.')

I love you.

And I love you . . . . I love you.

(The question now is whether he will make love to her or go back to reading his book. This question has no answer because the scene is an amalgam of scenes, one each week since they got married a few years ago. But before they do, one little exchange remains.)

Well then, if you didn't feel like saying, 'I love you,' why did you say it?

It's better to say it even if it is a technical lie.

What an old funny you are.

Anyway, I love you.

I love you.

See, the way I look at it, your problem is that Joe Yank is the biggest kid on the block. Now I know you're pretty friendly with him—him being your cousin and all—but someday he's going to say, 'Johnny Canuck, my boot is dirty. Lick it.'

Now then, are you going to get down on your hands and knees and lick or are you going to say, 'Suck ice, Joe Yank'? Because if you do say, 'Suck ice,' he's going to kick you in the nuts. And either way, you're going to lick those boots. It just depends on how you want to take it.

Of course, you can always kick him first.

Maybe we could just stay here.

I suppose.

I mean, I like Canada, really. It's not a bad place.

It *is* home.

Perhaps, though, we could go to Montreal for a change.

Could we?

Why not? Drop your school Parisian accent and unify Canada.

Oh!

We'll have to wait till Expo's over, or we'll never get an apartment; we already have friends there . . . . I don't see why not . . . .

I love you!

Me too!

The internal walls of an octagonal room are covered with mirrors. In the room stands a man naked. He is an ordinary-looking man; other people would say so if they could get in to see him. They cannot get in to see him because they do not knew where the entrance to the room is, or, if they did, how to open it. Likewise the man does not know where the exit is nor how to open it. Possibly he would not use it if he could. Likewise back again, possibly those outside would not enter if they could.

In any case, the man is ordinary looking; but at times he thinks himself surpassingly beautiful and at times surpassingly ugly. The man acts out these conflicting feelings, all the while watching himself in the mirrors. With one hand he strokes his beautiful body; with the other (it holds a whip) he lashes his ugly body. The times when he does these things are, it would seem, all times, and they run concurrently.

The situation lends itself to various interpretations. We might consider them; but let us not.

For Centennial Year, send President Johnson a gift: an American tourist's ear in a matchbox. Even better, don't bother with the postage.

On Training Therapists

Michael Glenn

The psychiatrist in training is embedded in a medically oriented matrix with a closed-guild tradition, whose model is master and apprentice. He is assumed to be inexperienced and naive, a stumbling creature whose every step must be watched and checked. The model of supervision approximates that of therapist/patient, and the supervision constantly resorts to unbeatable ploys, like commenting on the trainee's psychological hangups. Mathematicians, businessmen, artists, actors, teachers, historians: all are acknowledged to have some sense of the world and of their place in it by the time they are thirty; yet the therapist in training is encouraged to see himself as grossly inadequate, ill-informed, and bumbling.

The professionalism of the medical model, with its aura and mystique, permeates psychiatric training. One is constantly mystified and perplexed. The completion of training allows the now-professional psychiatrist to begin mystifying others, even though he usually has no idea how he does it. He seems to become mature, capable, and a member of the guild in good standing the moment the diploma enters his hand.

Its model makes psychiatry invincible. Attempts to change are readily discredited as psychopathology, delayed adolescence, and acting out. The trainer rarely encounters the trainee as another person, a brother or sister. Training is marked by psychological put-down, intimidation, and guilt-invoking techniques. Its graduates then repeat their experience with their clients. Such a dehumanizing, destructive system must be changed.

Szasz, Laing, and others have shown how psychotherapy dehumanizes both patient and therapist. Goffman has shown this in asylums. The same is true for therapist training, which effects the professional annihilation of trainees by incorporating them into a corrupting structure, which they must accept to succeed.

They must play the game correctly. But learning to play the game correctly often ties them to its rules for life. It is a Medean shirt which cannot easily be removed once it is put on.

There are several features to this.

Professional mystification and the psychiatrist's role

Psychiatrists, being physicians, have endured years of psychological brainwashing called education. They have learned that, to be able to make an exorbitant income, they must assume a social mask of Responsibility and Omniscient Doctor. They are our society's shamans, though lacking in the latter's sense of true drama.

Medical training has certain values: 1) it lets the young psychiatrist see the system as it really is; 2) it helps him learn to act decisively in emergencies; 3) it gives him experience with ultimate, profound situations; 4) it provides him with a range of human experience—albeit as observer—usually forbidden others not in the guild; 5) it gives him status in the system.

In return, however, medical training tyrannizes the young psychiatrist in several ways: 1) it foists an image of the physician on him; 2) it keeps him an observer, not a participant; 3) it makes him seem/feel infallible; 4) it inculcates in him values of sacrifice and responsibility, while at the same time insisting he owes himself all the luxury he can later obtain, thus encouraging him to accept materialistic values as the true measure of his worth; 5) it estranges him from others.

Medical training supports the conventional values in this society: the status quo, traditional sex roles, the search for profit. The physician becomes a petit entrepreneur. He has to behave the correct way. He becomes a defender of the church, the family, the community, the nation. His role today is a far cry from what it was in the nineteenth century, when physicians were often, as skeptics and scientists, in the vanguard of social change. Now, comfortable and fat; they challenge little and accept much. They hang on to what they've got.

In addition, medicine is mystifying. Doctors have kept their numbers down. They conceal facts from patients. They hide behind the garb of their professionalism, as if they possess arcane secrets. The public goes along with them and attributes all kinds of knowledge and power to them which they do not possess. Use of drugs, treatment of illness, prognosis of common maladies: all these are kept as secrets for the medical profession only. Mystification augments their status. But, based on a lie—that only they are capable of holding the secrets—it makes the "profession" ever paranoid, ever watchful, ever more secretive. Of course physicians resent pressure "from below" to demystify.

The doctor's morality is conventional: thus oppressive. Physicians act to heal and patch up: not to challenge the fabric of the system which sustains them. Psychiatrists, at the top of the "mental health" heap, may indulge in liberal causes without fear, especially in a liberal university or town setting; but they run into trouble if they become politically concerned beyond that. (I can cite five known instances of therapists being dismissed after becoming involved in community politics.)

The psychiatrist in training learns to treasure his elite identity, to pull rank on "ancillary" and "paraprofessional" personnel. His lengthy training lets him charge higher fees in private practice. He is a ubiquitous authority, assured prestige if he only behaves right.

The same is true of other therapist professionals. Each pecks on those beneath him; and all peck on the clients. Mystification of their skill maintains their invincibility.

Who needs medical training?

What is the rationale for psychiatrists—or any therapists—being physicians? How relevant is medical training?

Four years of medical school followed by an internship give the young psychiatrist the following: months of anatomy and biochemistry, histology, pathology, urology, surgery, cardiology. But he receives *no* sociology, psychology, anthropology, politics, or notions of human interaction. To be a physician, he endures all kinds of special training, which he only forgets later. Indeed, he has to *unlearn* his taught bias later on.

If the medical model is really important, all therapists could receive training in it. Certainly notions of public health, emergency care, and common maladies are useful to everyone who works with people. But the bulk of medical school's professionalism, formality, and specialization is irrelevant to the therapist's work.

The usual arguments for psychiatrists having to be physicians—thus distinguishing them from psychologists, nurses, social workers, etc.—are rationalizations for historical accident and caste privilege. Emotional difficulty was defined by physicians as a *medical* illness; thus it had to be treated by a physician specialist in emotional illness. The medical model makes psychiatry oppressive: people are defined as "patients"; they are told they have "diseases"; they are locked up, shocked, socially denigrated, and ostracized because they are "sick." The psychiatrist becomes society's cop.

Do people with problems in living really have an "illness"?

The medical model makes psychiatrists a healthy elite. It makes the patients an oppressed class. Other therapies too, insofar as they participate in the one-up, one-down relationship, join psychiatry as oppressive.

The issue of prescribing drugs is a red herring. Because only physicians can prescribe the drugs needed to treat emotional "illness," they maintain a monopoly on their role.

This issue is so contaminated with drug-company commercialism, "diagnostics," and mystifying guild elitism that any sensible discussion of it is impossible. The simple fact is, if drug use is important, most people can learn about it in a rather brief time.

Others argue that psychiatrists need medical training to "catch" brain tumors and other "organic" diseases which might masquerade as depression, conversion reactions, etc. The argument is weak. If such training is important for a therapist to have, it can be taught most therapists in a rather brief time. It doesn't take five years of medical training to recognize organic disease.

Medical school is about 80 percent a waste of time for the young psychiatrist. It should be scrapped.

Repression of trainees

In most psychiatric training centers, the residents, young adults, are powerless. Their curriculum is not theirs to make; their routine is set up for them to follow. "Others wiser than they" determine what they shall and shall not do. Resident advisory councils are false fronts.

The ideal therapist in training is intelligent and afraid; indecisive and obsessional, he can be made to feel inadequate and guilty with ease. Over and over again, in my own training, administrators and supervisors would push residents down, dismissing their grievances as adolescent psychopathology, criticizing their efforts at assuming responsibility for their own education. The amazing thing is how readily the residents accepted this image of themselves. They got themselves into therapy. They forswore social activism to uncover the "causes" of their rebelliousness within themselves. A more thorough job of mystification and brainwashing was never achieved!

Here, at random, are some incidents from my own experience:

1) An activist resident who organized the community against the university's "mental health center"—an imperial-

istic fraud—was fired for "clinical incompetence." The other residents refused to create a stir to defend him.

2) The director of the emergency room service decided that third-year residents would have to see every patient the first-year residents saw. This rule had not been observed for years. Rather than discuss the situation, the director insisted his will would be followed. Residents' arguments could not move him. Yet the residents would not consider a strike or collective action to dramatize their opposition. Their attitude was: Why make waves; we'll soon be out.

3) A resident rotating through a state hospital criticized its program to its director. The latter complained to a supervisor, and the resident was severely upbraided for "unprofessional behavior."

4) A paper written about the state hospital system was bottled up by the administration and refused imprimatur.

5) An anonymous letter circulated among the supervisory staff which demanded higher salaries for residents and threatened to call the press unless its demand was met was angrily denounced by several of the staff at a residents' meeting. The unknown author—it was unclear to the residents if any of their number had ever written it—was called "seriously disturbed" and told to get himself into therapy. The issue of salaries was not discussed, except when the director advised any resident who wanted more money that he could go elsewhere. The anger and fear of the staff was incredible.

6) The grapevine in the program proclaimed that, so long as a resident didn't rock the boat, he could leave the program and make $40,000 a year. Most of the residents swallowed the bait. What earthly incentive could they then have for challenging the system!

Our program emphasized one-to-one treatment, psychoanalytic insight, and hospital care. Family and group work was almost nonexistent; and the "community program" existed in a vacuum, whose instructors never discussed what was going on in the actual community outside but instead prepared the residents for administrative posts.

It was frightening how few residents saw any value in opposing a system which they all agreed was oppressing them. Their attitude was to wait until they were out and on top themselves. Their salvation, in other words, lay in their future capacity to bilk, brainwash, co-opt, and alienate others. They preserved the illusion that, so long as they disagreed inwardly, they could go along with the outward demand and still preserve their integrity.

Unless training programs are changed, therapists will continue to serve their own interests, not that of the people. They will be men of good will in an oppressive structure.

Therapy and politics

Therapists are politically naïve. They come through a professional education which gives them little understanding of social and political issues. Psychiatrists probably suffer the most through their long isolation in medical school, where they remove themselves from their society and give themselves the illusion they are gods. They are ignorant of their place in society; they are ignorant of what is going on in the real world; they are victims of a narrow horizon.

Many therapists go into debt to complete training. Making money to them is important. Staying within the system they can rise out of debt and become affluent in a matter of years. It is no wonder they guard their possessions jealously and are angry at those who "impatiently" press for change.

The life style of the therapist—certainly the psychiatrist —proclaims his place in the status quo. He lives comfortably off in the suburbs or in a town house. His children are in private school. He has a maid to free his wife. He owns color TV sets, cars, boats, land in the country, stereos, tailor-made clothes, season opera tickets, a fine portfolio of stocks; and takes vacations around the world. *HOW CAN HE EVER BE AN INSTRUMENT OF CHANGE, THEN?* He owes allegiance to the system in which he prospers.

Thus it is that he becomes an oppressor, an enemy of the people. While he eats high off the hog, others starve. Even when he is "liberal" he rarely risks his security for his ideas. Within the present system, it seems, he has no choice. That is why the system must change.

Therapy is not a branch of medicine, nor is it a social science

Therapy is a discipline in its own right, dealing with human feelings and human relationships in a human society. It was a historical accident that therapy became incorporated under its various disciplines.

If we accept this, it then becomes clear how unfortunate and divisive are the distinctions between the various therapy fields. For some therapists to have medical training and others social work training and others experimental psychology training, etc., means that the field of therapy is being partitioned like Poland in the eighteenth century. Therapy demands its own institutions, its own training programs, its own practice. The therapy fields belong together, brothers and sisters under one roof.

Current training programs prepare young therapists for roles which already exist in the system: institutional roles, private practice roles, research and teaching roles. But they don't prepare them for reexamining and challenging the system itself.

The young therapist may see this, but he isn't sure how to deal with it. Staying clean has its advantages. Going outside the system is a hardship. Only a few will take the risk, and they can be easily isolated.

New training programs are needed if any change is to occur.

Alternative training programs

Alternative institutions have risen dramatically in recent years. Spurred on by Goodman and others, free universities, free clinics, and new life styles have emerged. Roszak documents the movement's strength. Berke presents its rationale. Domhoff underscores its political importance.

Rather than confront the present system head on and be massacred by its flunkies, many today are working "to let grass push through cracks in the concrete": putting energies into new forms and new ways and letting the system collapse of its own dead weight. Some attempts have already been begun. Others will soon arise and solidify. The following is a sketch of what they will involve:

1) Training will not divide people into categories such as "psychiatrist" and "social worker." All people in the program will be therapists. They will be trained as such. Further skills can be obtained elsewhere.

2) Training will be open to all people, not made a class privilege. Those from poorer communities and minority groups will have ready access to the training their communities need. There will be an end to hunky experts who come as colonialists to tell people how to live.

3) Training will be funded by local communities.

4) Training will be demystified and deprofessionalized. What is necessary to know will be taught, straight out. What is unnecessary will be trashed. Therapists will be workers in their communities, like any other worker. Their skills are needed for the common good. But their skills will not make them a "professional" elite.

5) Training programs will be interdisciplinary, dealing with psychology and politics, sociology and art, the mass media, the analysis of power, theories of interaction, and contemporary history.

6) The model of training will change from hierarchical, obsessional, master/pupil interaction to a more open, popular, democratic form. All whose ideas and insights are valid will be heard. Age itself will carry no guarantee of wisdom.

7) New techniques will be evaluated openly, without fear of change. Therapy training centers will be like free universities, not trade schools. Free inquiry and dissent will be encouraged, not put down as "pathology." Therapists will become politically involved in the overall struggle against oppression.

8) The number of therapists trained will increase, thus benefiting the people by more available, more adequate, more relevant care.

9) Incomes for practicing therapists will be appropriate

to their work. No one will grow wealthy from the people's suffering.

10) Modes of collective practice and communal living will be tried, in the belief that the therapist's life style strongly affects his work. Therapists will not live aloof from their clients, distanced by class and interest, elite oppressors helping only from "above." They will be part of their community.

11) Therapy will be available to all, not sold to those who can afford it like fried chicken or any other commodity. It will be geared to the needs of communities, not the needs of professionals.

Let us push ahead, toward a radical therapy.

Das Hip Kapital

Craig Karpel

"Every revolution's got to have its gunrunners. . . ."
—Jim Fouratt, Goddard College, Vermont, June, 1970

On the night of the *Woodstock* premiere, Fred Weintraub, Warner Brothers' Vice-President in Charge of Creative Services, was a bit uneasy about the degree of enthusiasm with which the audience would greet the film. He wasn't taking the bomb threats *seriously*, mind you, but he asked Lieutenant O'Neil—just kidding around, you know—whether there was a way to keep anybody from walking out after only a few minutes. Not that there's much of a *likelihood*, of course, but you can never be too—

"Make better movies," said the lieutenant.

Weintraub professes not to have been concerned about the threatening letters and phone calls occasioned by Warners' release of *Woodstock*. The threats were generated by an undergroundswell of resentment toward the road-show price of $4 and $5, pretty hard for soft tickets. Kids who appeared in the movie, it was said, wouldn't be able to see it. Why should a kid who had fronted $18 for three days of peace and music not now be willing to spring for $5 more? But that was the point: most of the kids who went to Woodstock didn't pay. Since they didn't pay, it was a "free festival," and if it was a "free festival," what business did Warners have charging $5? Protest against the ticket price for the festival could take a direct form: thousands of kids coming

First published in *Esquire* (December, 1970). Copyright © 1970 by Craig Karpel. By permission of the William Morris Agency, Inc.

in over, under, around, and through the fence. Movie the-
aters are better fortified against the annoying tendency of
countercultural types to try to ride easy, so the freebies
were reduced to picketing. Perhaps there would have been
fewer pickets if the movie hadn't been rated R (got to
have a parent with you if you're under seventeen). If you're
old enough to ball in the grass, the kids reasoned, you're old
enough to see yourself do it in Techniscope.

Weintraub sits in his red, white, and blue sox, all forty-
two years of him, charcoal-gray head of hair, music-execu-
tive beard that you shave around the edges of, at an onyx-
topped walnut desk, grass cloth on the walls, shag carpet,
velvet couch rubbed the wrong way, fake Impressionist paintings in gilt frames—the sort of office they move you into and
out of in Hollywood.

"Just do me one favor," says Weintraub, who bought the
Woodstock movie for Warners. "Don't write anything about
how I've been running The Bitter End in the Village for
nine years, giving Judy Collins and Peter, Paul & Mary and
Joni Mitchell their start. Don't say anything about how I
was giving new acts a break and supporting them when these
kids were watching the Mickey Mouse Club on the tube. I
got a reputation to maintain, after all. Just say that I'm a
capitalist pig schmuck rip-off artist dirty old man and leave
it at that. No, tell them I *like* ripping off the people's culture,
that's how I get off."

More than a year working for the Establishment, and
you still don't feel the need to be defensive. Amazing!

"Within the so-called Establishment," Weintraub says,
"there are people who are as concerned as the young people
are. Right now the young people are ineffective—once they
learn to *use* the Establishment, changes will come faster
than anybody anticipates. What they need is somebody who
can sit down with the bankers. If the bankers think they can
profit, they'll play your game."

Was the $5 bite on *Woodstock* the bankers' idea?

"Man, they had to do something to make up for *The
Good Guys and The Bad Guys* and *The Madwoman of
Chaillot*, right? I mean, really."

How is *Son of Woodstock Returns* coming along?

"I haven't bought any festivals this year," says Weintraub. "Nineteen-seventy has been a bad year for festivals. Local authorities have obtained injunction after injunction against what The New Haven *Register* calls Aquarian Robber Barons, who threaten to conduct massive experiments on the effects of the music of Sly & the Family Stone on dairy-cow productivity. Even when festivals do come off, the kids have an alarming tendency to walk in without paying. What I have bought is a bus caravan, traveling across the country giving free concerts in different cities."

What cities?

"Oh, no, if I tell you and you print it, we'll have a hundred thousand kids at each one. We're not looking to have this thing ripped off. We want nice, small, peaceful concerts."

A lot of the kids think they're making a revolution.

"Yeah, but they take it too seriously. The revolution's gonna be an attrition kind of thing, if enough kids turn out like my daughter. She's married to a draft resister in Canada. That's her in the picture on the right. The way you can tell a real revolution's going on is, nobody who's involved in it takes it too seriously."

You seem to know a lot about revolutions, stranger.

"Are you kidding? I was with Castro *before* the revolution. I was arrested by Batista and sentenced to death."

For what?

"Running guns."

"To prevent possible misunderstanding, a word. I paint the capitalist . . . in no sense *couleur de rose*. But here individuals are dealt with only insofar as they are the personifications of economic categories, embodiments of particular class-relations and class-interests. My standpoint, from which the evolution of the economic formation of society is viewed as a process of natural history, can less than any other make the individual responsible for relations whose creature he socially remains, however much he may subjectively raise himself above them."
—Karl Marx, *Capital*

It is a point of honor with Paul Krassner that he has never taken a salary from *The Realist*.

That is because in the old days—*The Realist* first occurred in 1958, and as far as the Great Bourgeois Cultural Revolution goes, that was the old days—there was something called "selling out" that you were supposed to avoid at all costs. Anybody who was earning a living from what he did was said to have "sold out." It was okay for a revolutionary to *have* money in the old days, of course, but only if your father had founded I.B.M. or you were the chairman of the C.&O. railroad or something.

But in the last five years we have consummated a characteristically American conjunction of revolution and capitalism. Like anything else in the system, revolution has been encouraged to stand the test of the marketplace: If you're so revolutionary, why ain't you rich?

But isn't it bad Marxism to try to make a capitalist profit from social change? No. On December 9, 1861, Marx wrote to Engels, commenting on the Trent affair, in which an American man-of-war had taken two Confederate diplomats off a British mail ship:

"War, as I have declared in the *Presse* from the first day, will not break out with America, and I only regret that I had not the means to exploit the asininity of the Reuters- and *Times*-swayed Stock Exchange during this fool period." Marx thought it was kosher to profit from capitalism *as long as you were selling it short*. Only unfortunately he didn't have the means.

The way to exploit the asininity of *this* fool period is to get into the revolution business, to become some kind of cultural gunrunner. Dig it—the Woodstock market, every long-haired trader loaded for Bear: sell America short.

But the antipathy toward the short sellers among the longhairs has been there for some time. "George Metesky" wrote in the *Berkeley Barb* of November 18, 1966: "Our salaried hipness blankets us in the warmth of security until we masturbate ourselves into an erection of astral rapaciousness and grab whatever pleasures we might in the name of Love, always quick to contrast ourselves with middle-class man."

Four years later, the sentiment is expressed more bluntly on a toilet enclosure at the oldest established permanent floating rock festival site in Stockbridge, Massachusetts, the

Music Barn: "HIP CAPITALISTS EAT SHIT." Do they indeed? Let us hear what hip capitalists have to say for themselves as they coin their gold from a system their customers would like to destroy.

The underground press often derides Michael Butler and Peter Max for being hip capitalists. They are not. People like Bill Graham, Mike Lang, Hilly Elkins, Peter Crowley, Bill Hanley, Panama Red, and David Rubinson *are*, because they actually reach into the youth culture for products and services to sell to those who identify with it. Max and Butler reach only ostensibly into the youth culture, and the market they want to sell to is overground. I call them *hep* capitalists.

Michael Butler, forty-three, an Oakbrook, Illinois, paper heir, has palmed off on out-of-town buyers in twenty-six towns the world over $20,000,000 worth of tickets to a shuck called *Hair, The American Tribal Love Rock Musical*, that threatens to do for *Cannabis sativa* what *The Drunkard* did for souse. At a "teen fair" last year in Cleveland, Ohio, a barker in a paisley shirt shouted into a lavaliere mike, "Come on in and see a love rock musical, just like *Hair!* A musical just like *Hair!* Just like *Hair!*"—Just like *Hair*. A musical that was as close to *Hair* as *Hair* is to real freak life would be a musical like *The Student Prince*.

"*Hair, The American Tribal Love Rock Musical* is about this kid named Berger, see—"

That alone rules it out of the counterculture: there are no plots to the lives of countercultural people. The way you become countercultural is to expunge from your existence any contingencies that might conceivably result in a plot. It is as fatuous to have a plot involving the interrelation of hippies as it is to have a plot involving the interrelation of ducks, mice, and dogs. *Hair, The American Tribal Love Rock Musical* is the youth culture Disneyfied, freaks with little white gloves. Galt MacDermot's music is to rock as Stephen Foster's was to spirituals. "Bridge the generation gap," reads the ad. "Take your parents to see *Hair*."

Bridge the race gap: Take your owner to see a minstrel show.

"All our things looked made on an assembly line, Peter Max told us. So we stuck all his decals on all our things. And now all our things look made on his assembly line." —*Life*, January 10, 1969

WMCA–New York radio personality Barry Gray is five minutes into his talk show when he hears *another radio station* broadcasting in his studio. He looks over in the corner and it is Peter Max's girl friend in a Peter Max dress, sitting with her broken arm in a Peter Max cast wearing one of those self-contained FM stereo headphone radios turned all the way up. Amazingly, it is not a Peter Max headphone radio at all, merely a Panasonic.

Soon Peter Max is explaining to Barry Gray about yoga. "Yoga," he explains in his sacher-torte-mit-schlag accent, "has such beneficial powers that I'm pleased to tell you the White House has shown a great deal of interest in it."

The White House? *"Now let me make one thing perfectly clear,"* says the President, radiant in a white tunic. *"Om shantih, shantih om. My fellow Americans, sat nam and good night."*

After the show, Peter Max points to the headphone radio gleefully.

"It's fantastic, really, but so . . . *utilitarian* looking, nothing but gray and black. I've got a manufacturer, we're going to put them out with *white* cans, and *red* pads, and a *yellow* headband, with *blue* edges with little-white-stars-on-the-front. . . ."

Next thing you know, you'll be licensing Peter Max yoga.

"I am! I am! We've got a comic strip coming out in three hundred newspapers in which I illustrate sayings of Swami Satchidananda. It's called 'Meditation'."

Oh.

Peter Max, thirty-three, has parlayed his faculty for visualizing mass merchandise as plastic "cosmic art" into a business that grosses $1,000,000 on the royalties—10 percent of retail, "Twice," Max likes to point out, "what Disney gets" —from the manufacture of:

Peter Max shirts by Van Heusen

Peter Max sheets, pillow cases, and towels by J. P. Stevens

Peter Max ties by Seidler & Feuerman
Peter Max (plastic—he's a vegetarian) shoes by Laconia
Peter Max magazine by Hearst
Peter Max body stockings by Burlington
Peter Max housewares by Ekco
Peter Max umbrellas by D. Klein
Peter Max gift wrapping by Reliance
Peter Max sweat shirts by Standard Knitting
Peter Max spiral and loose-leaf notebooks by Westab
Peter Max vegetarian patchwork belts by Canterbury
Peter Max sleepwear by Hansley
Peter Max radios by Lloyds
Peter Max jump suits by Jumpsuits, Inc.
Peter Max wallpapers by Clopay
Peter Max animated feature film by Teletronics
Peter Max candy by Lotte
Peter Max infant coveralls by Pilgrim
Peter Max map by Rand McNally
Peter Max flatware by Oxford Hall
and
Peter Max himself by Peter Max Enterprises.

He recently bought a building on New York's East Side to provide working space for the forty-five operatives who translate his designs into mechanical art and a p.r. lady who offers the following: "People ask me, has Peter Max sold out. I tell them, look at *Shakespeare*—he was a financial success in his time, too."

The wrath of the underground press has ascended upon Peter Max for being a hip capitalist rip-off artist, "stealing the people's culture." This is probably the first time an assertion of propriety has been made with respect to closed-eye hallucinations. Peter Max owes his visions to deep, rhythmic breathing and what appears to be an RNA-DNA skew toward pastels. His designs borrow more from his former boss Milton Glaser and each other than from "the people's culture." They are so benign, trite, and repetitive that it is foolish for the underground to levy claims against them.

Max and Butler are hep capitalists because their concoctions are meant for people who want to be with it. Countercultural people don't want to be *with* it. They want to *be* it. Hip capitalism tries to get them to *pay* to be it.

The bedrock value of the counterculture is community. Long hair, dope, and rock music have become means to that end. The hair is a way people who want to get together have of recognizing one another. Smoking dope occasions a ritual, dissolves the membrane that separates one consciousness from another. Rock music provides a shared body of experience, or a pretext for gathering.

The bedrock value of hip capitalism is black ink on the bottom line. Long hair, dope, and rock music have become means to that end. The hair is a way of identifying the market. Smoking dope sensitizes the consumer to the product. And rock music is what is sold. Among the hip capitalists most responsible for making the bottom line rather than community the dominant value, for turning the counterculture into an over-the-counter-culture, are entrepreneurs like Bill Graham.

Recently an associate of Bill Graham's wrote the Department of Defense offering the services of his organization in arranging rock concerts for the troops. Graham, he explained, "created the rock scene in San Francisco and New York."

This might seem like an arrogant claim, but it isn't. Of course, the rock scene in San Francisco and New York wasn't created by musicians and songwriters. It was created by a concert promoter. Bill Graham indeed created the rock scene in San Francisco and New York, and Los Angeles, and Chicago, and Seattle and Kansas City and Billings, Montana, and Bemidji, Minnesota, and places he has never heard of. He created, by the magnetic—attractive and repulsive —power of his personality, the model for subjugating the music of the new culture to the economic dictates of the old.

Graham's act of creation began in Autumn, 1965. The former German refugee (né Wolfgang Grajanka), tractor executive, and actor was managing the business affairs of the sometime insolvent San Francisco Mime Troupe, the radical *commedia dell'arte*. In October, a rock group called the Family Dog had rented a ballroom and staged what would go down as the first San Francisco "community" dance. In November, Graham put on a Mime Troupe Benefit along the same lines and was overwhelmed by its success—the Jefferson Airplane flying, Fugs fugging, Allen Ginsberg howling, three thousand wired individuals working it out, and—money. And then, suddenly, Graham got a *brilliant* idea. Why not run a benefit for . . . *me?*

He found an empty ballroom in the Fillmore ghetto and proceeded to do just that, one benefit after another. It was Graham who produced the three-day Trips Festival to culminate Ken Kesey's twenty-four electric-Kool-Aid Acid Tests. A few weeks later, the Fillmore ballroom was advertising dances "with the sights and sounds of the Trips Festivals": the first authenticated instance of hip cultural rip-off for profit. From that point on, Graham's Fillmore and the Family Dog's Avalon became the forum and agora of hip culture, respectively. The Fillmore was run like the Cuckoo's Nest with Graham as Big Nurse, it stayed open and turned a profit. The Avalon was run loose as a goose, plenty good vibes, but constantly shutting down for want of cash. As the San Francisco scene became progressively less beautiful, Graham made progressively more money, manufacturing Fillmore oh-wow posters, setting up a management company, leasing a theater on New York's Second Avenue as Fillmore East in partnership with Albert Grossman, whom he later bought out. The more money he made, the more the underground grew to despise him. He could give benefits for the Panthers or the Haight-Ashbury Free Clinic, he could throw monster potluck Thanksgiving dinners, but there was still his . . . *attitude*.

"Say, Bill," says the writer, "I'm sure you can help me. Your p.r. people said they'd have complimentary tickets for me at the box office, and they do, only they won't give them to me because they spelled my name wrong. Can you straighten it out?"

"Can I straighten it out?" asks Bill Graham. He is standing in the lobby of the Fillmore West, tall, pale, wearing a Beethoven sweat shirt and *trousers*—the only hip capitalist in the world who wears trousers. "No, but I can straighten *you* out, buster. You pay like all the rest, support the musicians, do you hear? *Support the musicians,* can you dig that?"

"But Bill, *your p.r. person* called *me* and tried to lay these—"

"Listen you piece of shitttttttt"—the kids are filing in for tonight's show; Graham is snarling at the top of his lungs, but they don't even bother to look: Bill Graham calls kid piece of shit with eight t's on the end; dog bites man; so what else is new?—"the day the scum who told you to come here wants to get in here for nothing it'll be over *my dead body!*" Mild interest from the zonkers going up the stairs— Bill Graham's dead body, hmmm, now there's a thought. . . .

"But Bill, they've *got* the tickets, only they misspelled my name."

"I *fuck* your name, I *fuck* your tickets, I *fuck* YOU. You want to go upstairs you *support the musicians* like anybody else. Here, you vermin, give me a dollar, give me fifty cents, give me a dime, I don't give a holy screaming damn what you give me but you *support those fucking musicians up there* or I'll wipe you all over the pavement." Eight-year-old Wolfgang Grajanka did not walk from Paris to Marseille to Lisbon with sixty-three other Jewish orphans to escape the Nazis so he could let some hippie with an answering service get into his ballroom for nothing.

Graham is accused of having snuffed the vibes that made the whole San Francisco music scene well up in the first place—the sense of community among bands and audiences. He is accused of having demonstrated to the record companies in New York and L.A. that money was to be made off San Francisco. Yes, of course, he puts on the best *shows,* but are guards in Captain Action uniforms patrolling the lobby really . . . Aquarian? However, Graham is acknowledged to be the only man in America together enough to run fifty-two-week-a-year concerts. The ballroom now operating as Fillmore West was taken over from the Grateful Dead and the Jefferson Airplane, who tried to run it cooperatively and failed. Graham is hated because he makes so much money—well into the five-figures-weekly net, at least $16,000 a week off the Fillmores alone, but neither drops his prices nor gives it all away. He is hated because he has beaten people who claim to speak for "the community" at their own game. The Up Against The Wall Motherfuckers demanded the use of Fillmore East free one night a week so he gave it to them—once on the premises they hadn't the slightest idea what to do with it. A group in San Francisco approached him with a demand that he give one percent of his gross to "the community." Done, he said, if you can get any other business in the city to do it. So much for that.

But Graham is vulnerable on his own terms. He had the power to build a complete, vertically integrated music industry in San Francisco, but instead he concentrated on doing Scrooge McDuck kip one-and-a-halfs into his money tank. It wasn't until February 1969 that he got around to setting up an independent record-production company, and by that time the colonization of San Francisco by the record giants was complete.

Recently Graham placed an open letter to managers and agents in *Billboard,* importuning them to lower the prices of rock acts lest the ballroom and small-concert business, which has fallen on hard times everywhere but in Fillmore Nation, disappears. So Graham has come to realize that the tyranny of the dollar has the potential of destroying the culture which incubates new talent. It is a shame that it has taken him this long.

Maybe Graham's only remaining usefulness to the cultural revolution is as a crotchety rich uncle. The Alternative Media Project conference held last summer brought together heavies from the underground press and progressive radio stations. For four days the participants got it off anathematizing Bill Graham and everything he stands for. As soon as the conference was over, its coordinator got on the plane to go hit Bill Graham for the deficit.

Bill Graham makes a show of relishing the low esteem in which he is held. "I just want to relate, man," he jives, sitting at his unmagisterial desk in Fillmore West's cramped office, hanging his pendant silver Mogen David on his nose and leering. "Like, I'm just doing my thing, you know? I mean, I love everybody, because they're all beautiful people. I want to be a groovy dude. I want to be a righteous brother. I want to be a fabulous furry freak brother. Anything else I can do for you? Do you need any pictures?"

And as you shrug and begin to walk out: "Let me leave you with these parting thoughts—spare change, and Hare Krishna."

Hip brokers turn up when two parties to a contract can't get together. M.G.M. is manifestly incapable of calling Abbie Hoffman to make a movie from his book—a middleman is needed. Two of the most prominent middlemen are Mike Lang and Hillard Elkins. They are trusted by overground business interests because each was the first to perceive a profit possibility in social change. Lang realized that the time had come to bring every freak in the Northeast together at one place and time. Elkins realized that the time had come for the cast of the musical *Oh! Calcutta!* to take off all their clothes on cue. They are the P. T. Barnums of the new culture: they take the freaks to the people. The only thing that is harder than getting a scam together is smiling when one is coming apart.

Mike Lang, twenty-six, coproduced the Woodstock Music & Art Fair, the *Gesamtkunstwerk* of hip capitalism, and is a partner in the record company Just Sunshine. Jerry Brandt, twenty-eight, founder of The Electric Circus, the East Village hippo dance hall, is helping Lang get together The Train. The Train will highball America's favorite rock bands across the nation, behind a funky old locomotive and who knows what else, giving free concerts along the right-of-way—free because the kids now refuse to pay. Money will be made when The Train rolls: the movie will be shot, the record cut, the TV sale made, the profit reaped. But to get The Train rolling, there has to be some refinancing up front.

That is where Eugene comes in. Eugene is head of the Find Out Who the Hell These People Are and What They Want and Send Me a Memo on It Dept. of a swinging investment-banking firm. Lang and Brandt have invited him to check out The Train. As he walks through the door they flash on his advisers: two young ladies in white heels and pastel silk shifts and straight seams—seams? *stockings?*—and peaches-and-skim-milk complexions. Eugene is the first Establishment money man they have interviewed who is followed by groupies.

But Eugene does not flash. He does not flash on the Wiener Staatsoper chandelier, no. Not on the French doors either, nor on the one wall green, the other yellow, the blue. Sunshine's two stenographic sylphs, braless in crepe, kneeling on the floor don't do it to him nor does the speaker-phone, nor the great big (real!) crystal ashtrays. Thirty feet across the room is Lang's Louis Quatorze hippie wig coiffure, and he must be taking in the polychrome appliqué butterflies fluttering on faded Wrangler denims. But Eugene flashes on none of these, for this reason: though his office is on Wall Street and this place is on Fifty-seventh Street, Eugene is very far uptown from Lang and Brandt. Uptown people do not ever flash. Rather, they knit their brows and press their lips together and nod several times.

Eugene sits in a chair while Lang reclines on a six-foot-square patch velvet cushion and runs down The Train. It is a simple matter. The Jefferson Airplane and the Grateful Dead and Creedence Clearwater Revival and The Band and whoever else wants to come in on it will be signed. Before the net is realized, there will be an estimated capital investment of $2,300,000, and that is where Eugene comes in.

"Tell me a little about yourselves," says Eugene.

Lang and Brandt exchange deep karma sighs. On some astral plane or other they once-twice-three shoot. Brandt loses.

"My mother lives in Brooklyn," he says. "She's been across the bridge to Manhattan four times in her life. She told me never to cross the bridge alone. I crossed the bridge alone, the shit hit the fan, I never went back."

Pause.

Mike Lang does not want to hear Brandt's résumé. That is why you become a freak, so you can stop with the résumé already. But to Eugene, "the shit hit the fan" is not a résumé. Eugene wants to know *how* the shit hit the fan.

Brandt reluctantly brings himself to explain that after a stint as an agent at G.A.C., he went back to William Morris, set up the rock-stars department there, quit at $40,000 a year to open The Electric Circus, which he sold last year, and not for a bowlful of brown rice either.

Having duly knitted his brows and pressed his lips and nodded several times, Eugene turns to Lang.

"I dropped out of NYU and went down to Coconut Grove, Florida, and opened a head shop and—"

"A—a what?"

One of Eugene's groupies tells him it is a place where people go "to buy the stuff you need to take drugs."

"Then I opened some more head shops, promoted some concerts, ending up with the Miami Pop Festival, I got sick of Florida, came to New York, and put Woodstock together."

"Mike," says an associate, sensing that Lang has left an important credential out of his *curriculum vitae*, "is driven around in a Porsche by a hippie chauffeur in an undershirt."

Eugene has a simultaneous climax of brows, lips, and chin. When it is over, he collects himself and gives his own unsolicited rundown on the firm he represents in a go-go fiduciary tone.

"In ten years our firm has developed a net worth of over $40,000,000. We manage over one *billion* dollars. We've donated hundreds of thousands of dollars to worthy causes."

Brandt and Lang exchange glances. Sooner or later all Eugenes get around to the worthy causes.

"The firm's partners all have liberal politics. My boss's greatest regret is that he more or less personally raised most of the money for Nixon's campaign."

Oh brother. Brandt stares at that butterfly on his thigh. Did it just move? Or did it stay still and everything *else* move?

"We move into wherever other people aren't." That is not the first time Eugene has used that phrase. "The *next* thing." That either.

"What do you want out of this?" asks Brandt.

"We'd like to see at least a portion of our investment guaranteed."

"No, I mean, what do *you* want?"

"We're looking for a more than competitive return on our money, naturally."

Brandt gives up.

"Well," says Eugene, "I guess that just about does it."

Lang and Brandt guess this too.

Eugene would have packed up his briefcase now, if he had brought one.

One of his groupies walks right up to Mike Lang. "I've got, sort of, an *idea*, oh I don't know, you probably—"

"No, go ahead," Lang says.

"Well, what about having like, *ads*. Getting people to *pay* —you could say people on the train endorsed such-and-such products and have *ads*—"

"No," says Mike Lang, "It wouldn't work. It doesn't sell that way. People don't buy that way." He says this calmly. After you have watched 350,000 people walk into your rock festival without paying you can say anything calmly.

As Eugene and his advisers leave, it does not seem to Lang and Brandt that the particular swinging investment-banking firm he represents is going to go-go for The Train. There is something in Eugene's manner that suggests to them that he cannot dig the *scale* of it.

On the way out there is a wall that visitors to Just Sunshine are encouraged to decorate with colored marking pens. Everybody has scrawled his name in ebullient letters three to four inches high. Jerry gives Eugene a purple pen. Eugene stands on tippy-toes and writes his name.

Using the Palmer Method.

In letters one inch high.

The way they do it uptown.

On producer Hillard Elkins's town-house office wall in New York's East Sixties there is something called a Program Control Board. One column is headed THE ROTHSCHILDS. The play's production progress is marked in green crayon. The next column is headed REVOLUTION FOR THE HELL OF IT. Its status is indicated in *red* crayon.

"The story of this *Revolution for the Hell of It* movie

that I'm supposed to be doing from Abbie Hoffman's book is a microcosm of what's happening in the film industry," says Elkins. He has the build of a man who, in his Brooklyn youth, was plainly able to punch a ball three sewers. "M.G.M. had its board meeting the other day and they flash on the last scene: the burning of the Bank of America. 'Omigod! That's our *financial structure* they're burning!' What the hell did they think they were buying, *Andy Hardy Goes to Chicago?*"

His secretary pops in: "Jerry Lefcourt on three-two." It was Lefcourt, a young attorney whose clients include the Panther 21, who sold the book to Hilly. Abbie took the first payment of $25,000 and immediately gave it to the Panther bail fund.

"Eavesdrop," suggests Elkins. I lift the receiver: me, Elkins, and the F.B.I. simultaneously listening to Abbie Hoffman's lawyer.

"So *nu?*" asks Lefcourt. "Abbie just read in *Newsweek*—"

"That M.G.M. passed."

"Well? Did they really?"

"They're not going ahead with the theatrical movie, no —why, you're not surprised, are you?"

"Well with *that screenplay . . . .*"

"Listen, Jerry, baby, *you* may think *that screenplay* is fascist pig oink, but out at M.G.M. they happen to think it's a freaking fag plot."

"Well, I'm not gonna argue that one with you now. So what do we do now?"

"Nothing."

"Does that mean M.G.M. owns the property?" Frantic scribbling by the F.B.I.: What a fantastic idea! Just get the studios to *buy* the rights to all that communistic propaganda and then *pass*—we'll call it Operation Pass/Fail!

"Well, they're not gonna give it back to you, sweetheart. I mean, unless you want to forfeit the last payment. . . ."

"No," says Lefcourt with resignation, "we want the money." Exchange of good-byes. Lefcourt hangs up. Elkins hangs up. Just me and the heat sitting on the line.

"A microcosm, what'd I tell you," Elkins says to me.

"If it's honest, they got to hate it. Those boards out there aren't exactly sitting around with long hair and peace beads."

But didn't your production of *Alice's Restaurant* help set some kind of trend in Hollywood?

"No, man. The distributors thought *Alice* was a bomb. Forget about that bandwagon bullshit. We did *Alice's Restaurant* because it was in Stockbridge and Arthur Penn lives there. There wasn't any *Easy Rider* when we started it."

I thought it grossed a lot of money.

"Six million dollars." Shrug. "That's better than being poked in the eye with a sharp stick." Then: "That R rating killed us. Here's a movie about a performer who's a hero to kids, but kids can't even get into the theater. Too much pot smoking, one or two shots in the love scenes. I don't know. We're thinking of making some cuts. I mean, being on a double bill with *Naked Lady* isn't my idea of heaven."

A fructuous young man is ushered in wearing a custom-tailored suit, slicked-back long hair, and a beard. Around his neck is a silver wine taster's cup on a chain. He wants to give Hilly six bottles of Mouton-Rothschild 1875 for the opening of his play. Also, there is a restaurant that is in trouble, and if Hilly could see his way clear to—

"No thanks, man. I've been trying to sell franchises for a chain of Alice's Restaurants and it hasn't gotten off the ground."

"A microcosm," says a capitalist between two cultures. "I'm still doing the documentary of the Chicago conspiracy trial. You should hear what the defendants say about that! It's elitist, racist, male chauvinist, I don't know. Jacques Levy, the director, was stunned at the reaction. I had to say to him, 'Jacques, are you a politician or an artist?' They want to do what they accuse the other side of doing—rewriting history. Well, they're entitled to take a shot at it, but there was only one way it was. At any rate, I'm hoping that the documentary will take me out of the hole on the theatrical movie. I'm going to try to get independent distribution for it, through colleges, something like that. Forget Hollywood. They're trying to figure a market they don't understand."

Hip capitalists who are engaged in providing vital services to Woodstock Nation are not required to identify with its values. It is possible for them to sell underground radio or amplification or hash pipes or dope without being called to account for their political or moral or existential position. The man who rigs the sound for rock festivals and concerts has not been unwilling to operate 180° away from the counterculture. The man who supplies the material envelope of the drug experience does not wish to be mistaken for one of his customers. Even the heavy drug dealer, the countercultural entrepreneur *par excellence,* operating not merely in the underground but in the under*world,* draws a line beyond which he does not apply the hip value system.

Peter Crowley's aunt is a D.A.R. His father once was an Elk. His mother's family has land grants in Manhattan dating to 1642. Presumably all the Crowleys were pleased when Peter stopped wearing that fool earring.

Crowley's Cosmic Truth Distributors grosses $1500 a day, wholesaling hash pipes and roach clips and cigarette papers and other cannabis smokers' accessories to shops like Sorcerer's Apprentice in Terre Haute, Indiana, and City's Edge in Sioux Falls, South Dakota, and even to The Free Spirit which is connected to the Appalachian Varsity Men's Wear Shop in Boone, North Carolina; 1100 of them, with six sales reps around the country. He is one of the country's heaviest suppliers of . . . .

"Novelties," explains Crowley, a finely built man who seems to be around thirty. "When we go to conventions, we go to *novelty* conventions."

You sure would be a sight at a novelty convention, man.

"You should have seen me when I had my hair below my shoulders and a full beard and a *ring* in my ear—then I really looked like a novelty!"

Why did you cut your hair?

"Because I don't want to be associated with those riffraff

out there," says Crowley in a chilly Vermont twang. I'm a *real* freak, you see. *Freak's* freak. I don't need long hair to prove it.

"During the early sixties I was in the coffee-house business in Greenwich Village. I managed five different coffee houses and owned one. I ran three apartment houses and a hotel on Haight Street from the fall of '67 to the fall of '68—nothing but speed freaks, I had to quit 'cause when I'd try to collect the rent they'd threaten to kill me. And I was in the button business. I followed R.F.K. in California and Washington and sold buttons . . . did I *ever* sell buttons! I knew McCarthy would never make it, just from the buttons. I'll never forget a speech he gave in Pasadena, so wishy-washy—*terrible* for the button business. I poured nine hundred McCarthy buttons into the middle of Haight Street, I got so sick of seeing 'em."

Are *all* of those longhairs out there riffraff?

"Of course not. But long hair used to mean something, used to be a sign that you'd worked out a way to be a free agent within the system. But most of those longhairs now aren't freaks at all—they're just hippies, and hippies to me are nothing but straight people with long hair. A New York University professor friend of mine put it very well recently. 'There seem,' he said, 'to be a lot of sheep running around in wolves' clothing.' "

So you're selling wolves' smoking accessories.

"Our products exploit middle-class people who affect the idea of hip. I'm not against exploitation, you see. Everything's exploitation. You just have to be careful whom you exploit and for what reason. In the process of the rip-off I want to come up with something in my pocket.

"In the coffee-house business, we made our living by selling coffee to tourists for a dollar a cup and giving it away to freaks so the places would always be full. Now we charge nearly everybody a dollar 'cause nearly everybody's a tourist. Freaks like me have a kind of carnival morality about business—so long as it's tourists, you can turn 'em upside down and shake 'em till they stop jingling."

There are a lot of longhairs who would like to turn all you capitalists upside down and so some shaking.

"I'm not a capitalist. A capitalist is a person who owns the means of production and doesn't work at them, a coupon clipper. I buy things from seven craft cooperatives. They're not stupid enough to think capitalism is *business*. Socialism has business. Syndicalism has business. Nobody has the right to own things they can't run themselves, that's all."

So you're a revolutionary.

"I want a revolution, yes. But I want it to bring everybody up to my level. I want everybody to be an aristocrat. But they're looking for a Fidel Castro, and Fidel Castro is nothing but a manipulator—just like Richard Nixon.

"I give the system fifty-fifty to survive. If it does, I'll prosper. Even if there's a depression. People will still be buying necessities and freaks think anything they like is a necessity so they'll continue to buy anything they like, and I know what those things are and I'll sell them. And if it doesn't survive? I'll prosper too. A friend and coworker has a house in British Honduras with two servants keeping it ready. If it gets too hot here, the kids who work here and some friends of my family will go down there. We can fish in the river, we've got an electric generator, we'll be absolutely self-sufficient."

The tear gas at last year's antiwar Mobilization in Washington didn't do my friend Peter Donaldson's asthma any good. He gacked and wharfed his way with me to a Federal town house in Georgetown, where there was a roaring fire and tumblers of sherry and paintings with lights attached to them. An instructor in English with very radical politics, Peter was busted during the occupation of Columbia's Hamilton Hall in May, 1968, but before that he was a Kellett Fellow at Cambridge for two years, so bourgeois surroundings have a pacifying effect on him. He sat there, quiet, mottled gray and purple, drinking and recovering from the gas.

Into the parlor in a tinkle of bells and a cloud of incense and much flailing of tassels and fringes and purses and sashes came two fabulously furry freaks. One, Tom Law, of beatific mien and super-Breck Rapunzel hair; the other, Tom Watson, a post-Halloween pumpkin lit by a strobe candle.

"What are you doing here today?" Tom Watson asked Pete.

"Excuse me?" asked Pete.

"How come you're in Washington today?"

"What do you *think* I'm doing here? It's the goddamned Mobilization. Didn't you happen to notice a few hundred thousand people on the Mall on the way here?"

"Sure."

"May I ask what *you're* doing here today?"

"Sure. We were flown in to the festival from New Mexico."

"The *festival?* Funny, a lot of those people seemed to think they were here for an antiwar march."

"We call it a festival."

"Well, why were you quote flown in unquote to the quote festival unquote?"

"To observe the behavior of crowds."

"To observe the behavior of crowds. *What the hell is that supposed to mean?*"

"Like, you know, what people do when they're gassed, which way they run, whether they do what the marshals tell them, things like that."

"And you were *flown in* for that?"

"Sure," says Watson's backlit orange strobe smile.

"I give up," Pete said.

Later it was explained to me, and I explained to Pete, that Tom and Tom were Hog Farmers, members of a commune that had been *flown in* to Woodstock in a chartered plane to organize a "free kitchen" for the festival. It turned out that the Hog Farmers were capable of cooling out the sort of vibes that could have led to an ugly scene at the festival. They were brought to Washington by Bill Hanley of Hanley Sound, an organization that sets up public-address systems for gatherings like rock concerts and political rallies. Hanley Sound, which grosses upward of $750,000 a year, set up the system at Woodstock. It consisted of semitrailers jammed with fragile, expensive preamps and equalizers and filters, precariously top-laden towers, miles of delicate cable snaking through the muck, a stage piled high with custom-made speaker boxes, nearly a million bucks' worth of sound in all. Hanley brought the Toms to Washington to indeed "observe the behavior of crowds" under actual crisis conditions so that he could offer their services to a festival coming up a month later in West Palm Beach. With the Toms on hand, enough ugly vibes could be cooled out so that Hanley Sound's gear wouldn't be.

I passed on to Pete one tidbit that I thought would have a vasodilating effect—that while the Toms were putting him uptight at the town house, Hanley was over at the Mall getting arrested.

But I didn't tell Pete one thing I'd found out—I hope he is within wharfing range of a tumbler of sherry and a roaring fire and paintings with lights on them as he reads this—that Hanley's "most prestigious" job before Woodstock was wiring the Agnew-Nixon campaign for sound.

I am buying a wastepaper basket in the housewares department in Sears in San Francisco. The kid who waits on me has longish hair and a bushy moustache. I take out my charge card and he smiles. "Do you live in Marin?" Maybe. What if I do. "Well, I could ask you a question, but I won't." No, man, let's hear it. "Well, it would have to do with how you earn your living. . . ." How do you think I earn my living? "Well, you could be a dealer." You're right—I could be. I could be a writer, too. "I don't run into many of those here, mainly dealers." What sort of things do they buy? "You know, scales and things." You mean that just because a person has long hair and lives in Marin, that means he's a dealer? "Well, ideally he should drive a Porsche."

In the Marin driveway, a silver Porsche. Through the glass doors of the living room, a floodlit pool among the eucalyptus trees. Two women and a man, swimming naked. The man climbs out, shakes himself, puts on a kimono, and walks dripping into the living room. A kid walks in with an armload of wood and begins to make a fire in an enormous free-standing copper hearth. Panama Red sits down crosslegged on an Isfahan carpet near the fire. He is a muscular freak in his midtwenties, clean-shaven, auburn hair to midback. The kid comes back with an open bottle of

Château Margaux '61. He walks over and puts on a record: $5000 worth of gleaming McIntosh, Ampex, and Altec sound—*presence*, and *brilliance*. It is Dave Mason's *Only You Know and I Know*.

"There are five Panama Reds in the Bay Area," says Panama Red with *presence*, and *brilliance*.

Which one are you?

A long draught of Margaux. Why sip it? There's plenty more. *"The* Panama Red."

Only you know and I know. . . .

"Dig it, if the Man picks up a runner for a dealer who has scored off my runner and they threaten to put him away for good unless he tells the name of his connection, say he cracks and says, 'His name is supposed to be Panama Red.' And they say, *'Which* Panama Red—there are five of those bastards.' So he says, 'I don't know fellas, *the* Panama Red, I guess.' So the Man is right back where he started from."

Dealers as heavy as Panama Red are never anywhere near the place at which physical transfer of drugs (soft ones like marijuana, hashish, or acid; righteous dealers never mess with addictive drugs, purveyors of which they call "pushers") and cash occurs. They act more in the capacity of brokers, arranging deals between suppliers and customers who do not know each other and never learn each other's names. They deal directly with acid laboratories and cannabis smugglers, and sell to distributors beneath whom there may be one to three echelons of dealers, only the bottommost of whom sell to heads who themselves do not deal professionally. Panama Red earns the equivalent of $50,000 and up a year, tax-free, and employs a full-time assistant at $200 a week cash, plus expenses and all the dope he can consume.

"I figure I'm doing better financially at twenty-five than I would have if I'd stayed in oceanography," Panama Red says without the hint of a smile. "That's what I was studying at the University of Minnesota. You should have seen me then—I was a fraternity man, I was a jock, I was a Republican, I had a crew cut, man, I was your All-American Boy. I got turned on to grass for the first time in my unior year—took the starch out of my chinos, I'll tell you. t really opened my eyes to a lot of things. I began to ealize that they were training me to support a system, and decided that I really didn't want to have anything to do vith that system. So I decided I would work against it. I got a job in a bar in Minneapolis to tide me over, and it urned out it was owned by a Mafia *capo*. I started doing little jobs for him, and that's how I got introduced to the idea of doing illegal things for a living. Working for him made it easy for me to develop connections, so I began to deal a little on the side. My boss asked me to go out on collection jobs—people who were overdue on loans. He wanted me for that because of my build. But when I had a look at some of the violence that was involved, I decided, I can't stomach this, this isn't for me. So I quit. All I had was the dealing so I began to build that up. Drug distribution was still pretty primitive in Minneapolis five years ago, so before long I had things pretty well in hand—I was one of the heaviest dealers in the Midwest. Until I got busted. That was three years ago.

"I jumped $25,000 bail—I guess $25,000 was less money to me than it was to them—and came out here and was able to establish myself here with a little help from my friends, like they say.

"This is a tough business. You're constantly in danger of being ripped off. There's a lot of creeps around who prey on dealers, who if they don't inform on you they rip you off. I've had $40,000 worth of cash and drugs stolen at one shot. The legal expenses are tremendous—I spend something like $7000 or $8000 a year on lawyers. The secrecy is incredible. My old lady is a dealer too, and recently she did a number that involved a friend of mine. He didn't know that she lived with me, and when he told me about the deal I didn't realize that the dude she'd been talking about was him. You get to be pretty careful about who you're willing to socialize with—I've gotten to the point where I just don't go meet anybody anymore. A friend of mine has to have a guard with a shotgun patrolling his grounds twenty-four hours a day, he's so paranoid.

"But it can be a gas sometimes. We flew to England for

the Isle of Wight festival, chartered a helicopter and landed right at the site. Man, we were wrecked the whole time! When you got to stay clear of the I.R.S., you find weird ways of spending your money.

"My lawyers tell me I'm living on borrowed time because of the unlawful-flight-to-escape-prosecution. But within a year I figure I should be fixed for life, and I plan to retire. I'm going to buy a farm in Holland and give the business to my apprentice. We'll split the thing down the middle."

You mean you can trust him to send money to you in Europe?

"Man, if I can trust him with a thirty-foot trailer full of Culiacán, I can trust the dude to send me $5000 a month. There can't be any contracts in this business. If it wasn't for the trust people have for each other, the whole thing would collapse tomorrow."

As we leave to go to dinner, Panama Red pauses at the door to set a switch.

"Got to do the burglar alarm."

But there are no houses near enough for anyone to hear.

"No, it's connected directly to the police station."

The police station?

"Oh, it's safe. They already know what I'm into, they just don't know who I am, that's all. They can't get any evidence on my dealing. Certainly not by coming into the house while foiling a burglary. It'd never stand up in court."

But how can you bring yourself to call the cops to protect you if you're a professional criminal?

"You know, if you're going to commit felonies," says Panama Red patiently, "you've got to have a healthy respect for the law."

There are a few hip businessmen who had attempted to leaven the crassness of the music industry with some degree of concern for the community it serves. They think of themselves as "working from within."

The walls of a recording studio are perforated with millions of tiny holes. Yet instead of acting as conduits for sound, they contain it. Any sound made inside is absorbed before it has a chance to reverberate. If you step outside, you can no longer be heard inside. You are separated from those in the control room by a double pane of glass. If the people in the control room don't want to listen to you they can shut you off. But they have only to flick a switch to make themselves heard to you and *you* cannot shut *them* off. You can step outside, of course, but once you do you can no longer be heard inside.

The hip capitalist who attempts to work from within soon finds himself within a metaphorical recording studio. The men in the booth—the straight executives—dote on him and humor him and send coffee and sandwiches in to him, as much as he wants and more. But they are not about to change the way the board is set up just because he asks them to, let alone invite him to try his hand at the controls. . . .

The party is for David Rubinson's twenty-eighth birthday and his son Adam's fourth. It's also sort of a housewarming for David and Martha's new $50,000 Eichler ranch house down the peninsula from San Francisco, and as Adam's friends' mommies and daddies mill around the pool with drinks in their right hands and cigarettes in their left hands they titter with relief—why, he may have an oh-well-there-goes-the-neighborhood horsetail of black hair down his back and a beard like a fur-covered sledgehammerhead appended from his lower lip, but he has little Japanese gardeners and a pool-service man and firewood delivered and a black maid and a blonde mother's helper *just like ordinary people.*

"But just what is it you *do*, Dave?" asks one of the daddies in the living room. This particular daddy, like so many fellow daddies at this party, is dressed as if he were on his way to play golf.

"I'm Bill Graham's partner in the record business," Rubinson says fiercely. David Rubinson is a very fierce young man. He became fierce while working his way through junior high school, high school, and Columbia as a club-date musician at bar mitzvahs and weddings. He discovered that by contorting his brow and flaring his nostrils and opening his eyes all the way and focusing them hard on a drunk second cousin, he could vaporize the clown before the words, "Say kid, whyncha play 'The Hucklebuck,' and I want my Sammy to sing it, c'mere Sammy," could pass his swollen lips. "I'm executive vice-president of Fillmore Corporation," he barks. His bark is worse than his bite, but *so much* worse that it is a thing to be reckoned with, in and of itself.

"Oh, you mean Bill Graham of the *Fillmore,* with all the *kids,* yeah. But what exactly does that *involve,* like on a day-to-day basis?" The daddy is plainly having a rough time imagining a grown man with a horsetail of black hair down his back sitting behind a desk and talking on a telephone with buttons and giving dictation.

"Sitting behind a desk and talking on a telephone with buttons and giving dictation, for openers. I produce rock-music records—I go into the studio with musicians, arrange the music, direct the session, mix and edit the tape, commission the album cover, get it on the radio. I negotiate contracts with record companies and score movies and stay in hotels and fly on airplanes and have business lunches and make speeches at conventions."

"Oh, I see," says the daddy weakly. "Sounds very interesting." And he pauses, waiting for Rubinson to ask him what *he* does for a living. Luckily, he does not hold his breath.

Meanwhile, out at the pool, a daddy named Jeff has begun to tell his fellow daddies, with the help of four glasses of Napa Valley Riesling, about how his boss called him in last week and explained to him that what with the state of the economy, and its effect on the advertising business in general, and this company particularly, certain measures would have to be taken. "We've got to pare expense accounts, and get rid of the company cars, and the p.r. department, and *you,* Jeff.

" 'And *you,* Jeff'! I mean, I was one of the *founders* of the friggin' company. I *sold* the motherfrigger to them, but now it's 'and *you,* Jeff.' So I say, 'Well, how much notice are you giving me?' And he says, 'Things are awfully tight—I don't think we can offer you any.'

"So I've been home all week, calling executive recruiters, and they all say the same thing—'Well, we don't get that many openings at a salary level high enough to suit your qualifications.' So I've been hanging around the house trying to make myself useful. Cleaning the pool. Doing some gardening. Taking care of the kids. Vacuuming a little, even. And you know what? I'm having a ball! I *love* being unemployed! Love it!"

"Can you imagine that guy," Rubinson said a while later, "the mortgage payment coming due and he's sending out *résumés?* The whole straight economy's going down the drain and these people are standing around getting drunk and giggling at each other over bullshit. The record industry is recession-proof and here I am making money so fast I don't even want to know about it. All of these people in their baby-blue mohair cardigans are going to be lined up at my back door applying for jobs selling rock music to freaks. Eventually all these houses are going to be foreclosed, man, and the only people able to afford to live in this neighborhood will be dealers and people who are selling rock music to freaks. I'll look out the window one morning and there'll be a family of straights moving in and I'll turn to Martha and say, 'Oh, well, there goes the neighborhood!' "

Rubinson takes his game of *épaterles*-straights with him to the office. He likes to appear in record-company executives' offices in white Ben Davis chimpanzee-brand coveralls, "Thurm" in red script over a breast pocket, "Staley's— Products from Corn/and Soybeans" across the back. More substantially, if less consequentially, he has tried to get his brother recording executives to understand that, as he puts it, "there's a war on."

When he first arrived in San Francisco last year, a refugee from Columbia Records, Rubinson was struck by the large number of freaks there who desperately wanted to get involved in the music business but had no access to it. So while he was getting Fillmore Corporation together, he lined up an expert faculty and set up a series of free seminars on every aspect of rock music, from drawing contracts to splicing 16-track tape, and enrolled more than four hundred people from the city's hip community. It turned out that the main hangup of the San Francisco rock scene was that it was impossible for a band to get into a recording studio to make a demo without an outlay of hundreds of dollars, far beyond the resources of the people who are making the music. Rubinson convinced Bay Area studios to let graduates of the seminars on producing and engineering run free demo sessions with more than ninety bands, more than three hundred musicians in all. The point was not to burden Fillmore Corporation—a fledgling independent record company —with the overhead and hassles of what amounted to a "free university" of rock music. Rubinson was hoping that having, as it were, cut a demo for such a school, the music industry would see the percentage in opening itself to young people. At last spring's convention of the National Association of Record Merchandisers in Miami Beach, the only record executive on the dais under thirty, the only one wearing white coveralls with a chimpanzee on the front, declaimed—fiercely—that it was incumbent upon the industry to pick up where he had left off if, indeed, it wanted to survive.

"Let me draw a comparison," he said. "The U.S. government has alienated and disenfranchised many of the youth in this country. Many young people feel, quite strongly, that they have no effect upon things which determine the way they will lead their lives. Rock is more than a trend in music—it has become a way of life. We have alienated our business from the community which supports it. This could lead to disaster. The rock community must be allowed a say in affairs that affect its way of life. Those people most disenfranchised and most alienated are the people who support rock music, young people who could be of enormous value to the industry but as of now have no way in. The young college student or the young ghetto-dweller must be recruited and trained to join positively in our business. We must find the best, and allow them entrance. We must pass the mantel of leadership on to those who will take it anyway; but we must train them and educate them, or the crisis will become a catastrophe."

Then, to the accompaniment of much shifting within shiny suits, Rubinson edged into an area never before broached at a record-industry gathering. "The government continues to stand for repression of pleasure and suppression of liberties." Much coughing and tapping of cigar ashes. "Let's forget any political issues—let's talk business. If something is a vital part of my life, and it is not only made illegal, but prohibitively expensive; if I am in danger of being put in jail for something that is a part of my life, and if I must spend huge amounts of money and time raising bail, I am not about to buy records. That's business." That's *dope,* that's what that is. "It is entirely possible that very soon the segment of the population most responsible for your greatest profits will be in jail or out on bail, in the army, in hiding, in Canada, or *dead.*"

There is a type of applause members of N.A.R.M. reserve for long-haired kids who make Paul Muni speeches in Miami Beach. You bend your fingers back slightly and flatten your palms and clap slowly. If you are smoking you grip your cigarette with your teeth.

So in 1970 the record industry politely declined to open a free university for potential melody-makers—"you can't teach that kind of stuff," one influential record-company chief told me. "It takes talent." Presumably, *really* talented people can learn to repair low-end equalizers without ever having seen one. The trades simply ignored Rubinson's political—that is, business—rap.

David Rubinson has not been able to get another series of seminars on in San Francisco. The recording studios in the area have tired of giving time to penniless kids, and many of the demos put down by hopeful bands will remain unmixed. Every so often a freak pops his head into Rubinson's office to ask when the next seminars are going to start and draws back, mistaking his datum level of fierceness for annoyance. "Oh, I'm sorry," one blurts.

"No man," says Rubinson. *"I'm* sorry."

A growing number of freaks are coming to understand that commercialization of the life style erodes it. But their analysis of the process is simplistic: Hip capitalists are "rip-off artists" who "steal our culture." They talk with the animus of a host for its parasite. But freaks should understand that they and the hip capitalist are symbiotes: the freaks supply the life style, the hip capitalist the life accouterment. Freaks simultaneously denounce hip capitalists and buy their products. And *be* their products: "A hip capitalist," says Jerry Rubin in *Do It!*, which has earned him more than $75,000 this year, "is a pig capitalist."

If hip capitalists were simply taking something from freaks and selling it back to them at a profit (cf. Rubin: "The money pimps take the best things our hearts and minds produce, turn them into consumer products with a price tag, and sell them back to us as merchandise." The merchandise in which this product of Jerry Rubin's heart and mind appears has a price tag of $2.45), members of the counterculture might end up with less cash on hand, but at least they'd be getting their culture back in one piece. They aren't.

Only property can be stolen. The countercultural value of community is the polar opposite of property. Hip capitalism is pernicious not because it "steals the people's culture" but because it has gulled "the people" into thinking that the culture is *their property*, susceptible to larceny, rather than their community, which is inalienable. It stunts the new culture to fit it into old-culture models of property. Jann Wenner, the editor of the rock-music newspaper *Rolling Stone*, calls the hip life style a "mirror culture." The hip capitalist gets paid for holding up the mirror, and neither he nor the fairest of them all realizes that the mirror distorts.

The cultural significance of the Woodstock festival lay in the simple fact of 400,000 kids hanging out for three days. The music was the draw, but the people were the event. On the last night of the festival, Alex Bennett's radio show on WMCA New York was deluged with phone calls from kids who had been there: "Oh, the people were so *beautiful*," each said. None said, "Oh, the *music* was so beautiful." Fred Weintraub bought a movie about Woodstock which is mostly music—three-way-split screens, rock stars on each, larger than life, filling the frame. There is no attempt to communicate what it might be like to *be* at a rock festival, where it becomes manifest that the performers, tiny hairy fringed dots at the far end of a field, are subjectively smaller than the people next to you, that the stars are not the be-all of the counterculture. The movie is the antithesis of the actuality, and it propagandizes values that run counter to the counterculture. Some personal managers of rock groups capitalize the performers themselves, encourage them to enmesh themselves in the institutional relationships of property. Rock music, magical and transcendent, is the freedom music of a generation of American middle-class white kids. Yet its makers are guided not by shamans and philosophers and freedom-fighters but by lawyers and accountants whose role is to shield the proprietors of the new music from the forces that music is setting in motion. Bill Graham and his fellow concert promoters turn rock, which is inherently participative, into a voyeuristic medium—pay TV without the bother of cameras and receivers, spectators getting a look-see at an attraction *quid pro quo*. Mike Lang perpetuates the notion that if you want to boogie you've got to play ball with investment bankers and leisure-oriented conglomerates. Abbie Hoffman says Woodstock Nation is in people's heads; Mike Lang's modus operandi suggests that you have to shell out to *put* it there. Hilly Elkins can hardly make a movie out of *all* of freakdom, so he must identify "properties" within the counterculture—the title of *Alice's Restaurant* or *Revolution for the Hell of It*—that can be purchased from individuals, developed, and sold at a profit. His identification and development of properties is creative and expert, but they are properties nonetheless. If he were to direct his ample energies toward identifying and developing "communities" instead of properties—I don't even pretend to know what that would *mean* in practice, but he's probably on the right track with the Conspiracy documentary—the counterculture would be better off.

Hip capitalists are increasingly finding that their market is becoming antagonistic because the kids who consume their product do not want to be consumers. Graham is constantly being confronted with delegations demanding lower prices at Fillmore West and his Berkeley Community Theater concerts. The Grande Ballroom in Detroit has been forced by pressure from the hip community to "donate" one percent off the top to radical causes. The Eagles ballroom in Seattle has been forced to lower its prices and lengthen its shows by a group of militant high-school freaks. The Winter's End

festival in Florida early this year had to promise to donate
three percent of its profits to "the community," the New
York Pop last summer, six percent. The activists are backed
up by a huge number of kids whose antagonism toward the
hip capitalists is inchoate but unmistakably expressed: you
rip us off, we rip *you* off. One hundred and fifty thousand
freaks came into the Atlanta Pop Festival this summer over
the fence, and it is apparent that if state legislatures and
local zoning boards haven't made it impossible for rock-fest
promoters to turn a profit, kids looking for freebies have.
Warners kept its caravan a secret in a successful attempt
to keep the freebie kids away.

But the more sophisticated hip capitalists do not believe
they are stealing anybody's culture, and do not honor claims
to that effect. They justify the profit motive to themselves
in terms of what passes for hip ethics. "I didn't buy this
Porsche," says an "underground" radio personality. "I *scored*
it. If movement people don't drive Porsches it's because
they're not as together as I am." "When the mirror comes
around," says a hip apparel retailer in the argot of a cocaine
snorter, "I take as big a hit as I can." If it could be demonstrated to these people that they are teaching the goose to
sell them the golden eggs for $35 an ounce, they might
begin to understand the magnitude of the error they have
fallen into. But political freaks who demand a piece of the
action seem to them to be merely gangsters between hair-
cuts, and can be dealt with peremptorily.

The Alternate U. in New York City conducts a weekly
seminar on "Rock & Revolution" for movement people. Last
July it assigned itself the class project of doing it to the
New York Pop festival—that is, of participating in a collective effort to demand that the concert's promoters divide
their profits with "the community," that they donate money
to the militant Puerto Rican Young Lords, that they allow
movement people to control access to the arena and stage,
and make a portion of each program available for a political rap and performances by "community" bands. No sooner did the promoter capitulate than rent-a-freaks were standing on street corners distributing flyers proclaiming that "the

New York Pop festival's decision to honor the people by re-routing proceeds to rock-community causes may turn out to be one of the most impressive precedents in popular-music history." The promoters were making hip capital out of the fact that they'd been ripped off by radicals.

The members of the Rock & Revolution seminar now sat sweating in the stuffy dinge of their loft-classroom, trying to calculate their next move. One member asked if he could hear the terms of the agreement the collective had worked out with the promoters, so that he could decide whether it was worth it for the movement people to continue to lend their good name to the festival.

"I can't tell you," said a kid named Jim, who had been delegated to the collective, " 'cause there's a pig in this room. Somebody here has been telling Bill Graham everything that goes on. Graham has been trying to undermine this whole thing."

Everyone shifted position and searched the room with his eyes. Trying to look innocent while doing this was not easy. Get thee behind me, Bill Graham.

Silence.

"Well, if we can't hear the terms of the agreement we're letting them hype, I'm for pulling out of the whole thing. Let them have their festival, at least they won't be dragging us into it."

"Listen," shouted Jim, and the room became quiet. "Listen. Capitalists will *always* try to co-opt you. *You* have to be able to co-opt *them!* You have to be able to carry the thing one step further."

Nobody said anything.

Three Wise Men of Gotham

William Irwin Thompson

I

One comes away from [Emanuel Mesthene's] book, *Technological Change* [1970], as from a scholarly conference: with an ever renewed amazement that so formidable an activity can accomplish so little. Mesthene's book could very well be a transcript of the chairman's remarks from such a conference, for it is full of the usual ploys: the framing of large questions that are left unanswered, the calls for more research, the name-dropping that shows little insight into the authors mentioned, the plugs for one's own university department. Here is a book published with the Harvard brand name, but it amounts to little more than a commercial for the Harvard University Program on Technology and Society. With its eighty-nine pages of text set in very large type, this essay simply does not merit publication in any form other than mimeograph distribution to the members of the Harvard Program; but since IBM is supporting the program, so unprestigious an expression cannot be countenanced, and so the work is shoved in our faces.

Nowhere is the banality of technocratic liberalism so compactly expressed as in this bloated pamphlet. "With the proper economic and political organization, we could derive greater benefits from our technology than we do," represents the extent of the work's contribution to existing knowledge.

Originally published as "Technological Liberalism." Revised, from *The Canadian Forum* (March, 1971). Copyright © 1971 by William Irwin Thompson. By permission of the author.

o much like a conference chairman, Professor Mesthene sks a few important questions, but drops them because they re too large, and other members of the Harvard Program re at work on them. We are to trust that the amount of cholarly production coming from the program will conince IBM to continue its support so that the answers will ome pouring out in a whole series of Harvard monographs n technology and society.

How is it that Harvard of all places can be so stupid? Vhy is it that for all the work of the New Left, Old Right, nd Red Tories the banalities of technocratic liberalism glide moothly over the cracking surface of American society? n works like Mesthene's and other Cambridge products like he *Daedalus* project on the year 2000, one can only surnise that Cambridge, U.S.A., is the capital of technocratic iberalism, and that those in the capital are always the last o find out. Professor Mesthene is supposed to be a specialist n technology and society, and, although he drops some names n page 23, he shows himself to be totally ignorant of the deas and implications of the work of Ellul, Mumford, Maruse, C. S. Lewis, Noam Chomsky, Ivan Illich, and George Grant. How is it after all that has been written in studies nd screamed in the streets an expert can write such senences:

> *Technology, as I have noted, creates new possibilities for human choice and action, but leaves their disposition uncertain. What its effects will be and what ends it will serve are not inherent in the technology but depend on what man will do with technology.*

The cliché is vapidly reasserted that technology is only a tool o be used for good or ill, as the user chooses; and since echnology gives the user a choice that he didn't have beore, it really is positively good while it is scrupulously neural. Since more distinguished writers have challenged this ssumption, I should probably not rise to the bait, but one nore time.

Technology is not a tool, it is a culture. As an environnent of symbols whose most important expressions are not

machines and buildings but the institutions they embody
technology is powerful enough to warp even starlight as i
passes through its field. When you live in such an environment you are not free to pick up one tiny tool and use i
as you choose. You are overwhelmingly constrained to perform according to the culture of rationalization and the
process-definition of values. Because the technocrat claims
that values are not eternal *a priori* forms of human consciousness, he is free to bend them to fit the requirements
of *his* time. The real thrust of this book, like the real transformation of the new M.I.T., is the call for a shift from
technological hardware to the implementation of whole
new managerial-governmental systems for the control of an
advanced technological society. And if such traditional values as religion or the Constitution stand in the way, they
must be modified in a progressive fashion. Values, as every
good liberal knows, are not Platonic or Kantian forms; they
are constantly changing accommodations to historical change:
since man is in process, he can be processed.

II

"If I'd as much money as I could tell, I never would cry,
'Old clothes to sell'" is the lament of a pedlar in *Mother
Goose*. Zbigniew Brzezinski is another sort of pedlar in a
similar fix, for Professor Brzezinski is a Hubert Humphrey
political scientist in search of a future presidential client.
Understandably, he looks back fondly to the good old days
of JFK: "John Kennedy caught the essence of America's
novel position in the world when he saw himself as 'the first
American President for whom the whole world was, in a
sense, domestic politics.' Indeed, Kennedy was the first 'globa-
list' President of the United States." In an act of imitative
magic, Brzezinski quotes Schlesinger and then transfers the
spell into his own words. Once Brzezinski came rather close
to the White House, when in 1968 he served as foreign
policy adviser to the Humphrey Campaign, but fate decided in favour of Dr. Henry Kissinger; and so Professor
Brzezinsky retreated to the silence of writing this book [*Be-*

ween Two Ages, 1970]. Now with 1972 only a year away
he has returned to hawk his wares for the next liberal presidential candidate who may come his way.

One can see why happy Senator Humphrey and his "politics of joy" would have use for Brzezinski, for he chases
away all prophets of doom with the power of positivist
thinking: ". . . an apocalyptic minded reader may find my
thesis uncongenial because my view of America's role in
the world is still an optimistic one." Brzezinski can afford to
be optimistic because most of his data is, in the technocratic
fashion of the times, solidly based upon the future. "Indeed,
by 1985 mass starvation, mass homelessness, and the ram-
pant spread of diseases that have historically decimated entire populations will be generally eliminated." If there is a
bright shine to all of this, it is that of the well-worn, shiny-
bottomed garments of Camelot. Rummaging about in the
attic of Brzezinski's mind, we are brought back a decade
to 1960 when the Space Program, the Peace Corps, and the
Alliance for Progress were about to begin. Now there was
a time for liberal political scientists!

But it is now 1971. If you've been away from the planet
for the last decade, and don't have time to catch up on the
designs of Marshall McLuhan, Harvey Cox, Herman Kahn,
or Daniel Bell, then Brzezinski's old clothes may help you
to get through at least one cocktail party. But don't risk
more than that, for these aren't really good old clothes;
rather, they are mail-order imitations of the original thing.
For example, here is Brzezinski's ready-to-wear McLuhan:
"The cumulative effect of the technetronic revolution is
contradictory. On the one hand, this revolution marks the
beginnings of a global community; on the other hand, it frag-
ments humanity and detaches it from its traditional moor-
ings." Evidently, the Director of the Research Institute on
Communist Affairs and Professor of Government at Columbia University is not aware that his original thesis is in *Understanding Media.* It would seem that he must be getting
his McLuhan through *Newsweek* or other popularizations.
How else can one account for the following misunderstanding of McLuhan?

"The new reality, however, will not be that of a 'global village.' McLuhan's striking analogy overlooks the personal stability, interpersonal intimacy, implicitly shared values, and traditions that were important ingredients of the primitive village. A more appropriate analogy is that of the 'global city,' a nervous, agitated, tense, and fragmented web of interdependent relations." [*Sic*]

Since Brzezinski is unaware of the conservative and tragic perspective built into McLuhan's analysis of retribalization, it is small wonder that he prefers to follow along with the chic liberal humanism of Harvey Cox. "The imperative need for both innovation and idealism is thus stimulating a rationalist humane outlook that is gradually supplanting both the liberal skepticism of some humanists and the conservative social indifferences of some modernizers." Brzezinski is no common technocrat or crass, manipulative "modernizer"; as a sensitive member of the managerial class he realizes that: "Belief is an important social cement. A society that does not believe in anything is a society in a state of dissolution." Unfortunately, he does not seem to have any idea of the kind of "cement" that is strong enough to hold America together in the transition "between two ages."

Professor Brzezinski is not to be blamed entirely, for the lack of imagination and knowledge is also present in his sources, Herman Kahn and Daniel Bell. "Growing anarchy in the Third World would very likely involve racist and nationalist passions. At the very least, this would create major pockets of disruption and chaos in the world." So much for the future of Canadian nationalism, and so much for the turned-over collar of Herman Kahn. Now on to Brzezinski's relabeling of Daniel Bell's conflict between the "apocalyptists" and "technocrats."

By focusing more deliberately on these qualitative aspects of life, America may avoid the depersonalizing dangers inherent in the self-generating but philosophically meaningless mechanization of environment and build a social framework for a synthesis of man's external and inner dimensions.

Such a synthesis may eventually result from the current intense conflict between the irrational personalism of the "humanists" and the impersonal rationality of the "modernizers."

This paraphrase of contemporary thinkers would be tolerable in a magazine weekly, and if the book were distilled down to its substance it would make a passable special for *Newsweek*. Trendy observations become blown up into major insights like: "Cultural change in our society may also be spurred by the growing female rebellion, accelerated by education and new sexual mores." Brzezinski is on the side of women, and we trust that, if he were at the side of some future liberal President, the next administration would be able to help all disadvantaged groups at the same time that it moved toward higher levels of research and development in the management field. For it is this peculiar combination of kindness and cost-efficiency-accounting that liberal political science is all about, and Professor Brzezinski is indeed a political scientist; that is, he is not a politician, like Humphrey, or a scientist, like Teller, but an adman who writes copy for both. Consider the following commercial for political science:

Within a few years the rebels in the more advanced countries who today have the most visibility will be joined by a new generation making its claim to power in government and business: a generation trained to reason logically; as accustomed to exploiting electronic aids to human reasoning as we have been to using machines to increase our own mobility; expressing itself in a language that functionally relates to these aids; accepting as routine managerial processes current innovations such as planning-programming-budgeting systems (PPRS) and the appearance in high business echelons of "top computer executives."

The periodic style of Brzezinski's prose gives him away; he imagines that he is writing a speech draft for some future leader. This is not political science, but political cosmetology, a covering of the ugliness of the American body politic of 1970.

Just as the cosmetician attempts to obliterate age in a person's character, so the modern behavioural political scientist attempts to obliterate history in his cosmetic "methodology." Brzezinski's statements about the religious past are historical nonsense: "By taking refuge in an autonomous, distant, divine future, man relieved himself of the obligation to struggle intensely with the present under circumstances he was neither intellectually nor practically prepared for." Since history has been modernized by turning (or twisting) it into an American behavioural science, it is understandable that a generation could be ignorant enough to accept these Sociology 100 generalizations. But professional methodology is no substitute for intelligence and knowledge. There is simply no period in European history in which Christians, Jews, or Moslems failed to engage in science, mathematics, art, or political activity because they thought the future was divine; on the contrary, those most convinced of the teachings of the prophets were the ones who sought to level all vain human institutions in preparation for the new order.

Another failing of the political cosmetician is that, whenever he makes a mistake, he attempts to make his error seem the trend of the future; if a hairstylist blights a woman's hair, he tells her that the very latest styles are all for blighted hair. So it is with Brzezinski: the technological managers damage the environment through "modernization" and then tell us we need to expand their program to include environmental management. In the terms of political science this comes out as the following: "The concern with ideology is yielding to a preoccupation with ecology." It is simply impossible for Brzezinski to realize that technocrats are not part of the solution but part of the problem. In point of fact, ecology is not a replacement for traditional ideologies; it is part and parcel of a radical ideological movement, "The Friends of the Earth," which is rethinking the whole relationship between the "technostructure" and human culture. In other words, it is a radical movement which is doing everything that Brzezinski fails to do in *Between Two Ages*.

The truly important questions are precisely those never brought up by Brzezinski, because these questions are not comfortable ones that can be answered with the banalities that would appeal to middle management. So he tells America what it wants to hear: that the flexible, pluralistic market system of American Free Enterprise is superior to the monolithic, bureaucratic, linear crash programmes of the Soviet Union. But the important question is what effect ecological planetary damage will have on these two different systems. Isn't it conceivable that planetary damage, more than the revolution of the proletariat, will express the internal contradictions of the system of the consumer-generated industrial nation-state? Nixon wants the SST, but the more jets the U.S.A. builds, the more irreversible is the high atmospheric climatic disruption. The Soviet Union does not have a Boeing, Douglas, and Lockheed to keep employed; it does not have a General Motors to interfere with pollution controls; but it does have exactly that kind of monolithic, bureaucratic, linear, crash programme operation that could exercise absolute control over environments and populations. Imagine a crisis in which the U.S.A. would move more toward a Soviet model in its attempts to cure the cancer of a growth economy.

Another important question that Brzezinski does not bring up is the matter of economics; he simply imagines bigger and bigger GNPs. Depression cum inflation seems to be an anomaly, and anomalies are what T. S. Kuhn, in *The Structure of Scientific Revolution*, tells us appear just as the old paradigm of normal science is failing. The liberal political scientists are, of course, prisoners of the old paradigms and textbooks, and so they cannot see the anomalies. America has to fight inflation by cutting government spending in the aerospace and academic industries; this creates unemployment which is good business but bad politics. Unemployment means people have less money, but pollution controls mean that the cost has to be passed on to the consumer, creating higher prices at a time when many people are living in a depression. Hence the dollar is pulled apart in the two different directions of depression and inflation, and, since the multinational corporations have to do a planet's business on a nation's currency, the International Monetary Fund is caught up in the internal contradictions of the system of the industrial nation-state. Clearly on the monetary, ecological, and military levels, we are being forced to think in planetary terms, but these terms are now absolutely impossible on the political level. Hence the real nature of the transition from the age of the bourgeois industrial nation-state to the technetronic era seems to be expressed in a condition of the "double bind." A condition of "Heads I win, Tails you lose" is not likely to ensure domestic tranquillity within the United States. More than likely the American people will give Brzezinski something to think about beyond R & D and PPBS.

In Gregory Bateson's theory of the "double bind," the condition generates madness. Many observers look at present-day America and say that it is indeed losing its mind. But since the lunatic and the genius "are of imagination all compact," let us try to look out through the optimism of the single unclichéd paragraph in Brzezinski's whole book:

> *There is something awesome and baffling about a society that can simultaneously change man's relationship to the universe by placing a man on the moon, wage and finance a thirty-billion-dollar-per-annum foreign war despised by a significant portion of its people, maintain the most powerful and far-flung military forces in history, and confront in the streets and abet in the courts a revolution in its internal racial relations, doing all this in the context of the explosion of higher learning in its rapidly expanding and turbulent universities, of rotting urban centers, of fumbling political institutions, and of dynamically growing frontier industries that are transforming the way its citizens live and communicate with each other. Any one of the above aspects would suffice to transform the values and self-image of a society, and a few might be enough to overthrow its system. All together, they create a situation that defies analogy to other societies and highlights the singular character of the contemporary American experience.*

If America is the country where the internal contradictions of the industrial nation-state are most acute, does that mean that America, the triumph of that historical moment, will become its victim, and that Russia or China will pass unencumbered into the planetary era? Or is it precisely because the dialectical contradictions are most extreme in industrial America that the technetronic synthesis will appear there first? Probably the latter, but in that probability Canada could be the part of North America which will make the shift most easily. Certainly it is part of the Canadian Dream of McLuhan that Canada has moved from the colonial nineteenth century to the technetronic city-state twenty-first century without ever having been a nation-state in between. It follows then that only Canadians are emotionally secure enough in their lack of a national identity to endure the transition between the two ages of the industrial nation-state and the planetary civilization of technetronic, multinational city-states. But the transition is going to be very hard on Americans. When Canadians become nationalistic, they lose their reserve; but when Americans become patriotic, they lose their minds. If Kennedy made the whole world domestic politics, it is time for the whole world to return the favour. Since the earth is too fragile to withstand the convulsions of a giant in a fit of patriotism, perhaps it is time for Canada to take America by the hand and gently lead it into the future.

If America is going to count on the Brzezinskis for international guidance, then it is obvious that the "double bind" is going to drive America crazy. Since 1967 a few have discussed the possibility of a Far Right military takeover, but, really, a Far Right military takeover has been going on for some years; the election of 1968 was simply a crystallization of a long-term process. This is not to say that things cannot get worse, but it is to say that the Right is publicly failing and that Nixon is showing himself to be totally inept in handling the problems of the double bind. With the return of the foreign scientists to their native countries, with the massive layoffs in the scientific industries in California, Florida, and Washington, Nixon has depressed the central nervous system of American society. It is quite possible to imagine that in 1972 or 1976 some strong man might arise who would want to overcome the stress-engendered "cognitive dissonance" of America by bombing China and eliminating the Left. But that is too neat. It is more likely that planetary damage, global famine, economic chaos, domestic terrorism, and the ideological splinterings of the old platforms of the Democratic-Republican consensus could create the right context for a Leftist-Rightist transformation, an American national socialism in which the New Left *jugend* and the I. G. Farbens of Boeing and Lockheed are simultaneously appeased. I really doubt if a Hitler could arise in America, but I do think a Peronist version of FDR would have a chance of becoming President. If America does effect a simultaneously Leftist-Rightist transformation, then the convergence in economic systems between the U.S.A. and the Soviet Union will be completed.

If the first National Socialism was a tragedy, perhaps the second will be a farce, or at the very least a comedy. The technology of 1971 makes death camps and torture unnecessary. Stone knives can only be weapons; steel knives can be scalpels. Primitive technology kills, but advanced technology "cures." Whatever the future holds, I doubt that Professor Brzezinski will ever secure the position of a Schlesinger or Kissinger, for the man most likely to be hired by the first Technetronic President of the U.S.A will be Dr. José Delgado.

III

The occupational redundancy of the liberal political scientist perhaps can best be expressed in the following scene taken from Dr. José Delgado's *The Physical Control of the Mind: Towards a Psychocivilized Society* [1970]:

Electrodes were implanted in her right temporal lobe and upon stimulation of a contact located in the superior part about thirty millimeters below the surface, the patient reported a pleasant tingling sensation in the left side of her body "from my face down to the bottom of my legs." She started giggling and making funny comments, stating that she enjoyed the sensation "very much." Repetition of these stimulations made the patient more communicative and flirtatious, and she ended by openly expressing her desire to marry the therapist. . . . The second patient . . . openly expressed her fondness for the therapist (who was new to her), kissed his hands, and talked about her immense gratitude for what was being done for her.

It would seem that Frazier, in Skinner's *Walden Two*, knew what he was talking about when he said: "What is love, except another name for the use of positive reinforcement?" Delgado's research makes even Orwell's 1984 seem out of date, for there torture was used to retrain the disturbed to love Big Brother. If Delgado's assumptions are correct, then the Future State will replace control through torture with control through pleasure:

A systematic analysis of the neuroanatomical distribution of pleasurable areas in the rat (164) shows that 60 percent of the brain is neutral, 35 percent is rewarding, and only 5 percent may elicit punishing effects. The idea that far more brain is involved in pleasure than in suffering is rather optimistic and gives hope that this predominance of the potential for pleasurable sensations can be developed into a more effective behavioral reality.

If more of the brain, rat or human, is involved in pleasure, then it seems likely that future behavioural managers will reason that it is absurdly wasteful to create a political technology based upon pain, force, and error. Perhaps the managers will feel that aversive therapy is counterproductive in public relations, but that "a convertive-affective therapy is humane to the subject and positive in terms of its feedback to the clinicians." If a therapist of the near future were ever to encounter an extremely disturbed, highly resistant, antisocial personality, it would be much easier to convert him through extreme pleasure than through pain. It is also highly doubtful that most character formations could stand up under the sweet burden of intense and protracted pleasure. If the momentary "total body orgasm" experienced when a drug addict injects methedrine is sufficient to alter the personality, then it is obvious that a total body orgasm protracted over a period of hours would be sufficent to alter a person's perception of time, his perception of his own life-history, and the self-image and character-structure derived from these. From the point of view of the behavioural scientists, this would be pleasant work in what could be amiable surroundings. If we now use toys and cartoon murals in pediatric offices and clinics, then the social clinic of the technological society would not have to look like a laboratory at all; instead, it could look like the interior of *Playboy* magazine.

Dr. Delgado's main purpose in his research is, of course, not to create salons of pleasure, but to discover cures for epileptic and brain-damaged persons who suffer from seizures of uncontrollable violence. In this he has been enormously successful and is deserving of the international fame he now enjoys. But like most human beings, Dr. Delgado is a contradictory creature. At one moment he is poohpoohing naive fantasies of a race of robots with radios planted in their brains by the CIA; then he goes on to tell us how we now can move "toward a psychocivilized society" by "conquering the mind." One side of the profile of Dr. Delgado is the smiling, deeply humanistic and widely read family physician; the other side shows the Faustian gleam of the laboratory technologist.

> *The chronicle of human civilization is the story of a cooperative venture consistently marred by self-destruction, and every advance has been accompanied by increased efficiency of violent behaviour. . . .*
>
> *Ours is a tragically imbalanced industrial society which devotes most of its resources to the acquisition of destructive power and invests insignificant effort in the search which would provide the true weapons of self-defense: knowledge of the mechanisms responsible for violent behaviour. They are necessarily related with intracerebral processes of neuronal activity, even if the triggering causality may reside in environmental circumstances. Violence is a product of cultural environment and is an extreme*

form of aggression, distinct from modes of self-expression required for survival and development under normal conditions.

Delgado takes issue with the behaviourists, for he is deeply concerned with the contribution of the organism to the Stimulus-response mechanism and would define mind as "the intracerebral elaboration of extracerebral information." But it is clear from above that his disagreement with the behaviourists is only one of degree. Like Skinner, Delgado believes that "violence is a product of the cultural environment." In his model of a successful social community, Walden Two, Skinner imagined that undesirable behaviour could be eliminated through superior cultural design. "We discourage attitudes of domination and criticism," says Frazier, and we are asked to take it on faith that they therefore do not appear in the community. I find it astonishing to see how scientists who are used to working with the binary codes of computers can make this naive claim. It should be immediately evident that the structural processing of information in man is binary: light and dark, good and evil, yes and no, this or that, 1 or 0. It follows this structure that any social rule or implicit agreement is set up so that its negative inversion is automatically brought into existence with its positive formulation. If one says, "Love Big Brother," he is also saying, preconsciously, "Do Not Love Big Brother." The very structures of behaviour at Walden Two are the very things that will bring the community down, which is a realization that all sophisticated thinkers from Heraclitus to Hegel have emphasized. Everything contains its own contradiction. Dr. Delgado's cure for violence and epilepsy contains the zombification of man. It simply does not matter whether or not the good doctor thinks he is only desiring the good; more crimes have been committed in the name of good than in the name of evil.

It must be an expression of the failure of the education of scientists that men like Skinner or Delgado can become so advanced in specialized areas and yet remain so linear and simple-minded in general areas. From the Iliad or the Old Testament, through Marx and Hegel, to Yeats, McLuhan, or Kolakowski, the dialectical and contradictory nature of consciousness has been described over and over again. The message is, in fact, built into the primary myth of our civilization. Yahweh points out, heightens, and attractively illuminates the Tree of Knowledge by negating it. The sin of tasting the fruit is a consequence of expressing the tree in consciousness. To be sure, Adam was free not to eat, but he was constrained because the tree was the only element in his environment that was negated. To be in a real Garden of Eden, man must be mindless; no opposites should be conceivable, no negatives should exist. Mind is binary; the no-mind is unitary. On Homer's terms: if each thing asserts itself and is not alone in the universe but shares a space with other things asserting themselves, then conflict is inevitable, and the space of the cosmos is a battlefield.

Violence is, therefore, not simply an expression of the cultural environment. Conflict is the expression of the tragic necessity in which the contradiction must exist if its positive is to be. In the fallen world of binaries, man knows by twos; joy and suffering, birth and death, good and evil. Put a *man* in a utopia and he is still a man thinking in terms of 1—0, kiss—kill, love—hate. Only by altering the very *structure* of consciousness can conflict and violence be eliminated, but to effect that alteration we would have to eliminate human nature. People who could never turn structures inside out, think in mirror-images, dream up Marxist contradictions, and deal in the values of positive and negative would have no minds at all. Thus in order to perfect man, science would have to create a society in which no science was possible. The rulers would have to be outside the rules by which they governed the fixed human beings. If these rules are to protect man from evil, and if the rulers are outside these protections, then eventually the rulers will come into conflict and the society will fall. The predicament is absolute: as long as we think in terms of humanism—democratic, scientific, or Marxist—the solutions multiply arithmetically while the problems multiply geometrically. As long as one thinks in the secular terms of norms and deviations, then, as Marx says, "The ruling ideas are in every epoch the ideas of the ruling class," and there is no way to avoid the clinical state in which some men *fix* other men. The fatuous liberal humanism of political scientists like Brzezinski will always fall before the greater strength of the behaviourism of scientists like Delgado.

When humanism breaks apart, it breaks into the opposites of mechanism and mysticism, and that is why the best critics of "the technological society" have been men of religious vision like C. S. Lewis in England, Jacques Ellul in France, Ivan Illich in Mexico, and George Grant in Canada. The importance of the religious vision of human nature is that it conceives of identity in terms other than instincts and politics. If one does not think in terms of certain inherent values, then there is no convincing argument against manipulation; technology can improve upon biology to eliminate the vestigial ape in man, and cultural design can eliminate the correspondingly primitive institutions. If mind is bestowed upon the organism by culture, and science is the most important institution of that culture, then the physical control of the mind is not the destruction of a preexisting entity, but a creative and scientific improvement upon parenthood. In order to justify the science of the brain, it is absolutely essential that the scientist feel that his work is only the last act in man's conquest of nature. The raw organic pre-mind is a jungle waiting to be cleared, developed, and civilized. What man has been able to do before to the environment is now about to be done within the brain.

> *The mind is not a static, inborn entity owned by the individual and self-sufficient, but the dynamic organization of sensory perceptions of the external world, correlated and reshaped through the internal anatomical and functional structure of the brain. Personality is not an intangible, immutable way of reacting, but a flexible process in continuous evolution, affected by its medium . . . .*

It is quite possible that Delgado is correct when he says that "human beings are born without minds," but one can draw two conclusions from this perception. One leads in the direction of genetic engineering and the physical control of the mind; the other leads in the direction of "the no-mind" of Zen Buddhism. Of course it depends upon what one means by "mind." Delgado feels that because there are "no detectable signs of mental activity at birth," humans have no minds until they are bestowed upon them by their culture. It follows quite naturally that the more scientific is the culture, the more mind there is to be bestowed upon neonates. However, not all of Delgado's data support his conclusions.

As the fetus grows, many organs perform something like a dress rehearsal before their functions are really required. This is usually referred to as the principle of anticipatory morphological maturation. The heart starts to beat when there is no blood to pump; the gastrointestinal tract shows peristaltic movements and begins to secrete juices in the absence of food; the eyelids open and close in the eternal darkness of the uterus; the arms and legs move, giving the mother the indescribable joy of feeling a new life inside herself; even breathing movements appear several weeks before the birth when there is no air to breathe.

Why then should we not suppose that the brain "thinks" before the culture has given it any thoughts to think? There is, of course, an arbitrary aspect to this: it is much like defining a sound as a vibrating body, a medium, and a receiver. Without a receiver, there is no sound; without a culture, there is no mind. But it is not all arbitrary, for if the organism develops before it encounters its environment, then it meets the environment *on its own terms*.

Some efferent motor pathways appear before any afferent fiber enters the cerebrum. Initially, the cerebral association system develops toward the motor system and the peripheral sensory fibers grow toward the receptor field. Significant conclusions from these facts are that "the individual acts on its environment before it reacts to its environment." . . . Total behaviour is not made up of reflexes; rather, "the mechanism of the total pattern is an essential component of the performance of the part, i.e., the reflex," and behaviour therefore "cannot be fully expressed in terms of S-R (stimulus-response)" . . . . this reveals that "the cerebral growth determines the attitude

*of the individual to its environment before that individual
is able to receive any sensory impression of its environment. Hence, the initiative is within the organism."*

The implications that derive from the observations made
by the scientists Delgado quotes seem to indicate that the
organism is like a magnetic field; what is magnetized into the
field in terms of sensory inputs is determined by the *a priori*
structure of the organism. Human nature precedes the encounter with environmental nature. Delgado seems unfamiliar with the work of Eric Lenneberg at Harvard and Noam
Chomsky at MIT concerning the biologically innate aspects
of language ability. Familiarization with this work would
help in giving some precise content to Delgado's vague definition of the mind as "the intracerebral processing of extracerebral information." Culture can shape the "sensory
inputs" of the surface structure of language by determining
whether the child is to speak Chinese or English, but it
cannot determine the deep structure of language which is the
species-specific aspect of language ability. Delgado's ignorance of the research done at Harvard's Center for Cognitive
Studies and MIT's Linguistic Acquisition Laboratory seriously weakens his attempts to generalize on the basis of his
own specialized research. He does not really understand the
nature of the argument between Chomsky and Skinner, and
so his vagueness tends to involve him in circular definitions:
"Behaviour is the result of motor activities which range from
a simple muscular twitch to the creation of a work of art."
Delgado is quite content to philosophize in a rather sloppy
form of empiricism and he blithely ignores Whitehead's
warning that "the order of nature cannot be justified by the
mere observation of nature."

But for all his philosophic vagueness, Delgado has made
an interesting point in his assertion that human beings are
born without minds. The fetus lives in the oceanic feeling of
oneness; his body temperature is matched to that of the
amniotic fluid so that he cannot sense where he ends and
the universe begins. In this primordial state all is one, and
since mind is two we can imagine that the fetus is mindless.
Then comes birth, the fall from unity into multiplicity, and

the beginning of twos in the self and the other. But multiplicity makes a new order possible in the segmental articulation of language, and so we find the Hegelian dialectic of: (1) Unity, (2) Fragmentation, (3) Reintegration. But the culture cannot create language any more than the wind can create sailboats; culture can only startle the brain into consciousness.

But a linguistic consciousness, a mind, is both a blessing and a curse; expression requires suppression. To regain the transcendental sentience in which the self is continuous with the universe, the verbal adult has to move out of words into the no-mind of Zen. Recent research by Dr. Robert Wallace into the alpha rhythm of the brain in meditation suggests that the meditational state of consciousness is no mere fantasy of the experiencing subject. And so in growth the dialectic repeats itself; verbal consciousness becomes Unity, concentration becomes the Fragmentation of mind, and logic mastery becomes the Reintegration. "First there is a mountain, then there is no mountain, then there is." The oceanic presentience of the fetus and the transcendental sentience of the yogi or *roshi* are thus structurally alike in that they exist at the opposite sides of the mind.

Dr. Wallace's research indicates that individuals can be taught to move into the alpha rhythm and that this deeper state of consciousness can be therapeutic in the treatment of mental and physical diseases. Through mysticism the individual can become what Abraham Maslow called "a self-actualizing personality"; through mechanism the individual can become a physically controlled, psychocivilized subject. The choice is clear; it is only the middle ground that seems treacherously muddy. The humanistic movement that began with the Renaissance has reached its limit, and at that limit Western culture has broken apart as *mechanism* and *mysticism* move in opposite directions along the circumference of human civilization. If the opposites are to meet in some future completion of the sphere of human culture, I do not think they will meet in the constellation of Delgado. Now as the oceans are filling up with mercury, it is time to have done with Western, Faustian Man. The conquest of nature, the conquest of space, and the ultimate conquest of the mind:

these are all the expressions of our old pathologically unbalanced culture. Dr. Delgado assures us that he is against aggression, but his conquering of the mind is only aggression raised to another order of magnitude.

"The once sacred rights of man must change in many ways," said H. Bentley Glass upon the occasion of his retirement from the presidency of the American Association for the Advancement of Science. What the good doctor had in mind was compulsory abortion, genetic control, and all that sort of thing. At the end of humanism it is the human body that has become the battleground where mechanism and mysticism fight it out toward the year 2000. Marx was prophetic, for impotent man now exposes himself to virile machines, and all the genitals and breasts of *Hair!* cannot put *Homo sapiens* together again. The justice is absolute and poetic: the North Americans who once rolled over the Indians with the railroads of the nineteenth century are now about to be turned into Indians by their own technology; it remains to be seen whether these will be the dejected Indians of the Plains or the elevated Indians of Rishikesh.

Why Users Are Losers

Stephen A. Kurtz

Noteworthy buildings tend to be evaluated but twice in their lifetimes—at birth or on their deathbeds. For architectural critics and journalists alike, the long span in between tends to hold little interest. In thus preferring the finished product to the processes of use, writers join their readers in a set of common prejudices.

Articles in most architectural journals are written, after all, for an audience of two—the architects themselves and the manufacturers of building supplies. In displeasing the one, a magazine risks the loss of readership as well as its prime source of new and exclusive material. In displeasing the other it risks the loss of advertising—its prime source of income. Whatever the personal integrity of editor or writer, these economic influences become all pervasive. They explain the consistent emphasis on esthetics (imagery), materials, and technology. They explain why adverse criticism, even in these realms, is so rare and, even more importantly, they explain why discussion should remain confined to such categories. Why not, for example, evaluate the building from the standpoint of the user? Of all approaches to architectural journalism, this is the least employed. And the reason is clear. *The user, especially in the case of urban housing, is seldom the client.* In the company of agents responsible for urban housing, he remains a passive onlooker, and his impotence is reflected in the absence of his opinions from the architectural press.

Large-scale sociological issues have been frequently discussed in design journals, but hardly with the specificity to clarify one concrete situation. Consequently, I set out here, in a random manner interviewing five not necessarily representative families, to find out how a particular housing project, widely praised for its design qualities, was evaluated by those who lived in it.

The project chosen, University Towers in New York City, was built by I. M. Pei and Partners in 1966 for New York University. It consists of three apartment towers of which the two considered here are owned and rented by the university, while the third, a Mitchell-Lama–funded co-op, has been excluded. The two rental towers were chosen simply because, of those buildings that seemed appropriate for such a study, these were the only ones in which I knew at least one resident, so that a relaxed introduction to other tenants might be more easily accomplished.

I was chiefly interested in determining how the space affected the living arrangements of the residents, what possibilities it opened or closed for them, to what extent they felt the need to modify the space, and to what extent such needs could be satisfied. I was also concerned about the tenants' relations with the landlord/administration as it influenced their attitudes toward the complex, as well as the general social/economic climate in which these attitudes were formed.

Apartment Plan

Perhaps the most influential factor in the physical environment is the plan of the apartment itself. Each of them, whether of one, two, or three bedrooms, is dominated by a large living room (23′2¾″ by 18′9¾″) whose one glass wall may offer dramatic skyline views. In the trade-off of space that made these luxurious and uniformly appreciated living rooms possible, bedroom, kitchen, bath, and closet space were severely reduced. The two-bedroom apartments,

for example, have but one bath, few closets, and, in common
with the others, very small kitchens (which vary, but
average about 10′ by 7′ *including* the space occupied by
utilities). Thus the "public" spaces used for entertaining
dominate over the private ones. Since most of the residents
are young couples with children, this means the near absence
of "retreat" or work space for adults. Moreover, even the
style of entertainment is dictated by this arrangement. Since
only the living room is suited to this purpose, it is impossible
for husband and wife to entertain separately at the same
time. "Togetherness" may thus become a forced thing, while
its avoidance becomes equally self-conscious and unsatisfac-
tory.

Kitchens and Closets

While the need to entertain is an important part of the
living patterns of these residents—amply met by the space—
the need to accumulate—an equally important part—is not
met by the skimpy closet facilities. The large numbers of
decorative and semiuseful objects that middle-class families
tend to amass simply cannot be accommodated. This lack of
storage space might impose a Thoreauvian restraint, but that
is hardly the architect's business.

Since the women uniformly felt that the kitchen lacks adequate storage space, they supplement it with pegboard
panels and an extra cabinet. The already tiny work space is
thus further reduced and the inclusion of a breakfast table
becomes impossible. All meals must therefore be taken at
the dining table, which informalizes a formal space, or for-
malizes what would otherwise be a casual activity.

In the case of the three-bedroom apartments, when two
bedrooms are used by children, neither one (BR I is approxi-
mately 9′ by 14′10″ and BR II is 9′3″ by 14′6¾″) provides adequate play space, so that the living room must assume this function as well. This can conflict, of course, with
the prime use of the room as an entertainment area, and
may demand a frantic end-of-the-day cleanup before guests

arrive. This might have been avoided had a sliding partition been used to separate the two children's bedrooms. These rooms could then be thrown together for play space in the daylight hours, and separated for sleeping at night.

More Work Space

But perhaps the most regrettable deficiency in planning was the failure to include work space for these academically employed people. Since a study has not been provided, when the resident is a parent he must often choose between using one bedroom for himself or for his child—a painful and unnecessary conflict. It could have been resolved by sectioning off part of the living room—perhaps an area that would include the window, perpendicular to the dining wall—for a study. The resulting living room space might be less elegant than the original rectangle, but it would permit a considerably more harmonious existence.

The plan and design of the apartment affect the tenants' lives in even more specific ways. The proportions of the living room, for example, are ideally suited to the sparsely furnished, stripped-down esthetic championed by fashionable designers in the mid 1960s. One resident's handsome realist paintings, set off by her husband's interesting collection of American nineteenth-century furniture, seemed to contradict the proportions and demands for openness this space implies. Although estheticians have claimed that it is neutral, the space applies subtle directives in the choice of furniture styles and arrangements. The typical dining room wall provides a less subtle directive. This wall, which offers most direct access to the kitchen/living room pass-through (itself universally regarded as a waste of space) and is lit by a tall, narrow window, was clearly meant for a dining table. Moreover, if the table is not a long rectangle or oval, bur rather is a circle or square, an uncomfortable leftover space results. Most residents follow this unspoken directive, while those that fail to do so create a low-level but nevertheless real sense of discomfort.

Space for Play

To the extent that communality exists among the tenants, it has centered principally around children—in the organization of a nursery and babysitting co-op. Pressure from these groups, via the University Plaza Tenants' Association, obliged the university to construct additional playground space. Simple usage brought about other changes to the surrounding grounds. For example, no direct access had been provided from the northeasterly block (100 Bleecker Street) northeast to Bleecker Street. Tenants, taking the shortest route through the lawn, beat a path that, over opposition, was eventually sanctioned by blacktopping. Although community spirit is severely limited by the transient, competitive, upwardly mobile character of the residents, it has also been discouraged by the complete lack of community facilities, such as meeting rooms and social halls. The architect's responsibility for some of these negative features may be mitigated first by the budget limitations imposed through the Mitchell-Lama–funded co-op, which served as model for the rental towers, and second by the fact that the buildings were originally conceived as much for apartment-sharing graduate students as for young faculty members, although the former have been almost entirely displaced.

Elegant Status

Two socioeconomic factors that influence the residents' positive attitude toward these apartments are the extreme scarcity of housing at affordable rentals in New York City and the elegant status image of the Pei buildings. But beneath the claims of esthetic appreciation, I heard and sensed considerable resentment that sprang, in large measure, from the tenants' relationship with the owner. The buildings constitute, in a very real sense, a "company town" in which landlord and employer combine in one institution. The university contends that a break-even policy governs rentals, but the residents, many of whom settled here on the inducement of relatively inexpensive housing, have felt swindled by rent raises (based on rising costs) to which pay raises (based on "merit") were not quite equal, and doubt the claims of a landlord/boss who refuses to substantiate them by making the books public. The tenants' distrust is increased by the university's award of a virtual monopoly to the Grand Union supermarket, which is universally excoriated by housewives for poor service, unhealthy conditions, and inadequate stock. It is the one most hated element in the environment.

A Gilded Cage

University Towers, however gilded, remains a cage. Within its sculptured walls a sense of victimization exists no less real, if less obviously justified, than that experienced in low-income public housing. And it even gets expressed, assuming the validity of such interpretations, in similar ways—by active defacement and (easier on the middle-class conscience) careless usage of public spaces. Here, as everywhere, prospective residents were not participants in planning, construction, or administrative decisions. The transient nature of the tenantry—and its changing character—may have made this impossible, even undesirable from a planning standpoint—yet exclusion from those processes has inevitable consequences in the "passive resistance" of people who were presented, after all, with a *fait accompli* simply to accept or to reject. Superficial modifications might be instituted with effort—but the basic decisions were made by somebody else. The passivity fostered by noninvolvement in planning and administration, coupled with the transient nature of many academics, prevents even the consideration of what creative alternatives are available. For these reasons, and perhaps because of simple ignorance in the ways of modifying space, tenants have not partitioned the large living room to gain needed private areas. Given the shortage of adequate housing and a host of bourgeois palliatives (doormen, high-fashion imagery, convenient garaging, and the sense of a safe enclave amid hostility), continuation of this benevolent despotism must persist. Not until tenants decide to demand as much responsibility (not merely privilege) for their housing as students do for their education, will they start to become the clients for whom apartment blocks are built.

Bank of Amerika: A Second Check

Richard Parker

> A bank is many different things to many different people.
>
> *—from the Bank of America's annual report, 1969*

> The bank was the biggest capitalist establishment around . . . an example of American capitalism which is killing people around the world and in the United States.
>
> *—a student, explaining why the Bank of America was burned*

When students in Isla Vista attacked and burned the local branch of the Bank of America, they unleashed an enormous amount of criticism. The *Santa Barbara News-Press* called it "mindless anarchy" and the bank itself, in a $320,000 nation-wide ad campaign, declared it a "criminal act of violent proportions and . . . an insurrection against the democratic process." The Establishment consensus was that the violence of the student insurrection had been completely purposeless, and the attack against the bank especially so. After all, wasn't the bank being run at a loss as a public service for the students? And how could a tiny Isla Vista branch bank, with little more than $100,000 in deposits, be responsible for "killing people all around the world and in the United States"! All in all, there seemed little explanation for the burning (and the attacks on other property), and the general surmise has been that the students blew whatever legitimate grievances they had totally out of proportion, under the influence of outside agitators, drugs, or both.

What they fail to understand is that the students' legitimate grievances may very well have involved and may still continue to involve the bank and the "capitalist establishment" it represented. What they fail to understand is that the tiny little branch of the Bank of America may have symbolized to the students something as distasteful and reprehensible as the few crates of tea dumped by the Sons of Liberty into the Boston Harbor in 1773. For, after all, the Boston Tea Party was never really concerned about tea, but about a tea tax, and the corrupt and detestable regime which that tax represented. If the papers of the time had viewed the Tea Party only as an isolated incident, then it too would have been "mindless anarchy," and George might well have rightfully condemned it as a "criminal act of violent proportions and . . . an insurrection against the democratic process." But then those papers and that ruler would have made the same mistake as have the *News-Press* and the Bank of America and most other contemporary commentators. For the burning of the Isla Vista branch had at its roots a sound understanding of where America is today and what the rebellion of the young is all about.

The Bank of America itself is not a particularly corrupt or dishonest or inhuman institution, perhaps no more than the university or the government. When charged with being a part of the "capitalist establishment," it reacted with righteous indignation: "If, by 'capitalist establishment,' the revolutionary left means a conspiracy designed to deny all people their rights, then we categorically deny that charge." However, "we at Bank of America are most certainly a part of the American economic system . . . we are also proud to be part of the establishment in the real sense of that word: established law and order, established orderly process, established principles of the sanctity of life and property, established democratic functioning for the redress of grievances." But today to be "part of the American economic system" and to believe that "establishment, in the real sense of that word" is "law and order" may stand as a more serious indictment than the spuriously fabricated charge of "conspiracy."

American Banking

What, in fact, is the role of the Bank of America in "the American economic system"? First, the Bank of America is the largest nongovernmental bank in the world. Its $25,-600,000,000 resources make it larger than its nearest competitor, the Chase Manhattan, by one-fourth. It has 955 branches in California and ninety-six overseas. Its loans in 1969 totaled over $14.6 billion and deposits over $22.1 billion. It employs over 33,000 people. Its profit last year was $152,000,000.

The Bank of America also sits on the pinnacle of a highly pyramided financial industry. The House Committee on Banking and Currency recently reported on the enormous growth of banks and other financial institutions: between 1900 and the mid-1950s "the assets of financial institutions increased forty times, as compared with eighteen times for nonfinancial corporations. Therefore, the relative position of financial institutions . . . has increased markedly during the last sixty years." Leading this increase has been the Bank of America. Along with nineteen other banks, it controls 51.5 percent of the trust assets in the country, totaling over $129 billion. The high cost of technological advances, as well as costs in general, have forced corporations to turn continually to financial institutions for expansion capital. Thus, for example, the same House Committee reported that the big banks and other financial institutions now account for 85 percent of the debt financing and, through their trust departments, for a major and rapidly increasing proportion of the equity financing. One specific illustration of this dependency of corporations on banking institutions can be seen in Litton Industries, perhaps the most spectacular of the conglomerate corporations. The debt of Litton reached $474 million in 1969, up from $275 million a year earlier and from a mere $14 million in 1964. And who was behind much of the debt financing? Bank of America. It is no wonder that Roy Ash, president of Litton, sits on the Bank of America's board, to ensure the proper relations between the bank and its big customer.

The House Committee on Banking and Currency considers dependency situations such as this highly undesirable, for the obvious reason that greater and greater power tends to be concentrated in fewer and fewer hands, hands that are able to act behind-the-scenes, and ungoverned by the public interest. Not only interlocking directorates but interlocking ownership by banks have aggravated this situation: banks and other financial institutions own directly or through trust departments 27.4 percent of the shares of 225 large corporations, a figure well above what is considered "controlling interest."

The Bank of America has been quick to defend itself against charges of its economic power. "To anyone with even a rudimentary knowledge of the banking industry or economics, such a charge," President Clausen told the bank's stockholders, "is an obvious hoax. The banking industry is highly competitive. . . . Moreover, the banking industry is not only highly competitive, it is excessively regulated. . . . This combination of competition and regulation makes it utterly impossible for any one bank, or the banking industry collectively, to wield the kind of power the radical left seems to believe we have at our disposal."

Nonetheless, the Bank of America, in consort with a number of other powerful U.S. banks, did have the power to block legislation in the House Banking and Currency Committee. A bill aimed at stopping tax evasion and frauds through the illegal use of secret foreign bank accounts could have saved taxpayers hundreds of millions of dollars. Officials of the Nixon administration who had originally helped to write the bill reversed themselves before a congressional committee. Six days earlier, a justice department official had testified in favor of the bill, but in the interim representatives of the Bank of America, Chase Manhattan, First National City, and Chemical Bank New York Trust Company had been meeting with Eugene T. Rossides, an assistant secretary of the Treasury, trying to persuade him to withdraw treasury support. In the meantime, foreign bankers were meeting with officials of the state department. Representative Wright Patman, chairman of the committee, knew nothing of these meetings; when he called his two government witnesses on the second day of hearings, December 10, 1969, he assumed that they would support the bill. However, both Assistant Secretary Rossides and IRS Commissioner Randolph W. Thrower testified that they could no longer support the bill because it "went too far."

Moreover, such incidents of the banking industry's lobbying ability are not unusual. Congressman Patman once told a National Press Club luncheon that "the banking lobby is the single most potent lobby that operates year-round in Washington . . . the behind-the-scenes stories of this lobby would fill pages. Members of the House Banking and Currency Committee have been offered huge blocks of bank stock—free of charge—and directorships on bank boards. Freshman members have been approached—within hours of their arrival in Washington—and offered quick and immediate loan service. . . . While I do not intend to name names here today, it is an open secret on Capitol Hill that many campaign chests are swelled by contributions from the banks."*

Almost simultaneously with Patman's speech, it was disclosed that another member of the House Banking Committee, Congressman Seymour Halpern (D–N.Y.), was more than $100,000 in debt to the First National City Bank, including one $40,000 loan granted at a prime interest rate reserved for only the bank's biggest corporate customers.

"I leave it to you," Patman concluded his remarks, "to judge what these contributions and campaign assistance might mean on a crucial vote on banking legislation."

Furthermore, in the past few years the banks have found a significant loophole that allows them to sidestep many of the regulations that congress created to limit their power: the one-bank holding company. The one-bank holding company neatly avoids the prohibition that banks move into the industrial or merchandising fields by making the bank a

*New York Times, August 1, 1960.

pseudo-subsidiary of a larger holding company. When a holding company is created, nothing changes except the title of the corporation: in the case of the Bank of America, on April 1, 1969, the official title became the BankAmerica Corporation. A few of the board members dropped off and a few others were added, but the corporate officers remained the same and Bank of America stockholders received one share of the new corporation for each share they held in the old Bank of America.

The former president, R. A. Peterson, made the bank's intentions in the move crystal-clear: "A one-bank holding company presents possibilities for greater participation in a number of profitable activities, particularly overseas. While we have no specific business in mind, such activities might include leasing, warehousing, mutual funds, financing land development, travel bureaus, and other industries closely related to finance."* The last phrase, "closely related to finance," was a deliberate concession on the bank's part to the fears of congress. The specter of a few banks possibly gaining direct control of the already highly concentrated industrial and merchandising sectors of the economy was a thought few congressmen liked to imagine, and a situation they might pass legislation to avoid. Thus the Bank of America, like thirty-five of the one-hundred largest banks which had made the switch, was making loud noises about its intentions to stay clear of such dangerous shores.

But, ironically, such decisions may not entirely be in the hands of the banks. Describing the mood of congress, *The New York Times* warned that: " . . . there is concern that should one or more industrial companies gain control of a major bank (through a tender offer, for example) the other banks would be forced to defend themselves by forming great financial-industrial alliances."* What such alliances could hold for the future is not only of concern to the congress, but to pro-business elites as well. In an article reveiwing the one-bank holding company, *The Harvard Business*

*New York Times, September 18, 1968.

*February 20, 1969.

Review was quite clear in its own concern: "There is a potential for excessive concentration and restraint of trade when a bank, with its privileged position, strength, and resources, joins in an organization with nonbank companies which can improve their market power through the availability of lenient bank credit . . . Banking might become too closely allied with nonfinancial functions and develop great financial-industrial combines with excessive political as well as economic power."*

Given the earlier remarks of Congressman Patman about the banks' present political power, such combines might in the future make the ruse of democratic representation entirely unnecessary. Congressional inaction about holding companies is a testimony to their present strength. After a year of study and debate, a bill regulating the one-bank holding companies has yet to clear Congress. Apparently the banks' power has not been completely destroyed at the hands of "competition" and "excessive regulation."

The Bank of America vs. The Golden West

> The only legitimate business in the world today is to fill the needs of people.
>
> —*A.P. Giannini, founder, Bank of America*

In California, the Bank of America is known in the profession's parlance as a "multiservice" bank, providing, thanks to its enormous size and diversity of interests, its leadership and hard cash to all sectors of the economy. The bank was purchased in 1928 by A. P. Giannini, a former fruit and vegetable peddler and self-made financier. The bank's growth was rapid, particularly during the Second World War and the sixties; and although forced to divest of the huge Transamerica Corporation by the justice department, it continued to grow until it reached its present premier position.

*May-June, 1969, p. 113.

Agribusiness

> Agribusiness is the biggest business in California, so the biggest bank should support it, shouldn't it?
>
> —*A. W. Clausen, President, Bank of America*

In agribusiness, of course, the Bank of America is the state's uncontested leader. Alone, it finances over half of the agriculture in the state, and until recently, through its Transamerica Corporation, controlled such massive holdings of prime land as the Kern County Land Company. It prides itself on its progressive attitude in this enormously wealthy business, and can point to the University of California's Giannini Foundation of Agricultural Economics, established in 1928, as an example of the bank management's philanthropic foresight in the agricultural field.

However, the Giannini Foundation is a perfect symbol of the double standard that the big banks, big corporations, and big growers impose on the California economy. The foundation, like the university's agricultural sciences division as a whole, is designed to do for the growers what the growers won't do for themselves. In general, California growers have been the most conservative voices in the state, loudly proclaiming the virtues of free enterprise and denouncing the vices of government intervention. But curiously enough, their moral code has never seen fit to denounce the tax-supported government services which the university and its agencies like the Giannini Foundation provide. Even *The Wall Street Journal* has been bothered by agribusiness's double standards. Asking the question "Couldn't and shouldn't agriculture foot more of the bill," the *Journal* provided its own answers.* "With few exceptions, growers aren't involved in their own research, relying instead on the university. And their contributions to the university are minimal. In the fiscal year ended June 30, 1967 (figures for fis-

*September 9, 1968.

cal 1968 aren't available, but they're expected to be quite similar), the university's State Experiment Station spent more than $25 million. Of this, more than $17 million was state funds and nearly $7 million federal funds. Less than $1.5 million was from industry." This poor showing [the *Journal* continued] certainly isn't because California growers are poor: "Growers say their earnings, compared with the steady increase in sales, are no higher than they were a decade or more ago. Yet this income is being concentrated in far fewer hands. California's farms currently total about 65,000 down from 81,000 in 1964 and 123,000 in 1954. The number of farms is decreasing by about 3000 a year.

"The average U.S. farm is some 350 acres and valued at $50,000; the California average is nearly 460 acres and $216,000." Yet, despite this amazing concentration of capital resources, and the enormous strength of the various grower's associations and the banks behind them, it apparently never occurred to them that in a *real* free enterprise system, when research is to be done, the businessman doesn't turn to the government. General Motors, for instance, when it designs a new car, designs *its own* new car. But in agribusiness, the university does it for you.

Just one example should illustrate how agribusiness, and thereby the banks, profit from publically financed research. In the middle sixties, the university's Ag Sci researchers developed a mechanized tomato harvester that almost completely does away with manual labor. The harvester was coolly received by growers, until Cesar Chavez's organizers and the possibility of having to pay decent wages to farm workers suddenly caused a boom in interest.† But did the University profit by its invention, and turn back its profits for other needs such as farm-labor housing? Hardly.

Fred Dutton, of the UC regents, when he discovered what was happening, screamed bloody murder. The two university inventors, Hanna and Lorenzen, had received only a few thousand for their work; the university was receiving royalties, it was true, but according to Dutton growers were saving at least $14 million a year because of the harvester

†c.f. *The Wall Street Journal*, June 17, 1968.

and tomato developments and the university deserved a far larger return on its work than it was getting. And lest anyone imagine that universities should not dirty their hands with such lucre, it is wise to remember that the University of Wisconsin has made $43 million on patents since 1925 and that MIT got $13 million from IBM for a single computer device in 1964. God forbid that free-enterprise agribusiness should have to pay for what it gets!

There is another significance to the tomato harvester and agribusiness's interest in mechanization: machines don't join unions. Tomato growers were the largest users of bracero labor in California, and tomatoes constitute the largest cash vegetable crop. With machines, growers have been neatly able to duck the problems of decent wages and decent housing for their laborers because they have disposed of the workers entirely. The university has been right in the midst of the process, developing harvesting machines, at last count, for cantaloupe, asparagus, grapes, olives, peaches, lettuce, and strawberries, and a praying-mantis-like contraption for citrus fruits. If the university, the growers, and the banks have their way, farm labor may disappear entirely.

This indifference to people's needs can be seen as a constant thread running through the relation of the Bank of America to agribusiness. It was no accident, for example, that under the Brown administration the chairman of the State Board of Agriculture was Jesse Tapp, president of Bank of America (and an *ex oficio* UC regent), nor that Tapp fought long and hard against the termination of the bracero program in California. When, in 1964, then-Secretary of Labor Willard Wirtz seemed ready to discontinue the labor importation program, Tapp announced that he was firmly behind Govenor Brown's proposed defiant use of the Immigration Act (P.L. 414) to bring in braceros as a "necessary supplemental labor force," although the Immigration Act was really designed to bring in opera singers, the Beatles, and the like, rather than provide more cheap labor for the growers. Apparently the Bank of America's decision on bracero labor followed the logic of *Animal Farm*, that, in deciding "the needs of people," "Some are more equal than others."

Even now, in 1970, the Bank of America refuses to give up on bracero labor. George Murphy has introduced a bill in the senate that would restore the bracero program. [Bank] President Clausen, asked to comment on the bill in a recent interview, said, "That seems to be a just bill. There is need for legislation to protect both sides in the farm question." Senior Vice-President for Agribusiness Robert Long, added that the Murphy bill is "better than what we have now." The bracero program is necessary because, Long says, "they provide a necessary labor force that is not available elsewhere." Long also thinks that "they [the farm workers] aren't so bad off . . . it's all been badly distorted . . . they're much better off than they were five years ago." As for the grape strike and UFW, however, Long says, "We're not a dealer in grapes. The bank is not a farmer. It would be improper and unfair for us to take a position on this." Long is, nonetheless, a member of the California Council of Growers.

Another indication of the Bank of America's indifference to the needs of people can be seen on the bank's board of directors. Representing agribusiness is Robert Di Giorgio, head of the Di Giorgio Corporation, big user of bracero labor and long-time battler against the unionization of farm workers. Although several of the corporation's divisions have finally signed with Chavez's United Farm Workers (after long and bitter strikes), the Di Giorgio table grape vineyards remain Chavez's chief opponents. Di Giorgio is joined on the Bank of America board by three other members of the Di Giorgio board: A.E. Sharboro, Marshal Hale, and C.F. Wente. Other representatives of agribusiness include: Harry Baker, who produces cotton oil; Louis Petri, Italian Swiss Colony Wine; Roland Tognazzini of Union Sugar; Theodore Von der Ahe of Von's groceries. As expected, no representative of the farm workers sits on the board.

After the Isla Vista branch was destroyed, the bank spent over a quarter million dollars to publicize its side of the story around the country. One of its releases, entitled "Bank of America Comments on: Academic Freedom/Students' Rights/The Rhetoric of Revolutionaries," was a series of excerpts from President Clausen's address to the stockholders.

In his remarks, Clausen dealt with charges leveled against the bank by students; among the charges was one that the bank had exploited farm labor and took antiunion stands. Clausen made himself quite clear:

"The facts are these. We have consistently maintained that there are problems on both sides of the farm labor dispute. Certainly the problems of the farm workers are real. So are the economic problems of the growers. . . . While we believe [that farm labor legislation is necessary], we have also steadfastly maintained our policy of not taking sides in a labor dispute." Presumably the also "uncommitted" Di Giorgio, Sharboro, Hale, Wente, Baker, Petri, Tognazzini, and Von der Ahe were sitting nearby as he spoke.

The farm workers' views of the Bank of America's impartiality differ a bit from Mr. Clausen's. In December 1968, the United Farm Worker's newspaper, *El Malcriado*, reported that on January 10, 1968, the Agribusiness Investment Company took possession of a piece of land at a sale, reportedly forced because of debts owed by the owner to Bank of America. In attempting to negotiate a labor contract, the UFWOC discovered that the AIC head was also a B of A attorney. On October 24, Cesar Chavez sent the bank a telegram notifying them that the UFWOC represented a majority of the workers and asking for negotiations. At first the bank denied owning the land, but then reversed itself. Vice-President Iverson admitted that the bank owned and controlled the land, but said the bank planned to sell it. Iverson agreed to meet with union representatives, but later they were notified by telephone that the bank would neither negotiate, recognize the UFWOC, nor permit elections for the workers. According to *El Malcriado:* "They [the bank officials] claimed they were not legally obligated to do so, since farm workers were excluded from the National Labor Relations Act. Second, claimed one high B of A official, 'We don't want to lead the parade . . . this is a social revolution.' Bank officials also reportedly said, 'We have more important business to attend to.' " Such as serving the needs of people? Or making sure the Bank of America was "not taking sides in a labor dispute"?

The bank is implicated in antilabor activities by its close

relationship with Dillingham Corporation. Lowell S. Dillingham, Dillingham president, is a long-time director of Bank of America. Rudolph Peterson, ex-president and current chairman of the Executive Committee of Bank of America, is a Dillingham director. Bank of America handles a major part of Dillingham's worldwide financing. Anyway, Dillingham mailed out on January 26, 1970, a letter from Vice-President Robert O. Briggs soliciting contributions for "Californians for Right To Work," a lobbying group that seeks a law prohibiting the union shop in California. A letter from the Californians for Right To Work was enclosed in the mailing.

The Bank and the Bombers, or, Good Germans Come in All Sizes

The Bank of America, as could be expected, is also involved in the defense industry. After agribusiness, the military-industrial complex is just about the biggest single industry in California, and it is only appropriate that California's biggest bank should be its friend. In 1968, California pulled down $6.5 billion of the total $42 billion defense department contract budget, and the Bank of America figured importantly in financing many of the giant corporations' activities. For example, it recently joined with other banks in creating a $200 million revolving credit arrangement for Boeing, seventh largest defense contractor in the nation, and manufacturer of such favorite weapons of destruction as the B-52 and Minuteman missile (as well as the great noise polluter, the SST). . . .

The Bank of America also enjoys special relations with the brains as well as the brawn of the military-industrial complex. Three of the bank's directors, including Chairman Louis Lundborg, sit on the board of Stanford Research Institute, a Palo Alto think-tank with a $60 million annual budget, half of which comes from the defense department. Stanford Research has or is holding contracts for such socially useful projects as the ABM, chemical warfare dispersion techniques, counterinsurgency warfare in both Thailand

and Vietnam, "reconnaissance surveillance and intelligence," and weapons systems analysis. Stanford Research personnel originated the "strategic hamlet" concept for Vietnam and also developed the CS tear gas sprayed by the helicopters at People's Park.

• • •

Finally, if the war in Vietnam is hurting the economy (as it undoubtedly is), the Bank of America is not feeling the pinch. Despite the tightest money policy in memory and the highest interest rates, the Bank of America's profits have climbed every year, up 50 percent since 1965, to $152,000,-000. If the Bank of America is not profiting from the war, it is not from lack of trying.

The Bank in Real Estate

Although most of its lending is commercial, the Bank of America nonetheless handed out over $3.4 billion in individual real estate loans in 1969. Since the building and buying of homes (and commercial buildings as well) was generally slowed by inflation, this sum constituted an important factor in the California real estate market. In general the bank claims to have a relatively enlightened attitude in this field, and proudly points to the $100 million loan pool it created for residents of minority-group areas. However, this is not the whole story.

The crisis in housing today is severe. *Fortune* magazine in December, 1969, carried a long article, whose first paragraph contained this warning:

"A housing crisis is building up in the United States. The shortage of acceptable shelter that has long been afflicting the poor and the black is spreading to the white middle class and even to quite affluent families. It may be that conditions are at their worst right now. But a real turnabout will not come quickly, for the housing industry is at present simply not well organized or well enough financed to make rapid solutions possible."

• • •

It is popular to attribute much of the rise in housing cost to the cost of materials and labor, pointing to the high wages in the building-crafts industry as an example of exorbitant costs. But, in fact, *Fortune* estimates that the expense of labor and materials adds up to only a 4 or 5 percent annual increase in the cost of housing; in contrast, land alone in metropolitan areas has increased 10 to 25 percent in little more than a year and, with the cost of financing, adds well over 5 percent to the average home cost. And, of course, it is the banks, saving and loan, and insurance companies which dominate the real estate and building-finance industries. Since most home mortgaging is going on now at between 8 and 9 percent, it is little wonder that half of America cannot afford mortgages on even a $20,000 home.

Clearly, the Bank of America is not alone at fault; the entire system is. In the inflationary spiral which is a necessity of the "New Economics" capitalism, it is the small and not the large who suffer the burdensome consequences. Thus enough money is always available for the big financiers, but not for the man who wants a home for his family. For example, Kirk Kerkorian last year obtained two loans from the Bank of America totaling $73 million, both *unsecured* except for Kerkorian's signature. This is an extraordinary sum of money to put in one man's hands just on the basis of a signature, but President Clausen reasoned Mr. Kerkorian was "a man of his word, a man of integrity." Had the loan been handled normally, the Federal Reserve Board regulations would have required collateral equal to five times the loan . . . a sum unmanageable, even for a wizard like Kerkorian. Although the country needs twenty-six million new homes, the major achievement of Kerkorian so far has been the International Hotel in Las Vegas. One wonders whether the country needs more homes in Harlem and Watts or hotels in Las Vegas.

Accused of such inequities, the Bank of America is quite fond of pointing to its $100 million loan fund for minority-group areas. It will speak of fulfilling its "social responsibility," and perhaps even repeat again for you the Giannini quote about "filling the needs of people." President Clausen saw fit to mention the program at length in his address to the stockholders, calling it officially the "New Opportunity Home

Loan Program," and even implying that it was a sacrifice for the bank because it "could have invested the funds more profitably in other endeavors."

A little more scrutiny, however, reveals a different picture. First of all, there is no "pool" of loan capital sitting idly waiting for some deserving black of chicano to arrive. The money is out and earning money in other fields. What Clausen means when he says $100 million has been "set aside" is purely nominal; the only substantial difference in this loan pool is that, when a minority member comes into a B of A branch to request a loan, the square footage minimum is reduced from 1000 to 750 square feet and the number of bedrooms from three to two. There is no mention in any of the bank literature of a reduced interest rate. Half of America cannot even afford mortgage payments on a $20,000 home, and there is no question in which half the majority of blacks and chicanos fall.

However, this does not mean that the loan "pool" has gone unused; Bank of America figures show that $31 million has been loaned out already. In its annual report, it features the Leslie family, a black family in Los Angeles, and the home the B of A financed for them. The story, after describing the $30,000 home of the Leslies, concludes, "And so after a dozen years of searching for a suitable home they could afford, the Leslies have finally found the shoe that fits and are wearing it happily. That, too, is what banking is all about."

With the prince riding off into the sunset, one gets the impression that the bank has done one more good deed for the day. But if it's a good deed, it's a good deed Urban League style. For the Leslies are no poor black family. Mr. Leslie is a municipal employee, with a good credit background and a middle-class income. What the Bank of America did was secure a loan they would have secured for any white family; the Leslies only happened to be black. Perhaps that proves the bank isn't racist, but more likely it means that the bank, like a lot of other businesses, has discovered that money is color-blind; that as long as there's enough of it, it doesn't matter whether a black or white is holding it. For Mr. Leslie and the 1900 other middle-class black or brown families helped by the Bank of America, things may be brighter; in the ghettos and the barrios, time moves more slowly.

The Bank Overseas

Because banks have been limited by law in their expansion within the United States, many of the biggest have turned outside for their future growth. The Bank of America is no exception. Begun originally as an outgrowth of the Bank of Italy, the B of A has returned to Italy and to seventy-four other countries and territories with almost one-hundred overseas branches. In 1969 alone, the B of A opened thirteen new branches, in spots diverse and as distant as England and Singapore.

Most of the international growth for the Bank of America has been in the last decade. In 1960, the bank had only nineteen overseas offices and $2 billion in overseas resources; by 1969, it had ninety-six offices and $7 billion in resources. This expansion is paralleled only by a handful of big banks —only Chase Manhattan, First National City, and Morgan Guaranty operate larger overseas networks. (But among the top ten banks are divided, at a conservative estimate, 75 percent of the foreign assets of U.S. banks.)

This growth in overseas finance closely parallels and reenforces the growth of U.S. corporations abroad. Indeed the financing forms much of the basis for that corporate expansion. By 1967 U.S. direct private foreign investment reached $67 billion, a fivefold increase since 1950. The actual far exceeds the official figure, surpassing $130 billion. With a 10 percent annual growth rate, these foreign investments are far outstripping domestic growth.

• • •

In general, American banks and corporations have been unwilling to work closely with those economies in which strong state control is exercised. Since there are few other sources of the needed capital than the big banks and corporations of America and Europe, most underdeveloped countries have been placed in the impossible position of

having to accept private investment with precisely the im-
balances it creates.

Tanzania, for example, allowed several foreign banks to
enter the country for exactly those reasons. But after several years, experience, Julius Nyerere, Tanzania's president,
announced in 1967 that he was nationalizing the foreign
banks, calling them "parasites" and "exploiters of Africa."
The Bank of America was one of the banks.*

Likewise, Argentina announced in early 1969 that it
planned to halt further penetration of the national economy
by American banking. Although ruled by a right-wing dictator who is definitely pro-American, Argentina placed severe
limits on foreign banks: half of the directors of any new
bank were required to live in the area of operation and
new foreign banks would be permitted only if they brought
new capital in the country and only if they would intensify
trade and financial relations with other countries.† The Bank
of America has four branches in Buenos Aires.

The bank's executive vice-president for international affairs, Roland Pierotti, was delightfully ingenuous in his discussion of the resistance to U.S. capitalism's intrusion. Explaining why even the Canadians, America's major economic
satellite, had refused to allow U.S. branch banks, he said,
"They're charmingly frank about it. 'You own all the industry
up here', they say. 'The least you can do is let us have our
own banks.' "‡ Venezuela and Chile have prohibited U.S.
branches, as has Mexico as well.

A perfect example of just what these countries have to
fear was offered by the bank itself as "the wave of the future" in its annual report. Featured was the Rio Tinto-Zinc
Corporation's copper mine in Bouganville, Solomon Islands.
The Bank of America organized the syndicate providing $350
million capital. To the bank, the project displayed "the mark
of a truly international bank in today's complex and interdependent world"; to the Solomon Islanders, it apprently
displayed something else:

*The New York Times, February 17, 1967.
†The New York Times, January 17, 1969.
‡Forbes, June 15, 1969.

"Sydney, Australia, Aug. 5—The police used tear gas and batons Tuesday to disperse inhabitants of Bouganville in the Solomon Islands who were trying to keep bulldozers from clearing land expropriated from them.

"A British-controlled concern in Australia will build a construction camp and storehouses on the land for a huge copper development on the island.

"The Papua–New Guinea administration, which is controlled by the Australian government, took over the land for the company after the villagers of Boro Vana refused to lease it. The bulldozers began work yesterday on the land, which is a mile from the village and covers 175 acres. The Australian government has said that the villagers have been adequately compensated for the land and its crops and that the copper project would be of immense value to the territory."†

• • •

The issue of Vietnam raises two interesting points about the Bank of America. President Clausen, in his address to the bank's stockholders, said, in effect, that the Bank of America opposed the war in Vietnam. "The war distorts the economy; it is a major contributor to inflation; it draws off resources that could be put to work towards solving imperative problems facing this nation at home . . . this bank has consistently pointed out that an end to the war in Vietnam would be good, not bad, for American business." But with the lure of profit, the Bank of America opened up a branch in Saigon in 1966, well after it was clear what was happening in that country. Moreover, it operates five military branches on bases in South Vietnam (and three in Thailand) to serve the military personnel. Presumably, had the Bank of America been a wee bit more firmly against the war, such things might not have happened. But then war and business-as-usual are not incompatible.

The second important observation also concerns Clausen's remarks. As well as "opposing" the war in Vietnam, he also tried to answer charges that the Bank of America helped exploit underdeveloped countries. He said, "It would be a

†*The New York Times,* August 7, 1969.

tragic mistake to take an exploitative position in any country's development. . . . In the political climate that exists in most lesser developed countries, the only passport to success is to help, not exploit, that country." Apart from the already-cited examples of Tanzania, Argentina, Bouganville, and South Vietnam, how do these noble words compare with the bank's other words and deeds?

The *U.N. World Economic Survey* has computed that the economic aid now being received by the underdeveloped countries totals no more than is due in interest on previous loans. The international aid situation is clearly disastrous. How to solve it? On March 1 of this year, President Nixon released his new study of foreign aid, the Peterson Report, so named in honor of the committee's chairman, Rudolph Peterson. Mr. Peterson retired as president of the Bank of America this year to become chairman of its executive committee. The report offers important insights into the thinking not only of President Nixon but of the Bank of America's top executive.

First, it is tart in its appraisal of internationalizing foreign aid: "The international organizations will have to take a less parochial view of their mission," although Senator Fulbright has condemned the alternative of bilateral aid for "becoming a vehicle for deep American involvement in areas and issues which lie beyond both our vital interests and our competence." The report also says a chief impediment is "unresponsive social and political systems," though it wasn't the unanimous conclusion of commentators that it wasn't the likes of Thieu, Chiang Kai-shek, or the Greek or Latin American juntas that the Peterson Report had in mind. The report goes on to predict that military aid will go up rather than down, since "as the United States reduces its forces overseas, increased security assistance may be needed for a time, to cushion the effect and to improve local security capabilities."

In addition, the report counsels, "Removing [legislative restrictions] would put the United States in a better position to work out with those countries, on a mature partnership basis, military equipment expenditure policies. . . ." Peterson, as the *New Republic* concludes, "is going to be a very

popular fellow in Athens, Rio de Janeiro, and Bangkok."*
The Bank of America is already a "popular fellow" in several of those countries, having opened branches soon after right-wing coups in Greece (1968), Indonesia (1967), and Guatemala (1957), for example, and maintaining banking facilities in Brazil, Rhodesia, and Paraguay.

The Peterson Report also offers hope of closer government cooperation with private industry and finance. Rejecting the earlier recommendation of the Pearson Commission that the advanced nations of the world use one percent of their gross national products each year to aid the underdeveloped countries, the Peterson Report prefers small quantities of aid, distributed in several ways. One of the chief ways would be through a federal foundation or authority that would place funds in the hands of "nongovernmental organizations" that "have demonstrated their qualifications and effectiveness in supporting social and political development." Translated, that means "nongovernmental organizations" like the Bank of America, who could administer aid programs, learn about infrastructures, and provide itself with enormous new leverage for private action, all while receiving a fee from the government.

Peterson wrote in June 1969: "The efforts of private development assistance organizations . . . to assist the modernization process are contributing to the atmosphere in which all business operates, just as the assistance of A.I.D. improves the climate for venture banking. With the end of the colonial era most European banks pulled back from Asia. The time is now ripe for their return with the new dimension of venture banking."

A sidelight: Peterson's remarks above were prepared for the Asia Foundation *Program Quarterly*. Peterson is a member of the board of trustees of the foundation, as is Russell G. Smith, the board's chairman as well as the Bank of America's executive vice-president for international affairs. Russell helped set up the foundation in 1954. The Asia Foundation was, until two years ago, a major recipient and conduit of C.I.A. funds.

*March 21, 1970.

Daddy Bigbucks vs. Mother Nature

Black Gold Goes North

Oil feeds industry, and industry needs oil. Contemporary America is a petroleum-based technology, and oil interests pack a wallop that few other groups can claim. The 27½ percent (now 22½ percent) oil depletion allowance is famous. The senators in Washington known informally as the "friends of oil" are legion. Even the presidency is subject to oil's pressure: when, after long debate by his own study group, reduction of the ridiculously high oil-import quotas was recommended, Nixon shelved the report. His decision costs Americans over $5 billion each year; but oil is stronger than people.

The Bank of America played a crucial part in the Alaskan oil drive. Appointed by the state, the bank was placed in charge of the $900 million Alaska received, investing it in treasury securities, where it has already earned over $50 million in interest for the state in a little over six months. The bank is very proud of its role—in its annual report, it declared: "Thus it was both gratifying and challenging that our bank was selected to do the job . . . perhaps no other event could have more graphically demonstrated our bank's capability in the money markets of the United States."

The Alaskan sale also "graphically demonstrates" several other things, about both the Bank of America and the mentality of profit. Well before the land was leased, it was clear that there were dangers involved, the biggest being transportation of the oil from the inaccessible North Slope to the markets. The oil companies' solution was a 800-mile pipeline; but now the federal government has an injunction on that pipeline, because pumping hot oil across frozen tundra, it turns out, melts the permafrost which then never refreezes. After Santa Barbara, the "Torrey Canyon," and the Chevron platform off Louisiana, the department of the interior has suddenly woken up to oil company promises about safety: the damage to the ecology of the region may prove greater than the money gained.

But the odds are that the pipeline will go through. Nine hundred million dollars is still nine hundred million dollars, and it will take a real natural disaster to stop its momentum. That's what is frightening about the Bank of America, and the big corporations: the bank's pride in its service is in the dollars it has made, both for itself and for the state of Alaska, not in a balanced picture of the needs of the state. The bank will tell you that it's not their responsibility but then Union Oil was saying the same thing when the well blew off Santa Barbara, as were auto manufacturers while cars were killing people because of faulty construction. Business and profit have an autonomy and logic all their own which they defend vigorously against outside interference; but since corporations function as part of the whole environment, and we are coming to realize that their actions affect us all, it seems nineteenth century to permit the kind of decisions which $900 million is able to dictate. In the old morality of the Church, the Bank of America is guilty of the sin of omission, rather than commission, hurting others by what it has not done and could have done.

The California Water Project

The bank has been one of the strongest supporters of the water project, designed to bring Northern California water south to the growers of the central valleys and the urban sprawls of the south. The bank profits in three ways from the project: (1) by underwriting the bond issues and holding a large percentage of the water bonds; (2) by the population growth in Southern California that the water system will allow; and (3) by the great expansion of agribusiness that will use the bulk of the water.

* * *

Among other things, the water project will enhance a trend already mentioned in agribusiness: consolidation. Robert Long, the bank's senior vice-president for agribusiness, admitted to a recent interviewer that the water project "is creating considerable turmoil . . . the water will not be available to medium and smaller operations (because of the high price) . . . it has to be a large-scale, very well financed company" to take advantage of the irrigation water. In other words, the water project will bring new lands under cultivation in a period of surpluses and overproduction, and will help drive the small owners out of business.

When Bank of America Vice-President Lee Prussia was asked about the potential ecological disaster the water project may hold for Northern California—the words might apply to Alaska as well—he replied: "A financial institution, historically and traditionally, has not been responsible for these kinds of decisions. We need not take a stand on issues of ecology."

The Bank and the Credit Card: Life by the Numbers

It was the Bank of America in 1959 which kicked off the "charge card" craze. Since then banks, with the B of A chief among them, have mailed out more than a hundred million of the cards, and the BankAmericard alone claims twenty-nine million holders. Not surprisingly, the charge card is a major part of the bank's annual profits. In 1968, the profit of this operation was estimated at $8 million and it has been climbing ever since.

The logic of the cards is quite simple: in the new technological age money is old-fashioned—so what we need is a substitute. And who better to offer the substitute than the banks, who, managers of money as well, can have their cake and eat it too. The Bank of America is fulsome in its statistical praise; in its annual report, it announced contentedly: "During the year, BankAmericard coverage expanded to forty-nine states and forty-eight foreign areas . . . cardholders increased from sixteen to twenty-nine million, and business outlets accepting the card rose from 397,000 to 646,000. Banks involved in the program increased from

1864 to 3350. National and international sales on the card are estimated to total over $2 billion for 1969."

In California alone, sales exceeded $500 million, a one-year, 25 percent jump.

What the bank does not like to mention is the effective interest rate on the BankAmericard: *18* percent per annum, on extended balances. What they advertise is the innocuous 1½ percent monthly rate, a seemingly small amount to pay for the "convenience" of a charge card. But if the bill is not payed within twenty-five days of purchase, it is compounded again and then again and again. It appears that among card-users this "extended balance" is more and more common: average indebtedness to the card is $185, according to federal reserve economists, and 78 percent of the cardholders use extended balance.* Bank of America officials say that in a "mature" Californian consumer area (saturated with cards), the bank realizes two-thirds of its profits from interest on the extended balances.

The bank is encouraging expansion of the extended credit system as well. Previously, it found small installment loans unprofitable, even at high interest rates—now the Bank-Americard is providing with computer technology and high volume, a convenient, extremely profitable substitute. Donald McBride, president of the BankAmericard Service Corporation (the bank's nationwide licensing subsidiary), furthermore foresees an increasing size to BankAmericard purchases—payment of income tax is already possible with the card, and McBride sees automobile purchases as the next big "breakthrough."

In the future, "in this century" says McBride, "everyone will have an ID card that will be the prime medium of exchange." Credit will be instantly checked by telephoning a computer. And at the end of the month, every cardholder will be able to take out an installment loan automatically by extending his balance—at 18 percent a year, naturally.

Life, March 27, 1970.

The Bank and Isla Vista

The Bank was on occasions less than honest in its dealings with the students. In December of 1969, the associated students of the university voted to remove student body funds from the Goleta branch of the Bank of America to protest the bank's involvement in agribusiness. D. J. Poulsen, B of A branch manager in Isla Vista, wrote to the student paper, *El Gaucho,* that he was "sorry you saw fit to take this action. . . . our bank is subsidizing a number of branches, such as Isla Vista, in university areas for the purpose of serving students." Four months later, however, in an interview with the college press service, Bank of America Vice-President Walter Hoadley said the Isla Vista branch was a special "test branch" for the bank's marketing research. According to Hoadley: "Isla Vista was one of our test branches, under my personal responsibility." It was "part of a long-range program to find out the financial attitudes of people age seventeen to twenty-five—what they know, what they want. . . . What we were doing there was laying the groundwork for financial services to be offered all over the state."

Like most college branches, the Isla Vista branch was not profitable. It was "an investment in future loyal customers," according to Barney Taylor, one of the bank's marketing research executives. As people grow older, they use more bank services. To help find out what the people want, the bank hired outside research firms to interview college students. In addition, the bank sponsored "focus groups" of six to ten college students who discussed banks and credit under the guidance of a moderator. The students didn't know who sponsored the discussions. The sessions were taped and sometimes a bank representative observed from behind a one-way mirror.

Afterthoughts

When the Bank of America was burned to the ground in Isla Vista, there were probably a variety of motivations in the crowd, some puerile, some wanton, but most with at least fundamental understanding of why they were there. It is becoming more popular now to concede that "some" of the students' protest was justified—more and more, people in the Establishment have recognized that the university is undemocratic, that the police have been violent, and that the realtors in Isla Vista have been charging excessive rents for apartments.

But to concede those failings, without conceding the centrality of the Bank of America, is to play a false and self-deceiving game. The students were selective in their attacks —one realty company was untouched because its owner had dealt fairly with the students; other stores likewise went untouched. Contrary to the *News-Press*, what happened in Isla Vista was not "mindless anarchy" but mindful rebellion.

For capitalism, and the economic and social life which it imposes on this nation, are what the students most bitterly despise. In increasing numbers, they are discovering that the minds of university bureaucrats, like the minds of the police, the minds of the Right, and the minds of our rulers, are conditioned by the capitalist society in which we live.

Capitalism to students is opposing a war by building branch offices in the war zones and providing the capital for weapons manufacturers.

Capitalism to the students is saying that you're helping poor blacks and browns when you're really making money off the middle class.

Capitalism to the students is saying, after the Santa Barbara oil spill: "We need not take a stand on the issue of ecology."

Capitalism to the students is helping the rich keep secret bank accounts that cost "hundreds of millions" while fifteen million people are malnourished in this country.

Capitalism is to the students driving natives from their lands to exploit more natural resources.

Capitalism to the students is saying you take no sides in a labor dispute, then refusing to negotiate with a labor union whose only goal is a decent wage for the working poor.

Capitalism to students is the duplicity of calling yourself a "public service" when you really just want to make money off students.

Capitalism to the students is a system which feeds on the weakness in man, strives to make him insecure, and then gives him security through the possession of *things* and the manipulation of *people*. It presumes that if each individual functions in his own interest the society will take care of itself.

Capitalism defines the value of a man by the money he makes, not by what he believes, or what he cares for. Gentleness, generosity, communities for people to live in, all these things *can* happen in capitalism, but only after profit has been satisfied. Farmworkers can be paid decent wages, but only after the growers have made their fortunes. Homes for the poor can be built, but only after hotels for the rich are in service. The poor of the world can be liberated from their misery, but only after the bank has made its money.

What the students in Isla Vista have demanded is not a bigger percent of profits for charity, nor even a voice in the administration of the capitalist empire; they have demanded its end. The accumulation of *goods* that demand our loyalty and destroy our environment, that place us in competition instead of cooperation with our fellow man, must end. The exploitation of blacks, of browns, of the students themselves must end. The unequal treatment of men because of the unequal sharing of property must end. At the beginning the Isla Vista rebellion was compared with the Boston Tea Party: an act insane alone but ultimately part of an organized resistance that made a revolution. William O. Douglas, associate justice of the supreme court, recently wrote these words:

"George III was the symbol against which our Founders

made a revolution now considered bright and glorious. George III had not crossed the seas to fasten a foreign yoke on us. George III and his dynasty had established and nurtured us and all that he did was by no means oppressive. But a vast restructuring of laws and institutions was necessary if the people were to be content. That restructuring was not forthcoming and there was revolution.

We must realize that today's Establishment is the new George III. Whether it will continue to adhere to his tactics, we do not know. If it does, the redress, honored in tradition, is also revolution.

POWER TO THE PEOPLE

Bill Buckley: Covert King of Rock Radio

Richard Reingold

A foolish consistency, the hobgoblin of small minds, is not one of William F. Buckley Jr.'s problems. As a major stockholder of what has become, while nobody was much noticing, a formidable chain of radio stations, the most engaging of American conservatives might have had them mouthing his own political and social views. Yet he has done nothing of the kind. On some of his stations, in fact, he has allowed a type of programming that even a Berrigan brother might look upon with favor.

Bill Buckley, the owner, editor, and chief moralist of the *National Review,* owns hard rock stations, soul music stations, underground screw-City-Hall stations. Where the audience has seemed to want them, Starr Broadcasting Group, Inc., of which Bill Buckley is chairman, has employed hippie disk jockeys and turned-on disk jockeys and announcers who, when not advertising head shops and skin flicks, read editorials deploring the war in Vietnam.

What has happened to our Bill? Has the plump little liberal sometimes thought to be hiding in every lean conservative at last emerged? Not exactly. What has actually emerged is the prospect of tidy capital gains and a gentlemanly six-figure profit.

In his magazine, his nationally syndicated newspaper column, and his TV show, the real Bill Buckley keeps churning

From *New York* Magazine (June 14, 1971). Copyright © 1971 by the NYM Corporation. By permission of *New York* Magazine.

out brightly doctrinaire conservatism for a sometimes eager and often amused public. Recently, for example, he tore into Carter Burden, a New York City councilman and principal owner of the *Village Voice*. Burden, like Buckley, is the child of wealth, but there any possible resemblance ends. Buckley was incensed at two articles of a hostile and gossipy nature on Henry Kissinger which the *Village Voice* had published, and he privately wrote Burden asking him to disown them. Burden refused to buy Buckley's position, and Buckley seemed to hit the ceiling and the typewriter, in that order.

The essence of Burden's reply, Buckley wrote in his newspaper column, is that "it is none of his [Burden's] business what runs in the *Voice*." With resounding disapproval, Buckley quoted Burden as saying: "It would be a grave disservice to the integrity of the paper and its staff if I were to presume that mere ownership of stock gives me a special right to protest its policies . . . . That is not to say that I do not recognize the responsibility which is inherent in any stock ownership—I fully accept responsibility for the *Voice*'s authors to write what they choose." Buckley found this view "absolutely novel in the theory of business."

"Rescued from the litotes," wrote Buckley, "that sentence says that the owner of a newspaper has a responsibility to publish anything anybody wants, never mind taste, judgment, the libel laws."

Buckley subsequently tore into Simon and Schuster for publishing Jerry Rubin's *Do It!*

"I want my dirty pictures sold to me by dirty little men, hidden in Russian Easter eggs," Buckley wrote, "not passed out ceremoniously by men and women who pride themselves on their contributions to thought and literature and who regularly publish great tracts of prose devoted to the maintenance of humane standards.

"So, Simon and Schuster will make themselves a hundred grand or so from the publication of this book, forever reminding us of Lenin's dictum that when the last of the bourgeoisie is hanged a capitalist will sell the rope. I shall think of Simon and Schuster when I think of Jerry Rubin. . . ."

If this kind of reasoning prevails elsewhere, certain citizens of Memphis, Tennessee, may think of William F. Buckley Jr. when *they* think of Jerry Rubin. WLOK, Buckley's funky Memphis radio station, seems not all that disdainful of the Rubin opus. In an editorial read over the air, it said: "The Memphis Review Board has found a book 'obscene' and brought pressure to prevent the sale of the book. . . . Members of the Review Board, the laughter you hear is not Jerry Rubin. It's your children."

WLOK's editorials, called Open Letters, do not seem to inhabit the same world, let alone the same corporation, that William F. Buckley Jr. bustles in. Their points of view differ in small matters as in large issues. "Seeing *Hair* makes me a little prouder of middle-class establishmentarian standards," Bill once declared. "WLOK heartily endorses the message of *Hair*, . . . Peace, love, and understanding. . . . May the Age of Aquarius soon be upon us," declared WLOK.

The schism between Bill Buckley, capitalist, and one of the stations that employs his capital includes Vietnam. "America's young men will die," WLOK editorialized. "America's resources will be committed to war. . . . Poverty, pollution, urban overcrowding, inflation . . . will all have to wait as we concentrate on a wider, winless, and unwinnable war."

"If Buckley ever heard one of our editorials, he'd drop down dead," says a WLOK staffer. Perhaps. Peter Starr, President of the Starr Broadcasting chain, says that his boss never sees editorial comments before they are aired. But he says that Buckley is aware of the programming at each of his stations, has approved of all the different formats, and has personally visited most of the stations. "His beliefs have nothing to do with the service of a particular station to a particular market," says Starr. "A station has to serve an area. There's an old rule in broadcasting that says: Don't program for yourself."

The man who so forcefully reminded Carter Burden of the responsibilities of ownership has been on occasion as permissive an owner as any iconoclastic employee could have wished. A few years ago Starr Broadcasting bought KCJC-FM, Kansas City, Kansas, then getting by as a "beautiful music" station. But shortly after the Buckley crew took over, a rival station, owned by the Mormon Church, began to out-Mantovani KCJC, and the ratings and profits fell. The Buckley management thought it knew what to do about *that* problem. They changed formats and for most of 1968 and 1969 programmed hard rock twenty-four hours a day.

"We had a bunch of freaks on that station," recalls Mike D'Arcy, Starr Broadcasting's national program director. "They were total freaks who were really into the scene."*

"The station was typical of all underground stations," says another Buckley employee, who has since left the station. "It had a lot of revolutionary talk going over the air. You know, the 'Let's blow up City Hall' kind of thing. But you can't tell people things like that. The [new format] was a financial disaster."

You win one, you lose one. The Buckley management shrugged off rock and revolution as being unprofitable at this time in Kansas City. In November 1969 the psychedelic posters came down from the station walls, the freaks were sent on their way, automated equipment was installed, and the station switched to bland music.

The public Bill Buckley is one of the rock scene's less hospitable critics. "I think the reason they hide in rock music," he declared of today's rotten kids on his TV show, "is because they are philosophically jejuned, and this is a way to make them sound sort of philosophical and heady and profound, whereas, in fact, they're just sort of a shallow recapitulation of pre-Adamite notions about personal hedonism."

One of Buckley's *National Review* editors, Frank S. Meyer —who should perhaps in his professional capacity have been given a crack at that particular sample of the boss's style —states the party line somewhat more crisply: "[Rock] is to be understood not as a form of pop music but as a constituent of the symbolism of revolt."

*That's what Mr. D'Arcy told me, and that's what my notebook, with notes taken during the interview, says he told me. At press time, I was advised that Mr. D'Arcy is prepared to sign an affidavit disclaiming and denying that he ever made these statements.—R.R.

The symbolism notwithstanding, it's not stretching the point all that much to say that William F. Buckley Jr. was one of rock 'n' roll's first popularizers. The first station Buckley ever bought, back in 1957, was KOWH in Omaha, which lays claim to being the first rock radio station in America. The price was $822,500, and the purchase came a year and a half after the founding of the *National Review*. In fact, National Review Inc., parent company of the magazine, was the actual licensee of the station. Frank Meyer recalls that the hope was that KOWH's profits would help sustain *NR*. "We kidded Bill a bit about it," Meyer recalls. "He just shrugged his shoulders."

The station's profits tapered off, however, due to a rock competitor. In fact, Buckley's broadcasting empire did not really get off the ground until 1964, when Peter Starr graduated from Georgetown University and went out to KOWH as a salesman. Starr was twenty-two then and had been a Buckley protégé for a decade, first as a newsboy delivering the Stamford *Advocate* to the Buckley home. At twelve, he called Bill and asked for a job on his yacht. "I got it, and I've been working for him ever since," says Starr.

Starr quickly proved to be the best salesman on the KOWH staff. Within five months he was general manager, and in 1965 gave the station its first profitable year since 1958. Starr Broadcasting Group Inc. was formed the following year. Buckley got two-thirds of the stock and became chairman of the board; Starr got one-third and became president and chief executive officer. In its first year, Starr Broadcasting bought a station in Sioux Falls, South Dakota. The following year it went into the Kansas City market. In 1969, it took over three black-oriented soul stations in Houston, Memphis, and New Orleans and a country-and-western music station in Little Rock.

To finance the acquisitions, Starr Broadcasting went public. Buckley's share of the company, as a result, is now about 13 percent, but he remains the second largest shareholder.

More recently, the company has purchased KEIR-FM in Dallas and is awaiting FCC approval to take over WCAM in Camden, New Jersey. In the past year, Starr Broadcasting has also begun to invade television. It now owns WCYB-TV, the NBC affiliate in the Bristol, Virginia, Johnson City and Kingsport, Tennessee, area. And the takeover of KHVH-TV in Honolulu is now pending FCC approval. All told, the Buckley radio and TV holdings cost over $14.5 million and are now probably worth considerably more, though how much more is hard to say. Last year, after a string of money-losing years, the company earned $376,000, several times the tainted profit Buckley prophesied for Simon and Schuster's *Do It!*

I visited three of Buckley's radio stations during one week in early March. First on the itinerary was the KUDL and KUDL-FM Kansas City operation. To get there you drive out on the interstate highway, turn off on a frontage road, then onto a dirt road which passes through the cornfield where the studio is located. The front door opens just far enough to bang into a sofa; the real entrance is around the side.

KUDL has been managed pragmatically. The FM operation, KUDL-FM, now plays soul music. In its acid rock days a couple of years ago it was called KCJC-FM. At about the same time the AM side, KUDL-AM, was billing itself, in a play on its call letters, as "Cuddle." Whether this curdled the sensibilities of the then chief stockholder more than the station's periodic lapses into freakhood is not known.

There was another such lapse last spring and summer, during the all-night show. As before, the motives were economic, not cultural. "We tried the heavy stuff because no one else was doing it," explains Bob Cole, who was then the program director. "The decision was made largely in the light of the economic climate. We were in the midst of a crushing construction strike that nearly killed this city. Though a lot of workers didn't have any money, the kids did." Once again, the station did not go about revolution half-heartedly. "We went the route, we went for the freaks," says Mike D'Arcy. "We had a couple of heads working for us. Some of our jocks became revolutionaries on the air."* Alas, the most recent revolution didn't pay off.

*See earlier footnote.

Now KUDL is back to conservative programming of the type you might hear in any American city. It calls itself Boss Radio and its disk jockeys—called Boss Jocks—have names like Weird Mitchell and J. P. Soul. They talk a lot about "getting it all together," and "Right on" is heard more often than the temperature. "Now," says D'Arcy happily, "our jocks sound like real cookers who just fell out of college or maybe never got there."

The commercials are zeroed in on the kid market—and occasionally on the kinky market:

"This week at the Astro Theater! The first *adult* movie in 3-D . . . so real that *you* think *you* are a part of the action.

"Woman's Voice: I felt like I was in there (BEEP) with that couple.

"Man's Voice: Oh . . . those girls!

"Another Man: If that's what 3-D is, I like it . . . I like it.

"Announcer: *Swingtail:* the first *truly adult* movie in three dimensions. . . ."

William F. Buckley Jr. wrote that the Rolling Stones concert at Altamont, California, is considered "the important event of 1969 in the Kidworld" because someone got killed there. "You can see it all in a movie just out, which they choose to call *Gimme Shelter,* which for all I know means something special in Kidspeak."

The important event of 1970 in Kansas City's Kidworld was something which might be called "Loose Park," which may or may not mean something special in Kidspeak, but which was most certainly the place where Buckley's KUDL cosponsored a concert. It was the most spectacularly successful free rock concert in the city's memory. The mammoth and well-behaved crowd particularly appreciated Brewer and Shipley, a locally known group that subsequently gained national popularity with their big hit "One Toke over the Line." A "toke," of course, is Kidspeak for a drag on a marijuana cigarette, and according to KUDL's Cole, many a toke was taken that night. "There was absolutely no trouble," he says, "but the air did smell a little funny."

Several months before "Loose Park," Bill Buckley was taking a somewhat less permissive view of marijuana and other drugs. "We are living in an age when the Secretary of Health, Education, and Welfare decrees that it is dangerous to drink Tab," he wrote. "Surely in such an age he owes us more than we are getting about the psychic consequences of using pot."

There was also a column that praised a New York doctor's clinic for young addicts and ended in a denunciation of the commercialization of the drug culture, as exemplified by the film *Easy Rider*. Buckley wrote: "I would not like to see Peter Fonda suspended on a meat hook, but I found myself less indignant at the sheriff [in the movie] the day after the evening spent with Dr. Baird [the clinic man] and all those haunted people. . . ."

Prothro Junction, Arkansas, looks about like it sounds, and one of its major points of interest is a deteriorated one-story building at the end of a trek through swampy fields which houses the studio of KXLR, Buckley's station in Little Rock. Starr Broadcasting bought KXLR as a country music station and it has kept the faith. The commercial messages continue to convey old-fashioned friendliness: "The friendly folks at Fairway Motors doesn't [*sic*] care what your credit record looks like, or even if you have no credit. All you need is a down payment. . . ." The only touch of modernization is the disappearance of the old disk jockeys, who used to have names like Pappy and Cousin. The new jocks have bland city names, and program director Larry Dean is pleased with them, with the station's financial record, and apparently with life in general. "We call ourselves All-American—you know, mother, God, country, apple pie," he says, shuffling a well-polished Oxford.

When Starr Broadcasting applied for KXLR's license, part of the programming proposal submitted to the FCC promised the beefing up of the local news-gathering efforts. But the station had no newsmen while I was there. There were only four full-time guys on the air, and they were all disk jockeys. KXLR made do with news from the ABC Entertainment Network and with local and state news ripped from the wire and served up by a jock assigned to cover news when not doing a show.

KXLR's general manager, John Doran, gave me a ride back to town and along the way told me of another Buckley success story at KISD, Sioux Falls, where he had been previously employed. "When Starr Broadcasting took over, the station was doing poorly in the market," Doran said. "The station was playing segments of music, a bit of everything." The Buckley team had the answer: rock it. "No one had been rocking before," Doran explained. "We took a Hooper after only thirty days, and we were already Number One. After ten months, we had gone from doing $8000 business a month to $30,000."

WLOK is Buckley's Memphis station, which likes Jerry Rubin, loves *Hair*, but gives the back of its hand to war in Vietnam. The back of its black hand, to be exact—or to be even more exact, the back of its *apparently* black hand. WLOK is a black-oriented soul music station, and its program director and afternoon disk jockey, Roger W. Cavaness, is the driving force. Cavaness seems to have the best of his own particular world. He is a white man who sounds black. Long-haired, hiply clothed, he has also greatly improved the station's ratings. "That young hippie over there is responsible for improving our sound," says general manager Eric Anderson with deep satisfaction, pointing at Cavaness.

Over the years, Buckley has occasionally been accused of having nothing to say to black Americans. WLOK confounds such criticism. In fact, not long ago the new and indubitably black ownership of an Omaha station called on white-managed WLOK for suggestions on how to run a black station. Walt "Baby" Love, who now holds down the afternoon drive-time slot on WOR-FM, New York, was given his first job on Starr Broadcasting's KYOK, Houston, and Love remains deeply grateful to KYOK, even though he was summarily fired in the middle of a show after he had given the standard two-weeks' notice in order to take a better job.

The newest Buckley radio property is KEIR-FM in Dallas. With an 1100-foot antenna and a 100,000-watt transmitter soon to be activated, the station will cover virtually the whole state of Texas. The freaks will not be around for this piece of the Buckely action. KEIR-FM is being programmed under the "Christian family" format. Instead of soap and psychedelia, the station sells time to ministers. According to Peter Starr, only the upright need apply; faith healers will not be allowed to buy time.

The only significant nonbroadcasting division of the Buckley company is Arlington House, a publishing company based in New Rochelle. Unlike the radio stations, Arlington's offerings are quite compatible with the public philosophy of the chief stockholder. The house advertises itself as "publishers for the silent majority" and among its recent titles is *Suicide of the West*, "the book that dissects Liberalism deep down to its rotten core." Another Arlington offering is titled, hopefully, *You Can Raise Decent Children* and its blurb goes: "Some spokesmen may laud 'the kids,' but most parents are worried sick. Is it still possible to raise children who won't turn into hippies, drug freaks, or subversives?" Thus far there seem to be no plans to push the book over the stations.

It is not clear exactly how aware the eminent conservative moralist is of the day-to-day affairs of his profit-making enterprise. His aides state that he knows the formats of each station, and it would seem that only by a great effort of will could he remain in total ignorance of all the goings-on at, say, Boss Radio in Kansas City or Funky Radio in Memphis. At any rate, if he is innocent of any close knowledge about the uses of his capital, he seems to be doing what he can to preserve it—his innocence, that is. After ten days of trying unsuccessfully to reach him in order to discuss the matter, I received the following telegram:

I HAVE ALWAYS MADE IT A PRACTICE TO REFER ALL QUESTIONS CONCERNING THE STARR BROADCASTING COMPANY TO ITS PRINCIPAL EXECUTIVE OFFICIAL, PETER STARR. MY HOLDINGS IN THE COMPANY ARE A MATTER OF PUBLIC RECORD. I DO NOT FEEL ANY OBLIGATION TO DISCUSS WITH ANY JOURNALIST ANY ASPECT OF MY ROLE IN THIS COMPANY. I AM ON MATTERS CONCERNING WHICH I TAKE PUBLIC ISSUES THE WORLD'S

MOST ACCESSIBLE MAN AND WILL BE HAPPY TO SEE YOU
TO DISCUSS NATIONAL REVIEW, OR THE SUEZ CANAL,
BUT NOT MY BUSINESS AFFAIRS.

                                    REGARDS,
                                    WILLIAM F. BUCKLEY JR.

Poor Carter Burden. Why didn't he think of that?

Kinder, Küche, Kirche As Scientific Law: Psychology Constructs the Female

Naomi Weisstein

Psychologists have set about describing the true nature of women with an enthusiasm and absolute certainty which is rather disquieting. Bruno Bettelheim, of the University of Chicago, tells us (1965) that "we must start with the realization that, as much as women want to be good scientists or engineers, they want first and foremost to be womanly companions of men and to be mothers."

Erik Erikson of Harvard University (1964), upon noting that young women often ask whether they can "have an identity before they know whom they will marry, and for whom they will make a home," explains somewhat elegiacally that "much of a young woman's identity is already defined in her kind of attractiveness and in the selectivity of her search for the man (or men) by whom she wishes to be sought. . . ." Mature womanly fulfillment, for Erikson, rests on the fact that a woman's ". . . somatic design harbors an 'inner space' destined to bear the offspring of chosen men, and with it, a biological, psychological, and ethical commitment to take care of human infancy."

Some psychiatrists even see the acceptance of woman's role by women as a solution to societal problems. "Woman is nurturance . . . ," writes Joseph Rheingold (1964), a psychiatrist at Harvard Medical School; ". . . anatomy decrees the life of a woman . . . when women grow up without dread of their biological functions and without subversion by feminist doctrine, and therefore enter upon motherhood with a sense of fulfillment and altruistic sentiment, we shall attain the goal of a good life and a secure world in which to live it."

These views from men of high prestige reflect a fairly general consensus: liberation for women will consist first in their attractiveness, so that, second, they may obtain the kinds of homes (and men) which will allow joyful altruism and nurturance.

Business does not disagree. If views such as Bettelheim's and Erikson's do indeed have something to do with real liberation for women, then seldom in human history has so much money and effort been spent on helping a group of people realize their true potential. Clothing, cosmetics, and home furnishings are multimillion dollar businesses: if you don't like investing in firms that make weaponry and flaming gasoline, there's a lot of cash in "inner space."

It is an interesting but limited exercise to show that psychologists' ideas of women's nature fit so remarkably the common prejudice and serve industry and commerce so well. Just because it's good for business doesn't mean it's wrong. *It is wrong,* and there isn't the tiniest shred of evidence that these fantasies of servitude and childish dependence have anything to do with women's true potential. The idea of the nature of human possibility which rests on the accidents of individual development or genitalia, on what is possible today because of what happened yesterday, on the fundamentalist myth of sex organ causality, has strangled and deflected psychology so that it is relatively useless in describing, explaining, or predicting humans and their behavior. Present psychology is less than worthless in contributing to a vision which could truly liberate—men as well as women.

Psychology has nothing to say about what women are really like, what they need and what they want, essentially, because psychology does not know. This failure is not limited to women; rather, the kind of psychology which has addressed itself to how people act and who they are has failed to understand, in the first place, why people act the way they do, and has certainly failed to understand what might make them act differently.

The kind of psychology which has addressed itself to these questions is in large part clinical psychology and psychiatry, which in America means endless commentary and refinement of Freudian theory. Here, the causes of failure are obvious and appalling: Freudians and neo-Freudians, and clinicians and psychiatrists in general, have simply refused to look at the evidence against their theory and their practice, and have used as evidence for their theory and their practice stuff so flimsy and transparently biased as to have absolutely no standing as empirical evidence. But even psychology which conforms to rigorous methodology has gone about looking at people in such a way as to have limited usefulness. This is because it has been a central assumption for most psychologists of human personality that human behavior rests primarily on an individual and inner dynamic, perhaps fixed in infancy, perhaps fixed by genitalia, perhaps simply arranged in a rather immovable cognitive network.

This assumption is rapidly losing ground as personality psychologists fail again and again to get consistency in the assumed personalities of their subjects (Block, 1968) and as the evidence collects that what a person does and who he believes himself to be will in general be a function of what people around him expect him to be, and what the overall situation in which he is acting implies that he is. Compared to the influence of the social context within which a person lives, his or her history and "traits," as well as biological makeup, may simply be random variations, "noise" superimposed on the true signal which can predict behavior.

To summarize: the first reason for psychology's failure to understand what people are and how they act is that clinicians and psychiatrists, who are generally the theoreticians on these matters, have essentially made up myths without any evidence to support these myths. The second reason for psychology's failure is that personality theory has looked for inner traits when it should have been looking at social context.

The first cause of failure is the acceptance by psychiatrists and clinical psychologists of theory without evidence. If we inspect the literature of personality, it is immediately obvious that the bulk of it is written by clinicians and psychiatrists, and that the major support for their theories is "years of intensive clinical experience." This is a tradition started by Freud. His "insights" occurred during the course of his work with his patients. There is nothing wrong with such an approach to theory *formulation;* a person is free to make up theories with any inspiration which works: divine revelation, intensive clinical practice, a random number table. But he is not free to claim any validity for his theory until it has been tested and confirmed.

Theories are treated in no such tentative way in ordinary clinical practice. Consider Freud. What he thought constituted evidence violated the most minimal conditions of scientific rigor. In *The Sexual Enlightenment of Children,* the classic document which is supposed to demonstrate empirically the existence of a castration complex and its connection to a phobia, Freud based his analysis on the reports of the father of the little boy, himself in therapy, and a devotee of Freudian theory. I really don't have to comment further on the contamination in this kind of evidence. It is remarkable that only recently Freud's classic theory on the sexuality of women—the notion of the double orgasm —has been tested physiologically and found plain wrong.

Those who claim that fifty years of psychoanalytic experience constitute evidence enough of the essential truths of Freud's theory should ponder the robust health of the double orgasm. Did women, until Masters and Johnson (1966), believe they were having two different kinds of orgasm? Did their psychiatrists cow them into reporting something that was not true? If so, were there other things they reported that were also not true? Did psychiatrists ever learn anything different from what their theories had led them to believe? If clinical experience means anything at all, surely we should have been done with the double orgasm myth long before the Masters and Johnson studies.

But certainly, you may object, "years of intensive clinical experience" is the only reliable measure in a discipline which rests for its findings on insight, sensitivity, and intuition. The problem with insight, sensitivity, and intuition is that these can confirm for all time the biases that one started out with. People used to be absolutely convinced of their ability to tell which of their number were engaging in witchcraft.

Years of intensive clinical experience is not the same thing as empirical evidence. The first thing an experimenter learns in any kind of experiment which involves humans is the concept of the "double blind." The term is taken from medical experiments, where one group is given a drug which is presumably supposed to change behavior in a certain way, and a control group is given a placebo. If the observers or the subjects know which group took which drug, the result invariably comes out on the positive side for the new drug. Only when it is not known which subject took which pill is validity remotely approximated.

In judgments of human behavior, it is so difficult to precisely tie down just what behavior is going on, let alone what behavior should be expected, that one must test again and again the reliability of judgments. How many judges, blind, will agree in their observations? Can they replicate their own judgments at some later time? When, in actual practice, these judgment criteria are tested for clinical judgments, then we find that the judges cannot judge reliably nor can they judge consistently: they do no better than chance in identifying which of a certain set of stories were written by men and which by women; which of a whole battery of clinical test results are the products of homosexuals and which are the products of heterosexuals (Hooker, 1957); and which of a battery of clinical test results *and* interviews where questions are asked such as "Do you have delusions?" and "What are your symptoms?" (Little & Schneidman, 1959) are products of psychotics, neurotics, psychosomatics, or normals.

Lest this summary escape your notice, let me stress the implications of these findings. The ability of judges, chosen for their clinical expertise, to distinguish male heterosexuals from male homosexuals on the basis of three widely used clinical projective tests—the Rorschach, the TAT, and the MAP—was *no better than chance*. The reason this is such devastating news, of course, is that sexuality is considered by personality theorists to be of fundamental importance in the deep dynamic of personality; if what is considered gross sexual deviance cannot be caught, then what are psychologists talking about when they claim, for instance, that at the basis of paranoid psychosis is "latent homosexual panic"? They can't even identify what homosexual anything is, let alone "latent homosexual panic"!

More frightening, expert clinicians cannot be consistent on what diagnostic category to assign to a person, again on the basis of both tests and interviews; a number of normals in the Little & Schneidman study were described as psychotic, in such categories as "schizophrenic with homosexual tendencies," or "schizoid character with depressive trends." But most disheartening, when the judges were asked to re-judge the test protocols some weeks later, their diagnosis of the same subjects on the basis of the same protocol differed markedly from their initial judgments. It is obvious that even simple descriptive conventions in clinical psychology cannot be consistently applied; that these descriptive conventions have any explanatory significance is therefore, of course, out of the question.

As a student in a graduate class at Harvard, some years ago, I was a member of a seminar which was asked to identify which of two piles of a clinical test, the TAT, had been written by males, and which of the two piles had been written by females. Only four students out of twenty identified the piles correctly, and this was after one and a half months of intensively studying the differences between men and women. Since this result is below chance, that is, this result would occur by chance about four out of a thousand times, we may conclude that there *is* finally a consistency here; students are judging knowledgeably within the context of psychological teaching about the differences between men and women; the teachings themselves are erroneous.

Ah, you may argue, the theory may be scientifically "unsound" but at least it cures people. There is no evidence that it does. In 1952, Eysenck reported the results of what is called an "outcome of therapy" study of neurotics which showed that, of the patients who received psychoanalysis, the improvement rate was 44 percent; of the patients who received psychotherapy, the improvement rate was 64 percent; and of the patients who received no treatment at all, the improvement rate was 72 percent. These findings have never been refuted; subsequent later studies have confirmed the negative results of the Eysenck study (Barron and Leary, 1955; Bergin, 1963; Cartwright and Vogel, 1960; Truax, 1963).

How can clinicians and psychiatrists then, in all good conscience, continue to practice? Largely by ignoring these results and being careful not to do outcome-of-therapy studies. The attitude is nicely summarized by Rotter (1960) (quoted in Astin, 1961): "Research studies in psychotherapy tend to be concerned more with some aspects of the psychotherapeutic procedure and less with outcome . . . to some extent, it reflects an interest in the psychotherapy situation as a kind of personality laboratory." Some laboratory.

Thus, since clinical experience and tools can be shown to be worse than useless when tested for consistency, efficacy, agreement, and reliability, we can safely conclude that theories of a clinical nature advanced about women are also worse than useless. It has become increasingly clear that in order to understand why people do what they do, and certainly in order to change what people do, psychologists must turn away from the theory of the causal nature of the inner dynamic and look to the social context within which individuals live.

Block's work (1968) established that personality tests never yield consistent predictions; a rigid authoritarian on one measure will be unauthoritarian on the next. But the reason for this inconsistency is only now becoming clear, and it seems overwhelmingly to have much more to do with the social situation in which the subject finds himself than with the subject himself.

In a series of brilliant experiments, Rosenthal and his coworkers (Rosenthal and Jacobson, 1968; Rosenthal, 1966) have shown that if one group of experimenters has one hypothesis about what they expect to find and another group of experimenters has the opposite hypothesis, both groups will obtain results in accord with their hypotheses. Thus, in a success rating task, where subjects were required to rate faces cut out from magazines on a twenty-point scale from —10, very unsuccessful, to +10, highly successful, the group of subjects whose experimenters had been told would rate the faces high had mean ratings, in every case, above the highest mean rating for the group of subjects whose experimenters expected the subjects to rate the faces low.

In all, about 375 subjects were tested; the results would have happened by chance about one in one thousand times. The experimenters were instructed to read the same set of instructions, and to say no more than was in the instructions; obviously, the cues which influenced subjects were nonverbal. Even with animals, in two separate studies (Rosenthal & Fode, 1960; Rosenthal & Lawson, 1961), those experimenters who were told that rats learning mazes had been especially bred for brightness obtained better learning from their rats than did experimenters believing their rats to have been bred for dullness. These results would have happened by chance one out of one hundred times.

In a very recent study, Rosenthal & Jacobson (1968) extended their analysis to the natural classroom situation. Here, they found that when teachers expected randomly selected students to "show great promise," these students' I.Q.s increased significantly from control group students, with the most dramatic increments in the area of reasoning ability.

Thus, even in carefully controlled experiments, and with no outward or conscious difference in behavior, the hypotheses we start with will influence enormously the behavior of another organism. These studies are extremely important when assessing the validity of psychological studies of women. Since it is fairly safe to say that most of us start with hypotheses as to the nature of men and women, the validity of a number of observations of sex differences is questionable, even when these observations have been taken under carefully controlled conditions.

Second, and more importantly, the Rosenthal experiments point quite clearly to the influence of social expectation. In some extremely important ways, people are what you expect them to be or at least they behave as you expect them to behave. Thus, if women, according to Bruno Bettelheim, want first and foremost to be good wives and mothers, it is extremely likely that that is what Bettelheim, and the rest of the society, want them to be.

There is another series of social psychological experiments which points to the inescapable overwhelming effect of social context in an extremely vivid way. These are the obedience experiments of Stanley Milgram (1965a), concerned with the extent to which subjects in psychological experiments will obey the orders of unknown experimenters, even when these orders carry them to the distinct possibility of killing somebody.

Briefly, a subject is made to administer electric shocks in ascending 15-volt increments to another person whom the subject believes to be another subject, but who is in fact a stooge. The voltages range from 15 to 450 volts; for each four consecutive voltages there are verbal descriptions such as "mild shock," "danger, severe shock," and finally, for the 435- and 450-volt switches, simply a red XXX marked over the switches. The stooge, as the voltage increases, begins to cry out against the pain; he then screams that he has a heart condition, begging the subject to stop, and finally he goes limp and stops responding altogether at a certain voltage. Since even at this point the subject is instructed to keep increasing the voltage, it is possible for the subjects to continue all the way up to the end switch—450 volts.

The percentage of subjects who do so is quite high; all in all, about one thousand subjects were run, and about 65 percent would go to the end switch in an average experiment. No tested individual differences between subjects predicted which of the subjects would continue to obey and which would break off the experiment. Predictions were far below actual percentages, with an average prediction that 3 percent of the subjects would obey to the end. But even though psychiatrists have no idea of how people are going to behave in this situation (despite one of the central facts of the twentieth century, which is that people have been made to kill enormous numbers of other people), and even though individual differences do not predict which subjects are going to obey and which are not, it is very easy to predict when subjects will be obedient and when they will be defiant. All the experimenter has to do is change the social situation. In a variant of the experiment (Milgram, 1965b), when two other stooges who were also administering electric shocks refused to continue, only 10 percent of the subjects continued to the end switch. This is critical for personality theory, for it indicates that the lawful behavior is the behavior that can be predicted from the social situation, not from the individual history.

Finally, an ingenious experiment by Schachter and Singer (1962) showed that subjects injected with adrenalin, which produces a state of physiological arousal in all but minor respects identical to that which occurs when subjects are extremely afraid, became euphoric when they were in a room with a stooge who was acting euphoric, and became extremely angry when they were placed in a room with a stooge who was acting extremely angry.

To summarize: If subjects under quite innocuous and noncoercive social conditions can be made to kill other subjects and under other types of social conditions will positively refuse to do so; if subjects can react to a state of physiological fear by becoming euphoric because there is somebody else euphoric, if students become intelligent because teachers expect them to be intelligent, and rats run mazes better because experimenters are told that the rats are bright, then it is obvious that a study of human behavior requires, first and foremost, a study of the social contexts within which people move, the expectations as to how they will behave, and the authority which tells them who they are and what they are supposed to do.

Two theories of the nature of women, which come not

from psychiatric and clinical tradition but from biology, can be disposed of with little difficulty. The first argument notices social interaction in primate groups and observes that females are submissive and passive. Putting aside for a moment the serious problem of experimenter bias (for instance, Harlow [1962], of the University of Wisconsin, after observing differences between male and female rhesus monkeys, quotes Lawrence Sterne to the effect that women are silly and trivial, and concludes that "men and women have differed in the past and they will differ in the future"), the problem with the argument from primate groups is that the crucial experiment has not been performed. The crucial experiment would manipulate or change the social organization of these groups and watch the subsequent behavior. Until then, we must conclude that, since primates are, at present, too stupid to change their social conditions by themselves, the "innateness" and fixedness of their behavior is simply not known. As applied to humans, the argument becomes patently irrelevant, since the most salient feature of human social organization is its variety; and there are a number of cultures where there is at least a rough equality between men and women (Mead, 1949). Thus, primate arguments tell us little.

The second theory of sex differences argues that since females and males differ in their sex hormones and sex hormones enter the brain (Hamburg and Lunde in Maccoby, 1966), there must be innate differences in "nature." But the only thing this argument tells us is that there are differences in the physiological state. The problem is whether these differences are at all relevant to behavior. Recall that Schachter and Singer (1962) have shown that a particular physiological state can itself lead to a multiplicity of felt emotional states and outward behavior, depending on the social situation.

In brief, the uselessness of present psychology with regard to women is simply a special case of the general conclusion: one must understand social expectations about women if one is going to characterize the behavior of women.

How are women characterized in our culture, and in psychology? They are inconsistent, emotionally unstable, lacking in a strong conscience or super-ego, weaker, "nur-turant" rather than productive, "intuitive" rather than intelligent, and, if they are at all "normal," suited to the home and the family. In short, the list adds up to a typical minority group stereotype of inferiority (Hacker, 1951): if they know their place, which is in the home, they are really quite lovable, happy, childlike, loving creatures.

In a review of the intellectual differences between little boys and little girls, Eleanor Maccoby (1966) has shown that there are no intellectual differences until about high school, or, if there are, girls are slightly ahead of boys. At high school, girls begin to do worse on a few intellectual tasks, such as arithmetical reasoning, and beyond high school the achievement of women now measured in terms of accomplishment drops off even more rapidly.

There are a number of other, nonintellectual tests which show sex differences: I choose the intellectual differences since it is seen clearly that women start becoming inferior. It is no use to talk about women being different but equal; all of the tests I can think of have a "good" outcome and a "bad" outcome. Women usually end up at the "bad" outcome. In light of social expectations about women, what is surprising is not that women end up where society expects they will; what is surprising is that little girls don't get the message that they are supposed to be stupid until high school; and what is even more remarkable is that some women resist this message even after high school, college, and graduate school.

I began with remarks on the task of discovering the limits of human potential. Until psychologists realize that it is they who are limiting discovery of human potential by their refusal to accept evidence, if they are clinical psychologists, or, if they are rigorous, by their assumption that people move in a context-free ether with only their innate dispositions and their individual traits determining what they will do, then psychology will have nothing of substance to offer in this task. I don't know what immutable differences exist between men and women apart from differences in their genitals; perhaps there are some other unchangeable differences; probably there are a number of irrelevant differences. But it is clear that until social expectations for men and women are equal, until we provide equal respect for both men and women, our answers to this question will simply reflect our prejudices.

References

Astin, A. W. The functional autonomy of psychotherapy. *American Psychologist*, 1961, *16*, 75-78.

Barron, F. & Leary, T. Changes in psychoneurotic patients with and without psychotherapy. *Journal of Consulting Psychology*, 1955, *19*, 239-245.

Bergin, A. E. The effects of psychotherapy: negative results revisited. *Journal of Counseling Psychology*, 1963, *10*, 244-250.

Bettelheim, B. The commitment required of a woman entering a scientific profession in present day American society. *Woman and the Scientific Professions*, The M.I.T. symposium on American Women in Science and Engineering, 1965.

Block, J. Some reasons for the apparent inconsistency of personality. *Psychological Bulletin*, 1968, *70*, 210-212.

Cartwright, R. D & Vogel, J. L. A comparison of changes in psychoneurotic patients during matched periods of therapy and no-therapy. *Journal of Consulting Psychology*, 1960, *24*, 121-127.

Erikson, E. Inner and outer space: reflections on womanhood. *Daedalus*, 1964, *93*, 582-606.

Eysenck, H. J. The effects of psychotherapy: an evaluation. *Journal of Consulting Psychology*, 1952, *16*, 319-324.

Fieldcrest—Advertisement in the *New York Times*, 1965.

Freud, S. *The Sexual Enlightenment of Children.* Collier Books Edition, 1963.

Goldstein, A. P. & Dean, S. J. *The Investigation of Psychotherapy: Commentaries and Readings.* New York: John Wiley & Sons, 1966.

Hacker, H. M. Women as a minority group. *Social Forces*, 1951, *30*, 60-69.

Hamburg, D. A. & Lunde, D. T. Sex hormones in the development of sex differences in human behavior. In Maccoby, Ed. *The Development of Sex Differences*, 1-24. Stanford University Press, 1966.

Harlow, H. F. The heterosexual affectional system in monkeys. *The American Psychologist*, 1962, *17*, 1-9.

Hooker, E. Male homosexuality in the Rorschach. *Journal of Projective Techniques*, 1957, *21*, 18-31.

Little, K. B. & Schneidman, E. S. Congruences among interpretations of psychological test and anamestic data. *Psychological Monographs,* 1959, *73,* 1-42.

Maccoby, Eleanor E. Sex differences in intellectual functioning. In Maccoby, Ed. *The Development of Sex Differences,* 25-55. Stanford University Press, 1966.

Masters, W. H. & Johnson, V. E. *Human Sexual Response.* Boston: Little, Brown, 1966.

Mead, M. *Male and Female: a study of the sexes in a changing world.* New York: William Morrow, 1949.

Milgram, S. Some conditions of obedience and disobedience to authority. *Human Relations,* 1965a, *18,* 57-76.

Milgram, S. Liberating effects of group pressure. *Journal of Personality and Social Psychology,* 1965b, *1,* 127-134.

Powers, E. & Witmer, H. *An Experiment in the Prevention of Delinquency.* New York: Columbia University Press, 1951.

Rheingold, J. *The Fear of Being a Woman.* New York: Grune & Stratton, 1964.

Rosenthal, R. On the social psychology of the psychological experiment: The experimenter's hypothesis as unintended determinant of experimental results, *American Scientist,* 1963, *51,* 268-283.

Rosenthal, R. *Experimenter Effects in Behavioral Research.* New York: Appleton-Century Crofts, 1966.

Rosenthal, R. & Fode, K. L. The effect of experimenter bias on the performance of the albino rat. Unpublished manuscript, Harvard University, 1960.

Rosenthal, R & Jacobson, L. *Pygmalion in the Classroom: Teacher Expectation and Pupils' Intellectual Development.* New York: Holt, Rinehart & Winston, 1968.

Rosenthal, R. & Lawson, R. A longitudinal study of the effects of experimenter bias on the operant learning of laboratory rats. Unpublished manuscript, Harvard University, 1961.

Rotter, J. B. Psychotherapy. *Annual Review of Psychology,* 1960, *11,* 381-414.

Schachter, S. & Singer, J. E. Cognitive, social, and psychological determinants of emotional state. *Psychological Review,* 1962, *69,* 379-399.

Truax, C. B. Effective ingredients in psychotherapy; an approach to unraveling the patient-therapist interaction. *Journal of Counseling Psychology,* 1963, *10,* 256-263.

The Nirvana Conference

Julie Baumgold

The sea slaps the rowboat around the Mexican bay, heaving and bucking in a cosmic tantrum. Two men in yellow shirts grip the starboard gunnels. Hugh Hefner, pale as an unsunned bunny breast, the hair whipping into his slightly vulpine face, and Bernie Cornfeld, the "King of Europe's Cash," are being reminded of their mortality a mile from the shore in this Plexiglas pod.

Oh, the insolence! The elemental disobedience! Their universe is out of sync. And they, who have always controlled their environments, great believers that all life can be customized, have lost dominion. This dinghy full of floating assets, centimillions, legal eagles, and attaché-case talent can be upset—plunged to watery vaults. The other ten men are playing, tossing boiled shrimp to each other, while jealous gulls circle above. An urchin in the prow laughs.

Hefner forgets to look at the shore. He stares into the void. White-fingered sea nymphs lap up at him . . . clutching. Possessive. Hugh Hefner cannot swim. Fear curdles his eyes. His white knuckles are soldered around his security symbols—a dead pipe and a forgotten Pepsi-Cola. His bare feet are curled in terror. Hefner has unplugged his sockets. Disconnected himself from the electric juice volts and push-buttons. Gotten out of his pajamas and exposed himself to the vital forces of sun and sea. Burst from the doors of his mansion, received life . . . and now this bitch sea is out of control, like a giant gadget he can't shut off.

Behind Hefner sits Cornfeld, his blue eyes developing real estate on the shore.

"If we capsize, who goes first, Bernie or Hef?" says one of the men.

"I'm on record," says Hefner. "The deal is off if I drown."

"How about walking on the water?" suggests Bernie.

"I never thought I'd see that beach again," Hefner mumbles as the boat scrapes onto the beach. He leaps into the water, fastened to his Pepsi and pipe, cradling his shoes and black anklets, a creature of shaken glamour.

The Nirvana Conference is almost over.

In the weekend when the moon passed across the sun and the planet Earth grew briefly dark, Hugh Hefner left his forty-room Chicago mansion and Bernie Cornfeld ("the Hugh Hefner of Europe") left his centrally heated twelfth-century castle to come together in a villa called "Nirvana" in Acapulco. A villa built because its owner had a hole in his heart.

They flew down, each in his private plane, each with his portable paradise, his dependents, toy girls, games, and monomania. First Cornfeld's white Falcon with the solemn Swiss cross on the tail, then the Big Bunny, Hefner's black DC9, crossed the skies, both carrying executive easy riders—outlaws to virtues that bring television studio audiences to applause. Classic disregarders of time and proportion. Two reveling divinities with a whole play universe.

They came to Nirvana, "a place or state characterized by freedom from or oblivion to pain, worry, and the external world" (Random House Dictionary), to plan a $15-million, thirty-two-story, 512-unit condominium between the new Holiday Inn and the El Presidente on the crowded Acapulco curve and to join in a kind of global covenant, Bernie to provide the capital, the Playboy organization to run the condominiums as semihotels with Playboy club units.*

---

*God knows, Bernie has the cash and Hef is getting the know-how. Through a heap of subsidiaries, Cornfeld's Investors Overseas Services manages more than $2 billion in mutual fund assets. And Playboy Clubs International, one of Hef's enterprises, now runs seventeen clubs and two resorts which last year grossed $41 million. Bernie, however, has his little worries lately. Earlier this month, shares in his fund management company plummeted 62 percent on European stock exchanges.

Two days earlier. Bernie Cornfeld's Carlyle Hotel living room is filled with unfed girls. All exhausted. They bisect the worlds of High Fashion and Constant Companionship and are usually excellent at waiting. In general they have up-swept hair, English accents, the elegant lines and snappish dispositions of ocelots, which Bernie also collects.

Lorna, who models lingerie for catalogs and plays young matrons in TV commercials, rises on her white boots, adjusts her Pucci to cover a ripple of thigh, and heads for the refrigerator, which contains only a package of saltines and two caramel eclairs. She walks past stacks of paintings of little dogs with imploring eyes which Bernie bought from a former girlfriend with similar eyes. The Darby, as she is known, goes with her. The Darby, like Lorna, is from Talent Management International, the model-talent agency Bernie has just acquired (he has a habit of owning what surrounds him). The Darby has been with Bernie two weeks, and she is drooping. Three hours' sleep a night, five trips back and forth from London to Geneva in a week.

"We go to all these great places and we only see airports and rooms," the Darby says.

"Ummm," says Jackie, a nineteen-year-old model from a Scottish town where the social life consisted of a monthly rugby dance. But she understands. Jackie's hair is pulled so tightly back from her scalp that it looks like it aches.

Didi, Bernie's German secretary, clips through, followed by Bernie's top girl, Cedric, whom he calls "Rattlesnake" because she is "spiteful as a snake" and once owned three vipers. Cedric is wan from the throes of starting the boutique which Bernie has bought her.

The talk about height, skin, and tooth decay ceases when Bernie enters. He moves like a man walking whippets over a quiet lawn who knows he is being stared at. His Guy Laroche (he has recently bought half of Guy Laroche) pants angle over the backs of his shoes, his long jacket is lined with Hermès scarves, and he wears a pink Cardin Indian silk scarf knotted around his neck as a tie. From his jacket there's a protrusion of peach shirt cuffs with man-in-a-hurry one-sided cufflinks. A carnival wheel of knife blades spins in his eyes.

He was to leave several hours ago for Acapulco, but as

Robert, his chauffeur, says, "You know Bernie, he never gets off on time." This inability to make scheduled flights is one reason for the cars that wait to whisk him to planes that wait. One reason for the television he installed in the front seat of the limousine was to keep his chauffeur from being bored.

Contempt for the temporal is an executive-easy-rider trait. In much the way that Peter Fonda tossed his watch into the dust, Hefner and Cornfeld cast off time—living their nights as days. So Bernie remains on New York time wherever he is, and Hefner lives his own electric days in the Chicago nights.

Bernie comes out of one of the bedrooms in a crew-cut mink coat and a lumberjack's cap, carrying his suitcase. "Here comes the Polish peddler," says one of his men. Bernie picks up a brown leather backgammon board by Gucci. He makes sure someone takes the little red set by Hermès. He leaves with only a Spartan number of girls (three).

We glide out of the gleaming Carlyle Manhattan heart that is now Bernie's New York. For Bernie has won the borough struggle: Brooklyn to Manhattan. He went through the enterprising deprivation of running an age-guessing stand on Coney Island, worked his way through City College, began to teach social work at Bryn Mawr, selling mutual funds on the side.

In the fifties Bernie and his mother lived in the Hotel Des Artistes on West 67 Street. There he would illegally park his Cadillac, accumulating over $5000 in tickets. Bernie left New York when Judge John Murtagh threatened to arrest him as a scofflaw. Since he didn't have the money for the fine, he left for Paris, taking with him a proven idea (the mutual fund), introducing it to a new market (Europe and the rest of the world outside the U.S.), selling it with aggressive American sales methods (door to door), and using American personnel techniques (constant retraining of his salesmen). Last night Bernie had dinner at Nathan's. "It's so much better than room service with all those maids running around."

Deep in the gloomy elegance of his Modified Car. Deep in

the tufted black leather. Secreted away in the privacy of blacked-out windows, Bernie feeds his tape decks. Bernie is sitting on the jumpseat (reversed to face the rear instead of the chauffeur) discussing his meeting with Hefner the previous weekend in Chicago. "I respect any man who will stay up until ten [a.m.] talking." Bernie was given the mansion's Gold Room with a water-filled mattress he wanted to experiment with "but all I could do was sit on it and bounce." After talking all night he swam in the romantic grotto—with his lawyer.

Finally the car arrives at the Westchester County Airport. Mexico in that? Bernie's plane is too small to take eight people and all the luggage, so Bernie leaves his own suitcase behind. (The rest of the weekend he is obliged to share Jackie's toothbrush.)

As we take off, Bernie is busy inserting an old videotaped Million Dollar Movie in his machine. The image appears on two TV screens. The movie is *The Catered Affair*. It is full of the eking drabbery of poverty, the fumbled happiness, the sacrifice of "If I spend on this, I can't have that." It depresses and fascinates Bernie. "I lived most of my life without money," he says. Bernie prefers fantasy. He says he is planning to do a movie about Oz. "Baum was a head, you know."

The backgammon sets are out and Bernie plays (for money). There will always be people to play with Bernie and Hefner. They walk inside their retinues like the little solid cores of Chinese take-apart boxes. Big Daddies with their false "kids" (as Hefner calls them) to answer the phones, to screen and shield and lower the ropes. By slightly raising their voices the Big Daddies can interrupt and immediately silence conversations until they have had their say. When they stand up to leave a place, suddenly it occurs to the others that yes, it's about time to go.

By the time we get to Brownsville, Texas, Bernie and Jackie (obviously elected as his weekend girl) are stretched out across a seat wrapped in an Hermès horse blanket and themselves. This public snuggle causes a mass averting of the eyes, which is hard in a plane of eight.

There are three ways to get to Nirvana. Buddhism, Hinduism, and on foot. Bernie walks up the marble steps etched out of the Las Brisas cliff, past the umber peasants hacking away at the parched rock with picks and shovels, stirring up lung dust. Below: the condemned. And Bernie is mounting. Up. Up. Up toward his host and Mexican adviser, Oscar Obregon II, who is leaning over the braided steel railing of the balcony, serpentine of face, with brows plucked into perpetual irony above conquistador cheekbones, something distinctly silken and rustling about him. A comprehension of decadence. A long red scar under his heart.

After being operated on by De Bakey in Houston he came to rest in Acapulco and decided to build "Nirvana," a blanched white multilevel sprawl bursting into rooms, one with a pool so that its occupants can make underwater entrances. Crystal sconces on stucco walls, foot-thick marble bathrooms with Sherle Wagner hissing-swan spiggots spitting blued water into sunken baths, porthole windows open to the palms. A huge indulged fantasy, a present to himself for not having died. Nirvana is run according to ancient Spanish custom: *mi casa, su casa*. Staffed by servants in hospital white, who look like they would lie for you in court.

Oscar disappears. Bernie organizes the rooms. He says to Jackie, "You room in with me." It is not a request.

The bodies are sprawled by the pool. New York white. Twitching every once in a while at the occasional dynamite blasts below (in the name of progress, not revolution). Bernie photographs everyone, snapping on his Nikon superlenses that magnify the anatomical perfections 100 to 300 times. Nirvana!

A pushcart-perfect dialect is coming from the pavilion by the pool: "Did you hear the story about . . . . This little Jewish man comes into the bar. 'I'll have a Scotch and soda, nigger,' he says to the Negro bartender . . . ." Now Bernie is telling a joke instead of talking. When Bernie talks business it is often with the long pauses of a former stutterer. Fluency always returns with his Yiddish accent.

Later that afternoon the Big Bunny darkens the skies. But Hefner doesn't appear at Nirvana. Bernie hears that because no one met Hef he went to Tres Vidas, the private club run by Bruce Leadbetter, the president of The Post Company in Dallas. At one time both Bernie and Hefner had independently contacted Post for sites on either side of Tres Vidas. The deal fell through in Dallas, but with Hefner at Tres Vidas it looks as if it's on again. Bernie in a panic takes Jackie and goes to fetch Hef.

Hefner is ready to come home to Nirvana. Bruce Leadbetter's card tricks have made him nervous. Bernie and Jackie and Hef and his inamorata Barbi return at dusk to Nirvana.

The living Hefner is not to be confused with the man who hosts *Playboy After Dark,* saying impossibly stiff sentences like "I hear you have just returned from the Continent" (it's hard to believe there's not a six-foot box of native soil in the mansion's basement). No, the living Hefner is fiercely charming. Witty. Kind of unaging. He says that if there were a portrait rotting up in his attic, "it would look like a large black-and-white rabbit."

Hefner! Has! Relaxed! He has just been through a clean re-creation of self. After a fifteen-year Howard Hughsian invisibility cycle which he spent revolving on his round bed in a Dexedrine frenzy, he got himself a passport, learned to delegate a little of his absolute authority, found love. The abused body is now cared for. He no longer looks like an unemployed magician. He belongs here.

"My success is not just business, but romantic," he says. Of course he is going steady. Pure teenage fulfillment. Nirvana. ("Hinduism. Salvation through the union of Atman with Brahma.") "I like to form things," Hefner once said. "I'm not attracted to dumb girls, just young girls."

Barbi, twenty, has the air of a lapsed cheerleader. "An outdoor girl by nature," *Playboy* calls her. "A nice Jewish girl," Hefner calls her. Her face is full of American Chiclet-chewing purity; her prepulchritudinous body stays thrust forward in the posture of a child reciting, as though someone had pushed her in the back when her bones were still soft. "Barbara is perfectly innocent, except in her relationship to me," says Hefner.

Hef met her on the third program of *Playboy After Dark.*

Now a regular on the show, she shoots him little sated-woman looks on the air. As "Barbi Doll," she was featured in a nine-page *Playboy* color spread in a series of bikini bottoms and wet or unbuttoned shirts. Barbi is the star of the Certs breath commercial ("if he kissed you once, will he kiss you again?") as well as the first German film to be shot in the USA, *How Did a Nice Girl Like You Get Into This Business?* (guest-starring Hugh Hefner). Hef changed her last name from Klein to Benton. "It's not that Klein is too Jewish, just too German. In Germany it's like the name Smith."

This August when she was filming in Scranton and Europe, Hefner delayed shooting his series to be with her. He says this gesture cost him a million dollars, "but I love the girl, she is most important."

The four Ionic poolside columns flame. Public Acapulco flashes across the bay. Oscar is giving a party. Don Miguel Aleman, who was once president of Mexico, brings the only man in Acapulco who wears socks—Kemmons Wilson, chairman of the board of 1600 Holiday Inns, and Mrs. Wilson, a woman of Lady Bird-like sweetness, who looks as if she collects fur-collared, jewel-trimmed evening sweaters. Mr. Wilson is shown the house. "Jeeee-imminy," he keeps saying. Mrs. Wilson is told Hugh Hefner is at the party. She is losing her gawk-control in this whole gawker-aimed environment. She looks around wildly, as though for Lucifer. They do not know who Bernie Cornfeld is.

The rest of the Hefner party jangles in. The men have that Buddy Greco–Trini Lopez resort look with sideburns and two-tone sweaters and a Keep-up-with-the-Chief air. With them are the stewardess bunnies, henceforth to be known by Playboy decree as "Jet Bunnies." The obligatory hank of hair covers each breast.

After the party the two sides meet in the stone pavilion lit by a mammoth silver candelabrum in the center of the white marble table. Bernie and Hefner sit next to each other, looking not quite ready to make cuts on their fingers and mingle bloods. On one side of Hef are his people and on the other side Bernie and his men. There are kicks under the table. One man tears at the flesh on his finger.

Hefner leans forward, the candles dancing on his etched face. He clutches his pipe (Dick Cavett, introducing him, once said, "We're going to snatch his pipe away and watch him roll up into a little ball"). He looks pretty interested for a man who has said, "I have no real pleasure with my money as money, like J. Paul Getty does, or in making conglomerates. Wealth does not mean that much to me. I can't even read corporate statements, I have trouble with a profit and loss report. All the same, I'm a very bright guy and good at business, at getting at the core and picking out flaws." Bernie looks pretty interested too. Almost fervid. ("Mr. Cornfeld says the money is not what keeps him going —it is helping people help themselves that makes it worthwhile."—The *Globe and Mail,* Toronto.) Do you think, Rattlesnake was asked, that Bernie would like to rule the world? "If there was a profit in it."

The pitch is high. All kinds of other land deals in New Jersey, Puerto Rico, Puerto Vallarta, Spain, Florida, are suggested. The men force themselves back to "priorities." Priorities in Nirvana.

In the middle of the meeting one of Bernie's lawyers gets up and takes the candelabrum off the table. "I know it's not as romantic, but . . ." and switches on the electric lights. The two resident romantics smile at each other: two men who worked very hard and are now building these monuments to the wasting of time—resort complexes, condominiums, movie production companies, model and talent agencies. Two men who share a complicity of power.

It's all right to be the American dream, but not to enjoy it. That's the vice of glamour. Grimy glamour, celebrated with tainted money.

"It's really amazing what some people are ready to believe about a normal heterosexual guy surrounded by all these goodies," says Hef. They say he's a fag, a Communist ("You can't tell these nuts that totalitarian regimes are more puritanical than America. . . . Besides, there's no night life in Moscow"), a Mafia hireling, totally work-oriented, "jaded to the point of not being able to enjoy myself with a girl."

Still, *Playboy* thrives on Hef's legend. Bernie is more truly the victim of the puritan ethic because he has a solemn business and a sultan's compulsion. Bernie has managed to enrage even the anesthetized Swiss government and the S.E.C. But cringe, all you puritans in your pebble tweeds. Weep from pique, all you beastly burghers. Shudder, all you frigid banks, as Bernie, the financial iconoclast and romantic experimenter, goes public and is underwritten by the Episcopal Rothschilds. Hires Franklin Delano Roosevelt's son James to improve his relations with foreign governments as well as assorted counts, hyphenated names, and ex-German vice-chancellors. It's the joy of being right against odds. Nirvana!

Hef, with the most successful premium-priced magazine of the twentieth century, knows the ecstasy. He has the pleasure "of seeing those [advertisers] who kicked us out of their offices crawling to us."

"The Billy Graham of investments," formerly of Bryn Mawr College, and the Crusader Rabbit of Sex, formerly of the *Esquire* mailroom, decide to meet the next morning at ten, the hour when the sun and moon and earth flip their noses at traditional order and the One True Way.

Ten, and Hefner is there, in the unfamiliar light known as day ("I bet you want to see if the Shangri-La myth is true," said Hef to a reporter who once urged him into the sunlight), wearing a black latex bathing suit with white racing stripes, a pair of black leather sandals that the poorest Aegean net mender would refuse out of pride, with Barbi Benton curled up in a little glowy ball at his side.

Behind Hef is a statue of a satyr grabbing at two nudes. One of Bernie's men dubbed it "Bernie and the Broads, or The End of IOS." Everything is so *faux*-connubial: Studs and bunnies, *huevos rancheros* and Coke, sun and moral turpitude.

"I'm going down to Tres Vidas," says Hef. "They promise to deliver a total eclipse. Maybe we could get the Black Bird and fly it around a bit." No one is saying, but everyone is thinking, "Where's Bernie?"

Bernie enters, his eyes to the prospective site: "Soon the mountains will be covered with hotels . . . our own total

eclipse," he says. The other eclipse begins. Through a pin-
prick punched in an envelope, Bernie glances at the sliver
which represents the moon covering the sun. He shrugs.
Hefner has decided to play backgammon, ignoring the cosmos.

"It's time," says Bernie, "to get the girls into the clothes."
This is Bernie's show—his girls wearing clothes from Cedric's, the boutique he owns. Jackie comes out first in a melo-
dramatic black satin jumpsuit. She reclines against pillars,
mounts one of the two stone lions that flank the pavilion.
Hefner pays no attention. Why should he? He is not producing this particular spectacular. It's not his turn yet.

The different shows drift by each other through the perfect
Nirvana set. The big game is impression-making. Oscar,
Bernie, and Hef all compete. There are Games of Chance
(backgammon and gin), Games of Time (subtitled "Who
Makes Who Wait?"). There are tests. The Absolute Loyalty
of the Retinue. The beauty of the girls.

English "supah" birds in Puccis saunter by young bare-
midriffed American rabbits. Nobility vs Nubility. Sexual
legends clang up against each other, part of the stud syn-
drome. At least twice during the weekend I am told that both
Bernie and Hef must make love three or four times a day or
they get physically ill.

Of course, the Big Two are limited by what they could import. Bernie, alas, is trapped with his plastic monastic Falcon, having left the Convair turboprop, the Jet Commander-
er, and "the helicopter to fly to my castle" at home. He takes
to joking. "My new plane is late; they're busy hooking up the
pool filter." He has had to leave behind his top girl, his Great
Danes, race horses, ocelots, vineyards; his Genevan Villa
Elma, which Napoleon built for Josephine; his French
Chateau de Pelly, where he keeps Mama Cornfeld; his Paris
flat, his London townhouse in Belgravia. Still he is the more
exotic: it's Europeana vs Chicagoiana. Bernie was born,
after all, in Istanbul. He "knows from" Cardin and Laroche.
And as he says, "Hef wears his pants too short."

This circus is performed before a trio of European guests,
marveling within their scorn at this American brassiness and

drive. The American struggle to relax. There are constant groupings and disbandings. Information-passing. Casual meets at poolside, dripping wet. Stroking Nivea on the eyelids, talking in heavy terms like "off the top" and "charging back" while the girls languor around and games continue.

Bernie's two lawyers are talking under a beach umbrella with *Playboy*'s director of international development. Bernie strolls over and says, "Of course we must make sure Pepe [the builder] brings things in on cost." At this point on Saturday afternoon, the Acapulco Deal is made (though not signed).

The *Playboy* contingent has taken off to see the site which Bernie scouted the day before. By 1 p.m. Bernie is annoyed, asking where Hefner is. "When we are in the country and he has nothing to do, he gets like an animal," Rattlesnake has said.

Hef returns to get in a few more Barbi backgammon defeats before lunch. Bernie plays with a friend, for money.

Hef: "The meeting of the giants. Result: two and a half dollars."

One of Bernie's men says, "We should maybe send out for delicatessen."

Bernie: "We have a delicatessen in Geneva on our ground floor next to our bank." (Hot pastrami and salami are flown in daily from New York. The local bakery is reportedly having trouble getting its rye bread right.)

Hef: "I can see it now: Bernie's Delicatessen, a whole chain." He is copying Bernie's stage Yiddish exquisitely by now. "We can put our clubs next door."

Bernie: "Are you kidding? That's the key to the whole empire."

Finally, there's the food. Barbi, whose appetite is God-Bless, wants a second plate of papaya ice cream. Hef frowns.

"But it's not the same as the other, it's a different color," she says vaguely.

"No, we don't want another portion . . . we'll get fat," says Hef, lifting the ice cream back onto the tray.

Already they're sorting out the plane situation. Hef and

Bernie and the advise-and-consenters are to fly to Puerto Vallarta to scout more land. Bernie's plane will fly Barbi to Los Angeles.

"Hey that's no good, we're flying without our girls," says Hef, panicked. "But whatever my girl wants she gets."

"Well, if you've got your own plane and all," says Barbi.

Sunday noon. The Big Bunny, a $5.3-million literal translation of the Philosophy of Modified Environment (that says let square beds be round, let silver planes be black, let anything straight-angled be free-form), waits to be stared at on the Acapulco runway. The perfect defiance. Airport sex appeal. When its shades are drawn, the windows are black from the outside, and in the night the floodlights aim back to light up the ghostly rabbit with the half-cocked ears on the tail. It has a semireclining, swiveling, and horizontal-under-the-fur capacity of thirty-eight. A sandwich of tan felt and orange plush, with white styrofoam and black plastic in between. And everything built-in, programmed, and push-buttoned. There are programmed tape decks and television screens that can show *Dr. Strangelove*, Charlie Chan, *The Ipcress File*, or *Playboy After Dark*. In the back is the "master bedroom," dominated by a huge, round, fur-covered bed ("the elliptical bed"), with a black leather headboard staring into a television eye with a side panel of instruments and buttons. One irresistible touch—a giant seat belt stretched across the bed. A shower and a pushbutton bathroom, and then ordinary wire hangers. Oh, well.

The three "Jet Bunnies," doubly trained to please, are dressed like flying French upstairs maids. They wear sky-watches with all sorts of dials they don't quite comprehend. Bernie refuses to use his seat belt for the takeoff; instead he goes to look at the bedroom. "My plane will have two bathrooms in the rear. And couches to sleep on. Who could lie down here?"

"Welcome to Puerto Vallarta." Bunny Marsha gives local time and temperature. "On behalf of our host, Hugh Hefner, it was a pleasure to serve you."

"I got chills when I heard that," Bernie says later. "I couldn't ever in a million years say, 'Welcome, you are the guests of Bernie Cornfeld.' "

A claque of imperialist gringos in patent leather boots and velvet pants, attaché cases in hand, walks through a tiny doomed peasant village on the Puerto Vallarta beach. They step over a dead iguana and draw the land curve in the sand with a stick, intent as any De Carlo lot buyer on finding the right place to "Enjoy Life."

Back on the Bunny, Hef and his men have returned to their gin game. They are talking about grass ("Our guys' stuff is good, but it's just not worth it"). And Antonioni being busted ("I mean, he's got the stuff wrapped around his legs"). Hefner is singing "Lady of Spain, I adore you . . . ."

"Jesus, you think I'm a nervous guy," says one of the men. "What about Bernie? In one weekend we have enough deals for the next two and a half years. Now Bernie wants to get us into some peninsula in Israel."

"We have to let them get this war over first," says Hef.

"Oh well," Jackie is saying about Bernie, "another chapter for my book. I can't figure him out. He makes me so uncomfortable. He just didn't talk to me."

The men shift to the back of the plane, and there in the "discotheque area," with the tapes and gadgets and games forgotten, Bernie and Hef deal. "A real marriage is going on," says one of them. "The world is theirs." The world in one sovereign gobble. In black-and-white condominiums with Playboy clubs in the basements run on Hefner's leisure ethic: fun is good.

In Chicago an awed customs official boards and allows everyone to make an oral declaration. No one has spent any money.

"When I think what we could have brought in," says Hef wistfully.

His big black Caddy is waiting at the ramp, ignition on. Hef puts out his hand to Bernie. "I think it has been a good weekend on both levels."

When the Master Rabbit and his avuncular pipe are gone,

ernie launches into a long diatribe on the plane, giving a
uided tour of flaws.

"My plane will be infinitely better worked out."

"Yes," says one of the lawyers, "but will your girls look
ke this?"

"I think the costumes are poorly designed," Bernie says,
eering into the cataclysmic cleavage of Jet Bunny Avis.
But then everything in the Playboy Mansion is essentially
cruffy. He charges the girls fifty dollars a month and they
ave to sign checks for everything they order, even a Coke.
ne of the girls brought me up to her room, and my God!
e has them in dorms. Eight to a room and bunk beds. Then
thought, it's not so bad at that. I might like to live there
or a month or so at fifty dollars."

They talk about the *Playboy* people. Garish.

"Yes, Garish Indiana," says one of the lawyers.

"At least they're not gangsters," says Bernie.

The pilot has phoned Bernie's car. But it's parked at the
rong end of Butler Field. Bernie goes off to get it, clutching
is mink together in the record cold. His eyes leak. His face
ches. The icewind chokes him. Pain enters Nirvana. It
aptures something fragile.

Up Against the Wall, "Big Bunny"

Claudia Dreifus

Playboy Magazine was about to go into the women's lib business. This is the magazine that has young men believing women have no pubic hair, the magazine whose masthead of seventy-one names includes four women, the magazine that turned down an article by Kenneth Tynan on masturbation, ("The *Playboy* man doesn't masturbate!"), the magazine that rarely hires woman writers, the magazine that presents to the world an image of womankind as brainless, mindless, dumb little chunks of tits and ass.

The first public sign of Hugh Hefner's interest in the feminist movement was flashed to the world on Dick Cavett's late night talk show. Hefner came on the air first: suave and soft-spoken, America's number one playboy, the man who owns a revolving circle bed and a jet plane completely equipped with bidets and bedrooms, wanted the world to know that he thought women's lib was an okay movement. Yes, he would agree that women have been discriminated against. What's more, the feminine population had been treated downright unfairly in job hiring, in business, and in the world of economics.

Cavett questioned Hugh a bit about his private life, whereupon he introduced his pretty Barby-doll girlfriend, Barbie Benton, and explained that he didn't think that she was at all interested in women's lib. Next came a psychiatrist. You should know that having a psychiatrist, psychologist, or sociologist involved in a discussion of female liberation is

From Liberation News Service. Copyright © 1970 by Claudia Dreifus. By permission of the author.

definitely a sign of trouble. The subtle implication is that any lady who is gutsy enough to fight for her own dignity has a "poor feminine self-image." (Do talk show hosts ever feel compelled to invite psychiatrists to discuss the sanity of movie stars or baseball players?) This psychiatrist, Rollo May, was too busy pushing his books to bother to indict the ladies, but his mere presence brought the sanity of liberated women into question.

At last, some fifteen minutes before the show was about to sign off, the exotic specimens were brought forth: two liberated women. The ladies, Susan Brownmiller and Sally Kempton, were from *Media Women*. Hefner quickly stated that he was in sympathy with their cause. "We probably agree more than you think," he leered in a careful attempt to undermine and co-opt debate. Susan just sneered. Hefner went on about how he thought job opportunities should be thrown wide open to women. Hefner's magazine *never* hires women writers unless they are big names, or in case of dire emergency. When Cavett naively asked Susan why she thinks Hef is her enemy, Susan responded that the man exploits and degrades women for a profit. Hef was offended. Susan asked him if he would like to walk around girdled into an absurd costume with a cotton tail stuck to his ass! The necessity for an answer was averted, because just about then the show ran out of time.

Several weeks later, the much heralded *Playboy* women's lib piece hits the stands. Called "Up Against the Wall, Male Chauvinist Pig!", the article is subtitled "Militant man-haters do their level worst to distort the distinctions between male and female and to discredit the legitimate grievances of American women." Illustrating the piece is a full-color Warren Linn drawing showing the five-part transition of a sweet loving chick from the kind of girl any red-blooded stud would happily have into a fearful castrating mean little man-hater. This Jekyll and Hyde transition, according to Linn, is the result of having read books like *The Feminine Mystique* and *The Second Sex*. The piece begins with the observation that "revolutions traditionally appear first as clouds no larger than a man's hand." Then it goes on to vividly describe last fall's Congress To Unite Women, complete with a scene in which one Congress participant cuts off her hair. Had you attended it, you also might never have noticed reporter Morton Hunt at the meeting, for the Congress was a "Women only" gathering. No men allowed. So how does the guy get to describe what people wore, what color and length their hair was, and whether or not their boots were custom-made?

Without shame, the article confesses that women have their gripes. But on the whole Morton Hunt sees the movement as silly, unnecessary, and potentially dangerous to the egos of American mankind. He rather subtly suggests that men are stronger than women and their strength gives them the right to oppress females. What's more, the family, as presently constructed, is the best possible way for people to live. Career women can't be good mothers. Little girls feel inferior when they see little boys throwing sticks farther than they can. Women are failures in their careers because they don't want to succeed. Hunt does concede that he'd like to see more ladies in the professions, but he qualifies his statement this way: *". . . and it might not be the best thing to have a Boeing 747, circling in the overcast, piloted by a woman during her premenstrual period."*

Morton Hunt *should* know better. After all, he makes his living off the backs of women. In January's *Redbook*—the magazine for "Young Mamas"—you'll find a piece by Mr. Hunt entitled "Money and Sex: Two Marital Problems or One?" It's an insipid article, offensive ultimately to both men and women, and clearly published because the author wanted some quick cash. Hunt can also be found in the April 1970 edition of *Family Circle:* "Unfaithful Wives: The Reason Why?" This gem, written up with leftover research from a book he recently published on adultery, includes a passage that asks: *"But why would a woman with so seemingly normal and satisfying a life* [a suburban housewife] *do anything so disloyal* [as to take a lover], *so dangerous, and so contrary to the standards of middle-class behavior?"* Morton Hunt makes his living off women and yet he understands so little about them that he places their freedom movement in "the discard pile of history."

There's an interesting history to how Morton Hunt originally received the women's lib assignment. Originally *Playboy* had broken with their discriminatory practices to hire a woman writer. The writer, a young woman named Susan Braudy, describes herself at the time as "not being very political and not very involved in the feminist movement." The pay would be $2000. "I think they understood," she said in a reluctant LNS interview, "that a man would never be able to interview any of the women. They're not stupid at all. What's more, I really thought I could do some good by writing for a male audience." So Susan-Girl-*Playboy*-Reporter sneaked into women's lib meetings by pretending that she was putting together a study for some scholarly Yale journal. Afterward, she put together what she considered a moderate but sympathetic piece on the women's cause. "I tried to talk to the question of male liberation," she explained. "I wrote that I thought this system imprisoned both men and women, that sexual roles had made it impossible for men to cry and be emotional and dependent. What's more, because I was writing for men, I mostly talked about the more moderate members of the movement."

When it was all done, Susan Braudy sent the piece to Chicago, where *Playboy* is headquartered, and received a note that the article had been accepted. Some time later she found herself in Chicago on assignment for another magazine. As a kind of goodwill gesture, Susan called her editor at *Playboy* to say hello and to thank him for taking her piece. Of course, he invited her out to lunch. When she arrived, Susan found that none of the male editors was attending—including the man who had given her the assignment. What's more, *Playboy*'s only lady editor was to be her hostess. It was a strained, but amicable meal.

The next few days were hell for Susan. Her presence in Chicago had caused a lot of stir in the *Playboy* offices. (Jokes: "I bet our ladies' lib writer shows up in combat boots.") Hefner, it turns out, never approved the idea of an "objective" article on feminism. Hef was furious that the piece had been commissioned, so he circulated a memo blasting the idea of an "objective story." The memo, which is presently circulating around media women circles in New York, was obtained through sources other than Susan Braudy.

"From a brief conversation with Jack K——of a couple of days ago, it sounds as if we're way off in our upcoming feminist piece. . . . Jack indicates that what we have is a well-balanced 'objective' article, but what I want is a devastating piece that takes the militant feminists apart. . . . Jack seems to think that the more moderate members of the feminist movement are coming to the fore. I don't know what he's been reading that brings him to this curious conclusion, but I couldn't disagree more. What I am interested in is the highly irrational, emotional, kookie trend that feminism has taken in the past couple of years. These chicks are our natural enemy. . . . The only subject to feminism that is worth doing is on this new militant phenomena and the proper *Playboy* approach is to devastate it."

Hefner had spoken and Susan was told her article was dead. However, *Playboy* was willing to give her $2000 if she agreed to let another writer use her research. Women have traditionally been used in publishing houses solely as "researchers." The Research Department is the female ghetto of any magazine. And here was Susan Braudy, a professional writer, degraded, niggerized, and returned to a woman's traditional place. That's how Morton Hunt was able to give such a vivid description of the Congress To Unite Women without ever having been there. And that's how Hugh Hefner was able to place ads in every important newspaper in the country announcing his exposé of the "man-hating feminists." "I felt used," Sue Braudy said later, "terribly used. I began to understand the rage that a lot of women feel."

Mush

Nora Ephron

> *". . . there may be a new trend gathering momentum. It is a return to romanticism, a yearning for years past, when life was simpler and values stronger."*
> —Time magazine

The media have been calling it a return to romance, but of course the return is only on the part of the media. The rest of the country never went away. The poems of Kahlil Gibran and books like *A Friend Is Someone Who Likes You* and *Happiness Is a Warm Puppy* have been selling hundreds of thousands of copies in recent years. Heart-shaped satin boxes of chocolate candy, single red American Beauty roses, record albums by Mantovani and the George Melachrino Strings, rhinestone hearts on silver chains—all of it sells to the multitudes out there.

What has changed, however, is that sentimentality is now being peddled by people who seem to lend it an aura of cultural respectability. Take Rod McKuen and Erich Segal. Both of them have hit the jackpot in the romance business: one is a poet, the other a professor. And each thinks of himself as much more than the mushhuckster he is. McKuen, the author of five slim volumes of sentimental poetry and countless songs, is the fastest-selling poet in America; Segal is the author of *Love Story*, which has sold almost 500,000 copies in hard cover, had the largest paperback first printing

From *Esquire* (June, 1971). Copyright © 1971 by Nora Ephron. By permission of Nora Ephron c/o International Famous Agency.

(4,350,000 copies) in history, and is on the way to being the weepiest and most successful film ever made. All of it is treacle, pure treacle, with a message that is perfect escapism to a country in the throes of future shock: the world has not changed, the old values prevail, kids are the same as ever, love is just like they told us in the movies. This optimism comes in nice small packages that allow for the slowest reader with the shortest concentration span and the smallest vocabulary.

To lump Segal and McKuen together here is not to say that they know each other—they don't—or that their work is alike. But there are some disarming similarities. Both appeal primarily to women and teen-age girls. Both are bachelors who enjoy referring to themselves as loners. Both belong to professions that rarely lead to commercial success. Both have the habit of repeating compliments others have paid them, and both do it in a manner that is so blatant it almost seems ingenuous. Segal, for instance, speaking on the prototype of his book's heroine: "Jenny exists and knows she is the inspiration for one of the strongest feminine figures in modern literature—honest to God, that's really what one critic wrote." Or McKuen: "There are a lot of people who take potshots at me because they feel I'm not writing like Keats or Eliot. And yet I've been compared to both of them. So figure that out."

More important, both of them have hit on a formula so slick that it makes mere sentimentality have the force of emotion. Their work is instantly accessible and comprehensible; and when the reader is moved by it, he assumes that it must be art. As a result, Segal and McKuen, each of whom started out rather modest about his achievement, have become convinced that they must be doing something not just right but important. Can you blame them? The money rolls in. The mail arrives by the truckload. The critics outside New York are enthusiastic. And to those who aren't, Segal and McKuen fall back on sheer numbers. Millions of people have read and loved their work. The stewardess on American Airlines Flight No. 2 from Los Angeles to New York loves every bit of it. "I'm so sick of all the crap in the world," she says. "All the killings, the violence, the assassinations. This one getting it. That one getting it. I don't want to read any more about that kind of thing. Romanticism is here to stay." She really said it. Honest.

I am a big crybaby. I want to tell you that before I tell you anything at all about Erich Segal. I cry at almost everything. I cry when I watch *Marcus Welby, M.D.* on television or when I see movies about funny-looking people who fall in love. Any novel by Dickens sets me off. Dogs dying in the arms of orphans, stories of people who are disabled but ultimately walk/see/hear or speak, having something fall on my foot when I am in a hurry, motion pictures of President Kennedy smiling, and a large number of very silly films (particularly one called *The West Point Story*) will work me into a regular saltwater dither.

One other thing about me before I begin. I love trash. I have never believed that kitsch kills. I tell you this so you will understand that my antipathy toward *Love Story* is not because I am immune either to sentimentality or garbage—two qualities the book possesses in abundance. When I read *Love Story* (and I cried, in much the same way that I cry from onions, involuntarily and with great irritation), I was deeply offended—a response I never have, for example, with Jacqueline Susann novels. It was not just that the book was witless, stupid, and manipulative. It was that I suspected that, unlike Miss Susann, Segal knew better. I was wrong to think that, as it happened. I was fooled by his academic credentials. The fact is that *Love Story* is Erich Segal at the top of his form; he knows no better and can do no better. I know that now. I know that I should no longer be offended by the book. And I'm not. What is it that I'm offended by? Perhaps you will begin to see as we go along.

> "Dear Mr. Segal: I realize that you are a busy man but I must tell you something that will probably make you inspired and honored. This past summer a very dear friend of mine passed away. She was seventeen and hardly ever unhappy or sad. Leslie had read your book. Not once but three times. She loved it so much. It was funny but everyone related Love Story with Leslie. She

cried and said the story was so beautiful and realistic.
When she was buried a copy of your book was placed
next to her. . . . I wish you knew her. She was so
unpredictable. That's what life is. She had an instant
heart failure, and thank G-d she didn't suffer. I hope
you don't think I'm a foolish college kid. I felt any
person who could capture young hearts and old must
be sensitive to life.

That is a typical letter plucked out of a large pile of mail
on Erich Segal's desk. There are thousands more, from old
ladies who say they haven't cried that hard since the Elsie
Dinsmore books, from young girls who want to interview
Erich for their high-school papers, from young men who
have read the book and want to go to Harvard and play
hockey and marry a girl who has leukemia. The mail has
been coming in in sacks since about Valentine's Day, 1970
(*Love Story* was published ten days before). The reviews of
the book were exultant. The movie is now on the way to
being the biggest film in history. And what has happened to
Erich Segal as a result of all this? "I always was the way I
am," he says, "only I was less successful at it. The difference
being that people used to think I was an idiot asshole
dilettante and now—you can find a nice adjective." Yes,
Erich was always this way, only now he is more so. You can
find a nice adjective.

"Erich, Erich, you're so pale," shouts Mrs. Jessie Rhine, a
lady from Brooklyn, as Erich Segal, the rabbi's son, signs an
autograph for her and rumples his curly black hair and stubs
his toe and rolls his big brown eyes. His aw-shucks thing.
Mrs. Rhine loves it, loves Erich, loves his book, and she
would very much like to slip him the name of her niece except that there is this huge group of ladies, there must be a
hundred of them, who are also surrounding Erich and trying
to slip him the names of *their* nieces. The ladies have just
heard Erich give a speech to eleven hundred New York
women at the Book and Author Luncheon at the Waldorf-
Astoria. Robert Ardrey, the anthropologist, who also spoke
at the luncheon, is hanging around Erich, trying to soak up

some of the attention, but it does him no good. The ladies want Erich and they are all asking him where they can get a copy of his speech.

Erich's speech. Erich has been giving his speech for months on the book-and-author circuit and he has found that it works. The audience especially responds to the way Erich's speech praises *Love Story* at the expense of *Portnoy's Complaint* and then rises to a crescendo in a condemnation of graphic sex in literature. "Have you any doubt," Segal asks the ladies, "what happened between Romeo and Juliet on their wedding night?" The ladies have no doubt. "Would you feel any better if you had seen it?" No, eleven hundred heads shake, no. "Fortunately," Segal concludes, "Shakespeare was neither curious nor yellow." Wild applause. Everyone loves Erich's speech. Everyone, that is, but Pauline Kael, the film critic, who heard an earlier version of Erich's speech at a book-and-author luncheon in Richmond, Virginia, and told him afterward that he was knocking freedom of speech and sucking up to his audience. To which Erich replied, "We're here to sell books, aren't we?"

The phenomenon of the professor as performer is not a new one: many teachers thrive on exactly the kind of idolatry that characterizes groupies and middle-aged lady fans. Still, there has never been an academician quite as good as Erich at selling books, quite as . . . you can find a nice adjective. He checks in with his publicists once or twice a day. Is everything being done that could be? What about the Carson show? What about running the Canby review again? What about using Christopher Lehmann-Haupt's quote in the ad? Is this anecdote right for Leonard Lyons? "I've been in this business fourteen years and Erich is the closest thing to what a publicist's dream would be," says Harper & Row's Stuart Harris. "All authors feel they have to make a publicity tour, but they don't know how to do it. Erich knows. He knows how to monopolize the time on a talk show without being obvious. *I* would know he's obvious, *you* would know he's obvious, but millions listening in don't know. So many authors don't know how to say anything about their books. They're shy. Erich knows how to do it without being blatant. He had to make a speech the week he was number one on the *Time* magazine best-seller list. He wanted to get that over to the audience, that it was number one, so he got up and began, 'I just flew down and made three stops. Every time the plane landed, I got off and went to the newsstand and bought *Time* magazine to see if I was still number one on the best-seller list.' The audience adored it."

We're here to sell books, aren't we? Yes indeed. And Erich knows that every book counts. One night in a restaurant, an out-of-town couple shyly approached Segal and asked him to autograph a menu for a neighbor who had loved his book. "Why a menu?" Segal asked. Because, the couple explained, it was all they had. "I'll tell you what," said Segal. "There's a bookstore around the corner that's still open. Go in and buy a copy of *Love Story*, bring it back, and I'll autograph that."

Erich has been around the country several times, giving his speech, talking about his book, never letting the conversation wander away from its proper focus. "My novel, *Love Story*, and Paramount's film of it mark, I believe, the turning point in the morals of the younger generation." Erich said that in New York several weeks after publication. Note how it is self-aggrandizing, but in the cause of public morality. Note how it is reassuring to older people. Note the way the name of the book is plunked into the sentence, along with a plug for the film and a plug for the film studio. Erich got so carried away with slipping these little factual details into his sentences that Jacqueline Susann, who is no slouch herself in the self-aggrandizement department, felt called upon to advise him against it. "Every time you mention the book's name," she told him, "you don't really have to add that it's number one on the best-seller list."

Exactly what has made *Love Story* so phenomenally successful is something of a mystery. There are theories, but none of them fully explains what happened. Yes, it makes readers cry. Yes, it has nothing whatsoever to do with life today and encourages people to believe the world has not changed. Yes, as Segal points out, the book has almost no description; people tend to read themselves into it. And yes, it has come at a time when young people are returning to earlier ways. As the critic for Yale's *New Journal* pointed out:

"Segal has perceived that the revolution we all talk of being in the midst of is in large part a romantic one, a movement not so much forward as backward, away from technology and organization and toward nature and people. . . . *Love Story* is a trick, a joke, a pun on those among us to whom an alliance with the fortyish-matron set would be anathema. Segal has tricked us into reading a novel about youth today that has little sex, no drugs, and a tear-jerking ending; and worse, he has made us love it, ponder it, and feel it to be completely contemporary. We are, deep down, no better than the sentimental slobs who sit under the hair driers every Friday afternoon. It's all the same underneath. Segal has our number."

When *Love Story* was first published, Segal himself seemed to possess a measure of self-deprecation. He admitted that his book was banal and cliché-ridden. But as time went on, he began to relax, the self-deprecation turned to false humility, and he took his success seriously. He acknowledged in a recent interview that he might well be the F. Scott Fitzgerald of his generation. He says that he has been compared to Dostoevski. He claims that his novel is in the tradition of the *roman nouveau* developed in France by Alain Robbe-Grillet and Nathalie Sarraute. He implies that people who hate his book are merely offended by its success. When *Love Story* took off in France, he called an associate long distance and said, "We are no longer a movement. We are a religion."

Can you blame him? Can you honestly say that you would have reacted any differently to such extraordinary success? Three, four years ago Erich Segal was just another academic with show-biz connections. "I lived for the day I would see my name in *Variety*," he recalled. He was born in Brooklyn in 1937, the eldest son of a well-known New York rabbi who presided over a Reform synagogue but kept a kosher home. "He dominated me," said Segal. "From the time I was the littlest boy I wanted to be a writer. My mother says that when I was two I used to dictate epic dramas to her. I believe her. I used to dictate tunes to my music teacher. I was that kind of spoiled child. But I came from a nice Jewish family. What kind of job was it being a writer? There was no security. My father wanted me to be a professional person." Rabbi Segal sent his son to Yeshiva, made him take Latin, and insisted he attend night classes at the Jewish Theological Seminary in Manhattan after he finished track practice at Midwood High School in Brooklyn: "I was always odd man out," said Segal. "It is true that I ended Midwood as president of the school and won the Latin prize, but those were isolated. What kind of social life could I have had? I spent my life on the subway."

At Harvard, which he attended because his father told him to, Erich was salutatorian and class poet. He ran every year in the Boston marathon and ran every day to keep in shape—a practice he continues. He also wrote two musicals, one of which had a short run Off-Broadway, and performed in the Dunster Dunces, a singing group that often sang a Segal original, "Winter is the Time To Snow Your Girl." Despite his activity, he always reminded his friends not of Larry Hart but of Noel Airman. (The influence of *Marjorie Morningstar* on Jewish adolescents in the 1950s has yet to be seriously acknowledged.)

Segal got his Ph.D. in comparative literature and began teaching at Yale, where no one took his show-business talk much more seriously than they had at Harvard. Yes, Erich was collaborating with Richard Rodgers, but the show never got off the ground. Yes, Erich had a credit on *Yellow Submarine,* but how much of that was writing anyway? And then came *Love Story*. Script first. Erich's agents didn't even want to handle it. Howard Minsky, who decided to produce it, received rejections from every major studio. Then Ali MacGraw committed herself to it, Paramount bought it, and Erich started work on the novel, the slender story of a poor Catholic girl named Jenny who marries a rich Wasp named Oliver and dies after several idyllic, smart-talking, poverty-stricken years.

Not a single eye was dry, everybody had to cry. Even Erich Segal burst into tears when he wrote it. "In this very room," Segal said one day in his living room at Yale, "in that very chair at that very typewriter. When I got to the end of the book, it really hit me. I said, 'Omigod,' and I came and sat in that very chair and I cried and I cried and I cried. And I said to myself, 'All right, Segal, hold thyself. Why are you crying? I don't understand why you are crying. When was the last time you cried?' And I said, 'The only time I've cried in my adult life was at my father's funeral.' Now it's stretching a lot to make any kind of connection whatsoever. So I finally concluded, after all the honesty I could muster after forty-five minutes of crying and introspection, that I was crying for Jenny. I mean, I really was crying for Jenny. I got up and wiped my face and finished the thing."

Segal's apartment, in a Saarinen-designed dormitory, is a simply furnished, messy one filled with copies of *Variety*, unopened mail, and half-packed suitcases—Segal is rarely at Yale more than three or four days a week. He spends the rest of his time on promotion tours or in conference in Hollywood. (Two other Segal scripts have been produced: *The Games*, about marathon runners, and *R.P.M.*, about a campus revolt.) His icebox has nothing in it but yogurt, and Segal is relaxing in his living room, eating a container of the stuff and saying that he is happy with the lecture on *Phaedra* he delivered that morning because it convinced one of his students that Hippolytus was in fact a tragic hero. Student opinion of Segal at Yale ranges from those who dislike his book and his huckstering to those who rather like it and envy him for his success in what is referred to in cloistered environments as the real world. But most agree that whatever failings Segal has as a personality are overcome by his ability as a teacher. He teaches classics with great verve— in suede pants, he paces back and forth onstage, waves his hands, speaks quickly, gulps down a cup of coffee a student has given him, and generates enormous excitement. Segal has written several scholarly works, one a book on Plautus called *Roman Laughter*.

"It's a tremendous relief to be able to walk into a classroom and speak freely," Segal is saying. "I don't mean your mind. I mean your vocabulary. I don't go in for Buckleyish sesquipedalian terms, but I do go in for *le mot juste*. Even to be able to say, 'Aristotelian catharsis'. . . . On a podium, if I said that, they'd say who is this pompous bastard. This to me is a normal way of speaking. This is the existence whence I emanate. This is the way I really am." But if this is the way you really are, Erich, who is that traveling around the country delivering those speeches? And why?

"What am I going to say to them?" he replies. "I don't know. I had to sell books. I mean, do you know what I mean? I'm embarrassed but I'm not sorry, because the end justifies the means, you know. Three or four *yentas* who buy the book will get it to the readers who have never bought a book before, and get the readership I really cherish, which is the readership of the young people." He paused. "Do you think I was pandering to them?"

No. Not really. Because Erich Segal really believes in what he is saying, is really offended by sex in literature, is really glad he wrote *Love Story* instead of *Portnoy's Complaint*, thinks that—however accidentally—he has stumbled onto something important. Don't be fooled by the academic credentials: a man who can translate Ovid cannot be expected to know better—or know anything at all, for that matter—when it comes to his own work. "You see, I wrote the book in a kind of *faux naïf* style," Segal explained. "And if you think it's easy to write as simply as that, well, you're wrong. But little did I know that I was creating a whole style that's perfect for the seventies. Let's face it. Movies are the big thing now, and this is the style that's right for the age— as McLuhan called it—electronic literature. Writing should be shorthand, understated, no wasting time describing things. I had no idea that I was solving the whole problem of style this way. But I like it. I'm going to keep it for all my other novels." Can you blame him?

It is a well-dressed, well-behaved group, this crowd of young men and women, lots of young women, who are waiting patiently in Constitution Hall in Washington, D. C., for the concert to begin. You won't see any of your freaks here, no sir, any of your tie-dye people, any of your long-haired kids in jeans lighting joints. This is middle America. The couples are holding hands, nuzzling, sitting still, waiting like well-brought-up young people are supposed to, and here he is, the man they've been waiting for, Rod McKuen. Let's have a nice but polite round of applause for Rod, in his Levi's and black sneakers. You won't see any of your crazy groupies here squealing and jumping onstage and trying for a grab at the performer's parts. No sir. Here they are not groupies but fans, and they carry Instamatics with flash attachments and line up afterward with every one of Rod's books for him to autograph. The kids you never hear about. They love The Beatles, they love Dylan, but they also love Rod. "He's so sensitive," one young man explains. "I just hope that he reads a lot of his poetry tonight."

They want to hear the poetry. They gasp in expectation when he picks up a book and flips it open in preparation. And onstage, about to give them what they want in his gravelly voice ("It sounds like I gargle with Dutch Cleanser," he says), is America's leading poet and Random House's leading author. "I've sold five million books of poetry since 1967," says Rod, "but who's counting?" As a matter of fact, Random House is counting and places the figure at three million. Nevertheless, it is a staggering figure—and the poetry is only the beginning. There are records of Rod reciting his poetry, records of Rod's music, records of Rod singing Rod's lyrics to Rod's music, records of Rod's friends singing Rod's songs—much of this on records produced by Rod's record company. There are the concerts, television specials, film sound tracks, and a movie company formed with Rock Hudson. There are the Stanyan Books, a special line of thirty-one books Rod publishes and Random House distributes, with *Caught in the Quiet* its biggest seller, followed by *God's Greatest Hits,* compiled from the moments He speaks in the Bible. McKuen's income can be conservatively estimated at $3,000,000 a year.

That literary critics and poets think nothing whatsoever of McKuen's talent as a poet matters not a bit to his followers, who are willing to be as unabashedly soppy as their bard and are not, in any event, at all rigid in their distinctions between song lyrics and poetry. "I'm often hit by critics and accused of being overly sentimental," Rod is saying to his concert audience. "To those critics I say tough. Because I write about boys and girls and men and women and summer and spring and winter and fall and love and hate. If you don't write about those things there isn't much to write about." And now Rod will read a poem. "This poem," he says, "is about a marvelous cat I once knew. . . ."

McKuen's poetry also covers—in addition to the subjects he lists above—live dogs, lost cats, freight trains, missed connections, one-night stands, remembered loved ones and remembered streets, and loneliness. The poem about the cat, which is among his most famous, concerns a faithful feline named Sloopy who deserted McKuen after he stayed out too late one night with a woman. Her loss brings the poet to the following conclusion: *"Looking back/ perhaps she's been/ the only human thing/ that ever gave back love to me."* McKuen's poetry, which he reads to background instrumental accompaniment, is a kind of stream-of-consciousness free verse filled with mundane images ("raped by Muzak in an elevator," for example) and with adjectives used as nouns ("listen to the warm," "caught in the quiet," etc.). A recent McKuen parody in the *National Lampoon* sums up his style as well as anything; it begins, *"The lone$ome choo choo of my mind/ i$ warm like drippy treacle/ on the wind$wept beach."*

Occasionally McKuen can be genuinely piquant and even witty. *"I wrote Paul this morning/ after reading his poem,/ I told him,* it's okay to drop your pants/ to old men sometimes/ but I wouldn't recommend it/ as a way of life. I didn't mail the letter." But for the most part, McKuen's poems are superficial and platitudinous and frequently silly. "It is irrelevant to speak of McKuen as a poet," says Pulitzer prize winning poet Karl Shapiro.

There was a time when Rod McKuen might modestly have agreed with Shapiro. Ten years or so ago, when he was scrounging in New York, living on West Fifty-fifth Street with Sloopy the cat and trying to make ends meet, McKuen might gladly have admitted to being just a songwriter. Even recently, after only two of his books had appeared, he told a reporter, "I'm not a poet—I'm a stringer of words." But then it happened: the early success mushroomed. "I don't think it's irrelevant to speak of me as a poet," McKuen says today. "If I can sell five million books of poetry, I must be a poet." Three million, Rod. "If my poetry can be taught in more than twenty-five hundred colleges, seminaries, and high schools throughout the United States, if it can be hailed in countries throughout the world as something important, I must be a poet. In France, one newspaper wrote, 'Rod Mc-Kuen is the best poet America has to offer and we should listen to him and mark him well.' "

The saga of Rod McKuen and his rise to the top is a story so full of bad times and hard knocks that it almost serves as a parody of such tales. Rodney Marvin John Michael James McKuen was born in 1933 in a Salvation Army Hospital in Oakland, California. His mother was a dime-a-dance girl; his father deserted her just before their son was born and Mc-Kuen has never met him. *"I remember hearing children/ in the street outside. . . . / They had their world/ I had my room/ I envied them only/ for the day long sunshine/ of their lives/ and their fathers./ Mine I never knew."*

McKuen's mother Clarice worked as a barmaid, scrubbed floors, and operated a switchboard to pay bills. Then she married his stepfather, who drove tractors to level dirt for highways; the family moved from one construction site to the next in California and Nevada. "My stepfather used to get drunk and come home in the middle of the night and yank me out of bed and beat me up," McKuen recalled. "That was kind of traumatic."

At eleven, McKuen dropped out of school and went to work as a lumberjack, ditchdigger, ranch hand, shoe sales-man, and cookie puncher. At fifteen, he received his first serious rejection from a young lady. At eighteen, he became a disc jockey with San Francisco's station KROW, dispensing advice to the lovelorn. After a stint in Korea writing psychological-warfare material for radio, he returned to San Francisco and was booked into the Purple Onion. A screen test followed and in the mid-fifties he worked at Universal on such films as *Rock, Pretty Baby* and *Summer Love*. In what must have been a move of some distinction, he walked out on the filming of *The Haunted House on Hot Rod Hill.* For his film career, McKuen had a dermabrasian, which par-tially removed his adolescent acne scars; he also has a long scar across his chin, the result of an automobile accident.

In 1959 McKuen moved to New York and before beginning to compose music for the CBS Television Workshop he sold blood for money and crashed parties for food. Then in 1961, after the CBS job folded, he helped compose a rock song called "Oliver Twist," which was noteworthy mainly in that it rhymed "chickens" with "Dickens." When no one famous could be found to record it, Rod did it himself; when the record took off, he began touring the country with a backup group (he does not play a musical instrument and has only recently learned formal composition). As Mr. Oliver Twist he played Trude Heller's, the Copacabana lounge, and did a twelve-week tour of bowling alleys around the country. "He was a pretty big act," said his then-manager Ron Gittman. "He wasn't your Ricky Nelson or your Everly Brothers, but he pulled people." The constant performing six nights a week proved too much for McKuen's voice: his vocal chords swelled, he could not speak, and after six weeks in bed the old tenor voice was gone and a new froggy one had emerged.

McKuen moved back to Los Angeles, played the Troubadour, and continued to set his lyrics to the simple music he composed in his head. In 1965 he opened at The Bitter End and was praised by the *New York Times* and compared to Charles Aznavour and Jacques Brel. Eddy Arnold, Johnny Cash, and Glenn Yarbrough began to record his songs of love and loneliness. The market had changed. "In the fifties and early sixties there were formulas," said rock publicist Connie de Nave, who handled Rod when he was doing the "Oliver Twist." "Your group wore certain colors, sweaters over pants, their hair had to be well-groomed, no smoking or drinking onstage. In the midsixties suddenly the individual could wear what he wanted. He didn't have to spend $18,000 on arrangements for nightclub acts. All the outlets where Rod had to do the "Oliver Twist" died. The college market began. The change made things ripe for Rod. Before lyrics had been simple and uncomplicated. Now they wanted depth. No one could come out and go, 'Oo, wa, oo wa.' You came out with your stool and you sang, and you didn't even have to sing that great.

You just had to feel. And as Rod was growing, the market came around."

Stanyan Street and Other Sorrows, McKuen's first book of poetry and songs, was an accidental by-product of a Glenn Yarbrough recording. When requests about the song began to pour into the record company, McKuen decided to publish a book containing it. With his own money, he paid for the printing, stored the books in his garage, and put the covers on and mailed them out in Jiffy bags. "I was very unsophisticated about it," McKuen recalled. "I didn't know what sort of discount you gave bookstores. I made them all pay cash and pay in advance. We had no salesmen, so I called the telephone company and got the yellow pages of all the major cities. We sent mailers to every bookstore. I knew people were asking for it and it wasn't listed in *Publishers' Weekly* or the guide to books. No one knew where it was from or how to get it." In a year, *Stanyan Street* sold 60,000 copies—about 120 times what the average book of poetry sells in a lifetime. Random House took over the distribution, signed McKuen to his next book, and gave him a Mercedes Benz.

Today Rod McKuen lives in a thirty-room house on a hill facing Beverly Hills with a pool, orange trees, four in help, several sheepdogs and cats, and a barbershop for Rod and his streaky blond hair. He spends about half the year on the road and in Europe; he has an illegitimate son in France whom he sees frequently. When he is in Los Angeles, he rarely leaves his house except for a recording session or a trip to his office on Sunset Boulevard. "I have about fifteen people who work for me there," said McKuen. "I don't like to think they work *for* me. They work *with* me."

McKuen is sitting now in the music room of this house. He is wearing a yellow pullover sweater and the ever-present sneakers and Levi's and he is talking about the return to romance he feels the country is in the midst of. "I paved the way for Erich Segal," he says. "It's been my strange lot to have preceded all sorts of things for some time now. I told everybody that folk music was going to come in very big three years before it happened and nobody believed me and of course it did happen. And I went around telling people there was going to be a romantic revival and nobody believed that either. I think it's a reaction people are having against so much insanity in the world. I mean, people are really all we've got. You know it sounds kind of corny and I suppose it's a cliché, but it's really true, that's just the way it is."

It is not entirely easy to interview McKuen, you see. Not that he isn't open and garrulous—but for one thing, most of his thoughts seem to end up in statements he supposes are clichés; and for another he tends to ramble. Ask him about his childhood and within seconds he will be off on a ramble about prejudice and the army. Ask him whether his poetry paints too sanguine a picture of the world and before you know it he will be telling you about capital punishment. Ask him about his new book:

"My new book has its roots in my childhood and in how I feel now, about getting back to basics. You notice in this house, I like lumber. I like wood. Frank Lloyd Wright was my favorite architect because everything he did sprang out of the ground. And even though you see a lot of gadgets and stuff like that I like them because they are gadgets. They don't try to be anything else. I don't like artificial flowers, for instance. . . ." Like that.

In any case, it really doesn't matter to Rod McKuen how the interview goes, because he is sick and tired of being written about and criticized for what he is doing. Rod McKuen, who in the old days would talk to *Stamp World Magazine* if they wanted to profile him, has now become what he calls "gun-shy." Writers describe him as a guru and he hates it. Critics confuse his songs with his poetry and criticize him unfairly and he hates it. Everyone is out to get him. "You know, it's pretty fashionable to knock me down," he says. "There's something criminal, apparently, about being a successful poet. Too many writers take umbrage at that. It's not fair. I don't think poets should starve. I don't think anyone should starve. That's another problem we have in this country that should be changed. . . ." And off he goes on a ramble about poverty in America, leaving the reporter to wonder about it all.

What does it mean? What does it signify? What is McKuen trying to say?

And the answer is probably best put in a poem McKuen himself wrote: *"If you had listened hard enough/ you might have heard/ what I meant to say.* Nothing."

Food Pollution

Daniel Zwerdling

> CANTERBURY, ENGLAND *(A.P.)—A twenty-three-year-old woman starved to death because she believed nearly all human food was produced by the suffering of animals, the Canterbury coroner's court was told. Miss Brenda Holton, an office secretary, had a horror of all meat and other foods that she thought had been tainted by chemical sprays. She tried to live on a diet of honey, cereals, and dandelion coffee, but her appetite faded and she wasted away.*

Brenda Holton, poor masochist, at least had a glimpse of the problem: namely, that the Western world, and especially the United States, is slowly eating itself to death as it stokes down nutty doodle snacks, hot dogs, balloon bread, chickens and steaks, canned orange juice, dehydrated soups, soft drinks, cakes made from mixes, and imitation whipped cream—all sodden with three thousand different synthetic flavors, colors, thickeners, acidifiers, bleaches, preservatives, package contaminants, antibiotics, and poison pesticides. Virtually no food on the grocery shelves is free from chemical additives which have no nutritive value, are probably harmful, and whose main purpose is to make eaters think they're eating something they aren't.

From *Ramparts* (June 1971). Copyright © 1971 by Noah's Ark, Inc. By permission of *Ramparts*.

Even Brenda's honey was contaminated with benzaldehyde, a toxic bee-repellent, her cereals tainted with preservatives and traces of grain pesticides, and her pathetic dandelions choked by herbicides and automobile exhaust fumes.

No one knows for sure whether synthetic additives in our food poison us in normal, everyday eating as many scientists suspect—traceable instances of human poisoning are rare—but there are well-founded suspicions, and no one knows that they *don't*. "We never know for sure whether additives are safe or not," warns Marvin Legator, chief biochemist at the Food and Drug Administration. "Long-term usage of additives can in no way be rated with safety. We have so many cases of common diseases like mental retardation and cancer, which we can't account for through epidemiological studies, for which we can't find a cause and effect." In other words, it might be chronic poisoning from food additives—but it will take years to find out. "The only reason we ever pinpointed thalidomide poisoning," Legator admits, "was because its effects were such gross abnormalities which are so damn rare. And even then it took us five years to find out."

Even if the ninety-three possible different additives in your daily bread aren't bad for you (and there's good evidence that they are), it is clear that they do nothing positive. At best you pay for synthetic color and taste, signifying nothing—except booming profits for the multi-billion-dollar drug and food industry. Food companies are beginning to devote themselves exclusively to processed, synthetic foods—and it's no surprise. "The profit margin on food additives is fantastically good," a top food marketer says, "much better than the profit margin on basic, traditional foods."

The word to the industry is out: the more additives, "the higher the potential profit margin, writes *Food Engineering,* a leading trade journal, which advises food corporations. "Shy away from price-oriented 'commodity' items and look to 'highly manufactured' products in the decades ahead." So much the worse for us and for our polluted inner environment.

II

Just before the birth of Jesus Christ, Pliny the Elder mentions that, in manufacturing groats, "an admixture of chalk is added which passes into the substance of the grain and contributes color and fitness." Today the food industry is more sophisticated: the nation's top drug and food corporations have parlayed synthetic additives into a $500 million a year business, churning out close to a billion pounds of it last year. Additive sales have tripled since 1955, and market researchers expect them to increase 25 percent by 1975.

Additives owe their phenomenal success to the boom in "convenience" foods, the expensive frozen and dehydrated stuff in pouches and trays which turn into meals when you add a little water or pop them in the oven for thirty minutes. It's a nice relationship: convenience foods wouldn't be possible without the marvelous things the chemical industry can muster. Convenience foods need every additive known: as *Chemical & Engineering News* noted in a special additive supplement: "They are prepared under more severe conditions of temperature, pressure, or agitation. Therefore they may require special flavorings, flavor enhancers, colors, and additives to make up for the partial loss of flavor, color, texture, and other properties caused by processing."

Additives are the vehicle for the mass food market; the two go together with an unpalatable symbiosis. Regional and local food producers are a thing of the past. The corporate food monopolies have taken over and are remaking food in their image. General Mills, General Foods, and Kellogg produce close to 75 percent of all breakfast cereals (most of them a feast of empty calories) among them. General Foods and General Mills alone manufacture the majority of synthetic foods; in all, ten huge corporations make the bulk of the foods sitting on supermarket shelves (and also export tons abroad). Additives play a crucial role in the maintenance of this hegemony. They allow high-speed production; they minimize costs and let the foods endure over thousands of miles of transportation and buffeting, keeping them fresh-looking and tasting for long periods of time.

For what has emerged in the period following World War II as a food-industrial complex, additives are a godsend. They've made possible ten thousand entirely new types of food products in the past decade, with four thousand new or modified products popping up on the market every year. All of them are convenience and synthetic foods, which, as a General Foods spokesman says, "will totally absorb the food industry's energies in the future."

It is one of those self-fulfilling prophecies. Additives mold the shape and taste of foods to come; and more and more companies get into the additive market by developing chemicals especially designed to get in on the synthetic need. Monsanto, the $2 billion chemical corporation, plunged into the food additive business in 1961; Pfizer entered the same year and now devotes almost half its research dollars to new food products. Union Carbide jumped into the fray in 1963, followed by the rest of the giants: Abbott, Allied Chemical, Atlas, Miles, DuPont and Dow among them.

And for compelling reasons: the food industry, with $130.6 billion in sales last year—a 63 percent growth since 1960—is the nation's biggest and fastest-growing business. Sales of convenience and synthetic foods are outpacing the traditional foods, and the consumer is paying for it. "Convenience foods have contributed more than anything else to the growth of the food industry," says Leonard Trauberman, managing editor of *Food Engineering*. "If you plot the dollar sales of food against the population growth, you'll find people are actually paying more dollars in the supermarket than ten years ago. And for the same amount of food. Those extra dollars the housewife is leaving behind in the supermarket are for convenience foods."

Additives cut costs for the manufacturers: Cakes that once needed eggs and butter need only tiny amounts of synthetic flavoring and coloring and emulsifier. Fruit juices no longer need fruit. But perhaps the biggest revolution in food is just beginning: the spun soy protein, a bland, tasteless creature of industry research which every additive in existence can turn into something resembling meat, vegetables, almost anything! One pound of isolated soy protein costs only 30 cents dry—but when it's hydrated, pumped with water, oil, flavorings, and other chemicals it's three times the size. Replace tomato mixtures with soy products "and save up to 30 percent," boasts an industry ad. One of the biggest sellers in the food industry lately is TVP—textured vegetable protein, which comes in granular, chunk, dice, strip, or chip style, flavored to imitate meat, nuts, even fruit. "Find out more about this fabulous new food," the ad says, "about the profit-making opportunities it affords."

It's a great future, this additive business; even aerospace companies like Aero-Jet General and TRW have put out industry feelers. This intimate union of drug and food corporations is paving the way for the monolithic food-industrial complex of the future which will make additives and the foods which need them. It's a field only for the giants who can muster the resources: like Greyhound's Armour and Co., which pumps out additives along with its dairy, poultry, meat products, and vegetable oils (buy them while waiting in Greyhound terminals); Beatrice Foods, whose subsidiary chemical companies find a ready market in its Aunt Nellie's, LaChoy, Meadowgold, and Dannon products; or International Telephone and Telegraph, the corporate king whose several hundred subsidiaries include, besides missiles and armament makers, food additive plants, Continental Bakery (the nation's largest, and home of Wonder Bread), Morton frozen foods, and candy companies. All IT&T food ends up in IT&T's Sheraton motor inns, restaurants advertised on communication networks built by—IT&T. It's a nifty package. The complete industry which manufactures the nation's guns—and its butter, too.

III

What do we need them for, these 33 preservatives, 28 antioxidants, 45 sequestrants, 111 emulsifiers, 39 stabilizers and thickeners, 24 bleaching and maturing agents, 60 buffers, acids, and alkalies, 34 food colors, 3 artificial sweeteners, 117 nutritive supplements (synthetic, to replace what processing takes out), 1610 artificial flavors—and new, imitation soy foods? The way industry tells it, convenience and synthetic foods—and the additives that make them palatable —are the answer to the twentieth century, the domestic revolution, the liberation of the consumer (synonymous in the food world with "housewife"). "The housewife of today, who may very likely have an outside job or be deeply involved in community activities, is no longer willing to spend three hours in the kitchen preparing dinner," writes *Chemical & Engineering News*. No one ever asked the consumer whether there might be other social means to liberate women —and consumers never *asked* for additives which might poison them before they can even adjust to "liberation." But the market doesn't work that way. "Consumers rarely demand anything," says S. Allen Heininger, director of food additives at Monsanto. "The only way to find out if there is a need for a product is to put the product on the market and see if consumers accept it. If the consumers accept it and buy it, then you can say they want it and, therefore, need it."

Food producers will argue that the consumer benefits from additives in food variety and cost. Variety means the thousands of different soft drinks and snacks and cereals which additives make possible each year: "Each of these products fills another piece of the consumer need," says John Mauriotti, a project director at Arthur D. Little, one of the nation's leading food research labs. "One snack might be crisper, one might feel different in the hand, one might have a slightly different flavor." Cost? When you buy soy protein "Beef Stroganoff" from the Thomas Lipton Company—via Unilever Corporation—"you're getting what you pay for," Vice-President Ernie Felicietti assures, "since a real meat product would cost four times as much." But once you realize that this soy protein costs Lipton about one-ninth what meat would cost, it doesn't seem like such a great deal.

The food industry has flooded the market's shelves with synthetic products, saturated the airwaves with their ads, and created a demand for additives which never before existed. They have succeeded in making it appear retrograde to eat plain old food. "You can say that a demand was created for convenience foods," *Food Engineering*'s Trauberman confides. "The function of advertising is to create a demand for a product and to point out its virtues. Of course, all the advertising in the world isn't going to make me buy a product I don't like. Ads tell the housewife over and over again that if she likes the product, it's still around to be bought."

With over $100 million per year spent on its advertising, a corporation like General Foods can keep its synthetic products going pretty well. Consider Tang, the imitation orange drink: When a severe freeze in Florida about six years ago decimated the orange crop, GF saw an instant opportunity for a new product: a simulated orange drink containing nothing but some citric acid, calcium phosphate, sodium citrate, hydrogenated vegetable oils, BHA, and some artificial color and flavoring. GF promotion did the rest. Do consumers want and need this kind of orange juice? Some never had a chance to decide. "My daughters won't touch natural orange juice," says Trauberman. "They drink only the packaged or canned concentrates. But it's only because that's what they're used to. Natural orange juice is unfamiliar."

IV

Geneticists like Nobel laureate Joshua Lederberg at Stanford and Bruce Ames at the University of California fret about the human gene pool. They think synthetic food additives may be fouling it up—only we won't discover what we've done to the human race for generations, when it's too late. "It's not that the food additive is a large individual risk, but it may be an epidemiological problem," says Ames. "If out of one million people one person's genes are mutant, that's a serious problem. Cigarettes were around a long time before we knew that they caused lung cancer. If we're filling ourselves now with mutant genes, they're going to be around for generations and generations."

But all chemicals in the food supply carry FDA's blessing, either because they are listed as GRAS—"Generally Recognized As Safe" (all the additives that were in use when Congress passed the Food Additive Amendment of 1958 and which *seem* okay after years of use)—or because food additive regulations restrict their use to levels which laboratory tests ostensibly have shown to be safe. Actually, less than half the additives on the market have ever been tested in a laboratory.

It's hard to eat with gusto when the FDA keeps bumbling over the toxicological surprises that keep popping up. FDA, poor, belittled, underpaid, understaffed agency that it is, has suffered its share of humiliations. In the past few years it has been forced to swallow earlier decisions and ban safrole, the carcinogenic flavoring ingredient in root beer; sharply restrict the use of Vitamin D in milk; strike the antioxidant NDGA from the GRAS list; fight to keep MSG—source of brain tumors in infant mice—on the GRAS list; and, of course, struggle through the cyclamate controversy. From 1950 on, the FDA continually ignored warnings by its own staff and the National Academy of Sciences that this most widely used artificial sweetener caused tumors in rat lungs, ovaries, kidneys, skin, and uteruses. It finally pulled cyclamates off the market in October 1969, only after the *industry* (Abbott Laboratories, Inc.) showed that cyclamates caused bladder cancer in rats. Then in a marvelous bureaucratic maneuver, the FDA allowed cyclamates on the market as long as they're sold as "nonprescription drugs" and if the label cautions that "medical supervision is essential for safe use."

Most soft drink companies have responded to the public furor and have taken cyclamates out of their mass market drinks and other artificially sweetened products, but only because of rotten publicity, not out of any commitment to healthy foods. (In fact, they immediately deported cyclamate drinks to foreign markets.) Now saccharin sales are booming—no matter that FDA's own labs produced tests last year showing saccharin may also induce tumors in rats. FDA's "independent" consultant, the National Academy of Sciences—which is dominated by industry representatives—reviewed all the literature on saccharin ("including some damaging evidence," says an FDA spokesman), but it saw no problem in current use levels. They did stress that saccharin needs intensive research and recommended restricting its use. Today saccharin is the biggest artificial sweetener on the market.

To fully understand how much protection the FDA is giving you, take a long, cooling swig of Mountain Dew, the tart beverage from Pepsi-Cola. Mountain Dew, like most tart soft drinks from the nation's $4 billion soft drink industry, gets its zip from brominated vegetable oils —artificial flavorings which have been stabilized in vegetable oil by a reaction process with poisonous bromine. Scientists at the Canadian Food and Drug Directorate discovered in 1969 that BVO causes liver, heart, kidney, and spleen damage in rats. Here's what different diet levels did to the rats:

"Growth retardation and impaired food utilization were observed in the 2.5 percent group, in which there was evidence of slight anemia. Enlargement of the heart occurred at the 0.5 percent level, and of the liver, kidneys, and spleen at the 2.5 percent level. All rats fed the brominated oil displayed thyroid hyperplasia, myocarditis, fatty changes in the liver, arrested testicular development, vacuolation of the renal tubular epithelium, and reduced liver glucose . . . activities . . . ."

In a well-publicized maneuver, the FDA swept brominated oils from the GRAS list in January 1970 and ordered food companies either to cease using them or to severely restrict their use. (Sweden *totally* banned BVOs as early as 1968.) But BVOs are still in your fruit drinks, since on the deadline day last July for eliminating BVOs the FDA quietly published a notice authorizing the use of BVOs on an "interim" basis until it finds enough toxicological evidence to exonerate or condemn them one way or another. Why? Because the Flavor Extracts Manufacturers Association, the powerful industry lobby in Washington, complained the Canadian experiment wasn't good enough and promised FDA it would carry out its own studies. Even though this is like commissioning ARCO to do a study of whether or not the Alaska pipeline should be built, the FDA asks the public to hold its breath and continue swigging brominated vegetable oils until the Flavor Association finishes its lab tests in 1973.

To fend off any public ruckus over potentially dangerous food additives, the FDA is beginning to review some, not all, of the chemicals on the sacred GRAS list—but only the ones which industry surveys indicate are used most, and which current research suggests are suspicious. That means that even more obscure additives which haven't already been thrashed around and questioned in food circles will continue to go untested. Even if it had the will, the FDA doesn't have the facilities or the staff to conduct many laboratory tests itself, so it farms out some of them to industry.

According to the 1958 Food Amendment's famous Delaney Clause, the FDA must ban outright any additive which induces cancer in laboratory animals. But as Dr. Lederberg points out, FDA tests geared toward detecting cancer (and perhaps mutations) won't catch more subtle chronic damage like brain retardation, allergies, or respiratory difficulties. That's precisely the kind of hard-to-trace poisoning we might have to worry about most.

GRAS list test results won't be ready for several years. In the meantime, you'd better look out for the following:

SODIUM NITRITE AND SODIUM NITRATE: The all-purpose meat color fixatives. Americans just can't abide brown hot dogs and bologna and breakfast sausage, food industry motivational research has decided, so it keeps the meat blood-red with nitrite and nitrate (which keep the hemoglobin in the blood from turning brown when exposed to air). Sodium nitrite and nitrate hold a firm place in toxicological literature as potent human poisons and as laboratory carcinogens and mutagens. Consider this unfortunate case reported in the *New England Journal of Medicine:* "A forty-eight-year-old factory worker was admitted to the hospital with intense cyanosis. . . . Twenty minutes earlier he complained of increasing nausea, became vertiginous, vomited three times, collapsed to the pavement, and turned a bluish color." Only one hour before he had eaten a pound of New York Polish sausage—a typical market sausage made of pork, coarse cereal filler, beef blood, artificial flavor and color, and sodium nitrite and nitrate.

Scientists worry particularly about sodium nitrate fertilizer residues in spinach and other leafy vegetables. Intestinal bacteria change the nitrates into nitrites, which then react with hemoglobin and turn children and babies blue in fits of methemoglobinemia, an acute blood poisoning. Medical journals are full of these cases. (California faces possible mass poisonings because it has an extraordinary nitrate level in drinking water due to fertilizer runoffs.) Nitrites, which are used to preserve smoked fish, like herring, salmon, and tuna, also react with certain substances (secondary amines) in the fish, and at stomach acidic levels form nitrosamines, which are powerful cancer agents. Or, warns Dr. Lederberg, if nitrite gets to the DNA in human cells as it does in laboratory tests with microorganisms, it will mutate the genes.

"Sodium nitrite is going to have to come out of our food sooner or later," says geneticist Ames. "If nitrite were coming up now as a new additive, FDA probably wouldn't let it on the market. But it's been around so long it will be hard to get it off. If the public can get used to brown hot dogs (even Germany, home of the wurst, eats its sausages without nitrite), it would be a lot better off."

PRESERVATIVES: No one in the United States government can get aroused by BHT and BHA, the most widely used antioxidants in the country—which Britain has heavily restricted, and completely banned from all foods intended for babies or children. American kids eat them every day in their Wheaties and Cheerios—every breakfast cereal and every packaged slice of bread on the market and countless other packaged fatty foods they eat daily. Rats fed BHT often show increased liver enlargement, and British scientists have found that BHA induces tumors. BHT poses a peculiar problem because although 75 percent of it is excreted from the body within twenty-four hours, the rest lingers and accumulates in body fats. None of the damaging evidence is conclusive—numerous tests have not found harmful effects—so the FDA takes the easy way out and leaves the additives on the market.

Sodium benzoate and benzoic acid, the most popular preservatives in margarine, fish, fruit juices, confections, jams, jellies, and soft drinks, have worried biochemists for years. The FAO/WHO committee on food additives reports that benzoates killed all the rats in one experiment—they died with convulsions, hyperexcitability, urinary incontinence, and loss of body weight. Benzoic acid, reports *Foods and Cosmetics Toxicology*, is "markedly toxic" in mice, reducing their survival rates and body weights and possibly contributing to cancer. That was enough evidence for the state of Wisconsin, which has banned sodium benzoate and benzoic acid from all its foods. From the FDA and food industry—not a murmur.

SYNTHETIC COLORS: They account for the color in 95 percent of the food on the market. Since Congress passed the Color Additive Amendment in 1960, a large number of colors have dropped from use because they are strongly suspected carcinogens. The last color to go, sort of, was FD&C Red No. 2, which causes cancer in laboratory mice. You'll still eat it on every maraschino cherry, though, because the maraschino lobbyists convinced the FDA that no one could possibly want to eat more than one or two at a time.

But the handful of synthetic colors left are making plenty of scientists uneasy—especially the coal-tar dyes. "Artificial colors are very suspicious," warns Dr. Lederberg, who says their molecular structures look like potent carcinogens. Laboratory tests by the FDA's own researchers show colors form skin tumors and ulcers on rats, and the Kaiser hospitals in California have documented numerous artificial color-caused asthmatic and other allergic attacks in children and adults. An FDA spokesman insists that "all artificial colors are continually under review"; meanwhile, almost every orange in the nation is dyed with sunshiny Citrus Red No. 2, which the FAO/WHO additive experts have flatly denounced as a potent danger—although the DA doubts that anyone would want to eat the peel.

CONDITIONERS AND BLEACHES: Virtually every loaf of bread or cookie or cake or doughnut you buy has been made with flour bleached and conditioned by poisons like hydrogen, benzoyl, and acetone peroxides, chlorine dioxide, nitrogen oxide, nitrosyl chloride—and they all end up in your stomach. If you swallow any one of them straight you will probably die. In trace amounts in the markets, "they might have a chronic mutagenic effect," warns Lederberg: "If bleach is going to change the color of flour, it's certainly going to produce other chemical alterations."

Chlorine, another potent poison, is also used in flour manufacturing—"it gets into the food abundantly," says Lederberg. "It's clear that chlorine reacts badly with DNA in microorganisms—the question is how it reacts in the body. These may be long shots," says Lederberg, "but there may be some bad surprises; I just don't want any surprises discovered late in the game."

But some surprises have already popped up. Like in South Africa, where flour with potassium bromate—a common ingredient in many American flours—caused poisoning outbreaks. The FAO additive committee has reported that potassium and ammonium persulfates, common flour strengtheners, give bakers dermatitis, and it warns that nitrogen oxides can form—nitrites again!—in the products. As far as anyone knows, Americans have been lucky with their bakery goods—up to fourteen pounds worth every week in every American home. But it's conceivable that our Wonder Bread, baked in the kitchens of Continental Bakers (of IT&T), is poisoning us—if not in twelve ways, at least in more than one.

An American dilemma! We're eating more than three thousand additives, most of them badly tested or unsuspected, and we scarely know where to begin. Chemical and radical journals give a tiny hint of the problem, a glimpse of what could be going on inside our bodies: Think about the 1610 artificial flavors, which Harvard University nutritionist Jean Mayer calls "one of the areas of greatest toxicological uncertainty at present." In the FDA's own tests several years ago, half of the flavorings tested caused retarded growth in rats; many of them increased mortality rates, degenerated heart muscle, decayed liver tissue. It's true the victims were only animals; as for humans, Kaiser hospitals have treated over one hundred individuals for allergies caused by artificial flavorings. Take methylcellulose: this all-purpose thickener in imitation jellies, jams, beverages, desserts, toppings, and low-calorie diet foods produces arterial lesions in rabbits, hardens and thickens their arteries, and paves the way for heart attacks.

Propylene glycol—which keeps all ice cream, candies, toppings and icings, baked goods, shredded coconut, even meats, moist—causes a high rate of limb malformations in chicken embryos, says *Food and Cosmetic Toxicology*. Or consider modified food starch, which thickens pie fillings and gravies: the FAO warns it "may harm the very young, the old, and patients with gastrointestinal troubles."

Most foods which contain shortening, including salad oils, use hydrogenated vegetable oils—supersaturated vegetable oil, which contributes as much as, or more than, animal fat toward heart disease. Even disodium salts of EDTA, which are used in canned vegetables and fruits to keep the juice clear and the color bright—FAO would discourage because they raise the calcium level of the blood in rats and erode their teeth.

The moral is not that all of these additives will poison you (though they *do* poison rats). But we can assume they won't do much good for humans who eat them every day in every food. One big area of concern to biochemists is how all of these different chemicals react in combinations in the normal diet. For they're always tested separately. But emulsifiers, the most widely used additives on the entire market, probably increase the chances that many additives which would normally be quickly excreted are instead absorbed in the bloodstream. Hydroxylated lecithin and the glycerides—the most widely used emulsifiers—all are enormous unknowns. The experiments aren't going on yet in the laboratories—but they're going on continually in your stomach.

V

When a New Mexico farmer fed some juicy, homegrown pork to his family last year, his children suffered irreversible brain damage. The hog had eaten some mercury-treated seeds. This sordid case got publicity, but almost every food on your table contains residues of pesticides—pesticides sprayed on growing crops, sprayed on animal feed, even sprayed as a fumigant on vegetables, fruits, and grains on their way to markets. FDA investigators have found that three percent of tested samples from the markets contain more pesticides than the law allows. It doesn't matter whether you're in Los Angeles, Kansas City, or Boston—the pesticides you eat are the same. The FDA tolerance lists, which prescribe just how much of each chemical can remain on market goods, reads like a dictionary of poisons: 187 pesticides (they're called "economic poisons"), including parathion (which last summer killed a boy in North Carolina when he breathed it in a tobacco field); chlordane (which gave a Philadelphia man bone cancer from its use in household termite spray); heptachlor, aldrin, and dieldrin (they've caused innumerable wildlife die-offs throughout the country); formaldehyde, arsenic, and of course the ubiquitous DDT.

The FDA argues that it sets tolerance levels at many times less than the levels required to poison humans outright, so even if some of your carrots have more parathion than they should, they can't possibly hurt you. The problem which every eater faces—and which the FDA ignores —is that one doesn't eat just one food with one residue at one meal: every food contains several different residues. And the levels add up.

Pesticides pose a nasty health problem because they destroy body enzymes and derange metabolism in the organs, and affect the body in other ways that even biochemists don't yet understand. Scientific literature does have disturbing cases of pesticides destroying the body's cholinesterase enzyme, which normally detoxifies certain toxins at nerve endings and synapses. The result: headaches, cramps, nausea, diarrhea, twitching, vomiting—maybe death. Scientists speculate that common chronic disorders, usually untraceable, are really due to chronic pesticide poisoning.

The problems aren't restricted to produce. The grocery store's plump chickens and steaks didn't get fat from corn meal—they've been primed with antibiotics and synthetic growth hormones which are passed on to you. DES (diethylstilbestrol), the super growth hormone, fattens 75 percent of the beef cattle in the United States. (Poultry used to get it, but that was outlawed—although hens still eat arsenic to make them lay more eggs.) FDA requires that all cattle be taken off these hormones, which are implanted below their ears, forty-eight hours before slaughter; therefore, meat should end up on your table without any residues. But in 1969, a random study found 0.6

percent of all beef livers still contained some DES residue—a small percentage, but in human terms it means twelve thousand people at any given time are munching beef hormones.

Antibiotics, lots of them, are mixed with all kinds of animal feed—drugs like chlortetracycline, penicillin, streptomycin, plus a little amprolium and arsenilic acid. By dosing the animals with potent drugs, meat producers can crowd them into filthy pens, get them fat quick, and send them to market before they succumb to profit-hurting disease.

The antibiotics usually end up in the food (they're even used as uncooked poultry dips, or on ice packed around fresh fish) and in our bodies. Chronic exposure to antibiotics immunizes the body against their useful therapeutic effects, so when bacterial infections strike, there aren't any drugs which can do the job. Antibiotics also disrupt the intestinal flora, fouling up the digestive system and body metabolism. Tetracyclines, as FAO additive experts warn, bind to teeth and calcium and inhibit skeletal growth in children. Or, as numerous medical journals point out, antibiotics will cause allergies. Some researchers speculate that the nagging allergies which so many kids suffer come from the same milk, meat, and fish which their school health textbooks promise will make them strong.

In a fitting ironic twist, a perverse salute to the last bit of technology to touch our food, contamination is also caused by polyethylene bags, cans, paper bags, and cardboard boxes—the sterile twentieth-century wrappings which smother our food in order to keep out dirt. Meats, crackers, soups, cereals, vegetables, fruits, crisp snacks: they all suck up several thousand additives used in the packaging, more bits of BHT and BHA, more sodium nitrite, methylcellulose, and potassium hydroxide—all in the wrappings this time—lime, zinc, chloride, soap, animal glue, shellac, peroxides—every additive that is also put directly into the food, and more. Rest assured (by the FDA) that the package-to-food migration is very small. Also remember that you get the additives from every package, from every wrapper, from every food. The levels add up.

You can forego all packaged food and spend the rest of your life munching fruits and vegetables which haven't touched a paper or polyethylene bag. A warning, though: they've all been rinsed with soaps and detergents to clean off the field dirt (which you could rinse in your kitchen sink); and in a last compulsive act to seal them for market, 75 percent have been soaked with mixtures of carcinogenic coal-tar waxes, paraffin, and petroleum naptha —the prime ingredient of napalm.

Caveat emptor. Let the buyer beware.

VI

"If we didn't eat anything we'd be 100 percent safe, wouldn't we?" laughs one FDA official, whose stamp brings new additives on the market or keeps them off.

In the food business, additives stand or fall on the risk/ benefit doctrine—industry's philosophy that since science can't ever guarantee that anything is *absolutely* safe, it's not fair to criticize an additive's potential dangers without emphasizing its market virtues. The whole issue of food safety, argues Richard Hughes of Arthur D. Little Laboratories—whose clients include the nation's top chemical and food producers—comes to this: "How do you define what is safe? Safety is relative. Water is dangerous in large amounts. Sugar can be a poison. Any substance you use, there will be some data showing that it has problems."

Food corporations see the risk of food additives, says Trauberman of *Food Engineering,* the same way General Motors sees the safety of its cars: "Fifty thousand people will be killed this year in automobiles," he says soberly. "I can produce a risk/benefit ratio and assure you that the public is willing to accept it."

The consumer seems so far to be willing to take the

chance, although he has never been told the odds against him. And the benefits? Hundreds of additives—if not most of them—do nothing to enhance food quality, and consequently do nothing for eaters. Nutritionist Mayer suggests we start eliminating the additives which industry puts in food purely for their "aesthetic" value. Start with artificial food coloring: orange peels may sometimes look greenish, tomato sauces won't always look vine-ripened red; eliminate color fixatives like sodium nitrite and nitrate, and hot dogs and salami will be slightly brown. Get rid of sequestrants like calcium disodium EDTA (which inhibits human blood coagulants), and canned kidney bean juice may turn cloudy instead of clear and each bean won't stay the same color. Consumers could adjust to this and also to less artificial flavoring.

Many preservatives could go; they do prolong food freshness—but who wants bread in their bin with eleven of its fifteen nutrients leached out by mass-production processing? Eliminating preservatives from bread means simply that manufacturers would have to deliver more often to groceries. Bleached, soggy American preserved bread runs a 10–15 percent spoilage rate even now—which suggests bread manufacturers are causing their own problems by producing too much surplus.

For any kind of additives you talk about there are foods which contain but don't need them, or new-fangled foods which need them but which consumers didn't ask for in the first place. And each category of additives (like emulsifiers or flavors) contains countless chemicals which only duplicate the same effects and compound the human risks. No one needs potassium sorbate (which can dangerously increase the body's potassium intake) or sodium sulfite (which destroys thiamine). Or hydroxylated lecithin, which, the FAO food additive committee warns, science knows frightfully little about.

When you put the squeeze on the industries, even they admit that most synthetic additives aren't really necessary in terms of food production. "There aren't very many additives that could not be eliminated without the food industry falling apart," Trauberman says. "The food companies could still be in business. The consumer would have less variety of foods; she'll [the American housewife again!] eat the same amount of foods even if there are no additives. The consumer may just have to change her eating habits."

There are only two reasons food additives are so crucial to the industry: high profits and market control. Without synthetic additives, a handful of centralized food corporations could never saturate the markets of an entire nation (and much of the Western world) at minimal production costs. Once the food industry controls the market, it totally controls what you eat. "The consumer always exercises the final choice of what she buys," proclaims an industry executive. But he means a choice not between nutritious (pollutant) foods and synthetic, plastic foods pumped with contaminants, but between Screaming Yellow Zonkers, Madison Avenue's most successful "mod" promotion job in years, and eight other varieties of artificially flavored and colored crackerjacks. Your local supermarket tells you where the choices and the profits are: lone shelves on the outer walls display meager varieties of (usually) wilted vegetables and fruits, dairy products, meat, and poultry; not much profit there. Then look at the rest (95 percent) of the floor space: hundreds of different brands of the same synthetic foods, artificially flavored, colored, and textured. That's where the additives are—and industry's greatest profits. Not just profits for the food producers, but for the chemical corporations as well. Add them together—and the food production business, thanks to synthetic additives, dominates the nation's economy.

Don't look to the government, personified by the FDA, to give you much relief. Fifty years of giving in to industry every time an additive is questioned—as Jim Turner documents in *The Chemical Feast*—shows that the agency's primary incentive is to keep good relations with the industry it is meant to regulate.

That explains why the FDA relies so heavily for advice on its "independent" consultant, the National Academy of Sciences, ostensibly an objective scientific organization whose food protection board formulates toxicological standards and passes judgment for the FDA on the safety of individual additives. The food committees read like a *Who's Who* of the food and chemical industry; in fact, the only people involved in the food market who are *not* represented on the NAS boards are the consumers. Just to make sure the FDA listens to the right advice, the food industry pumps millions of dollars into trade lobbies which guarantee that the predominant voice in Washington is the industry's. It's not hard to find cause and effect: If you wonder why MSG is exempted from labeling requirements only on salad dressing, French dressing, and mayonnaise, you'll find the answer at the Mayonnaise and Salad Dressing Association.

When you understand what the food business is all about, you can't escape the conclusion that living is a matter of politics: merely eating to keep yourself alive involves political decisions every time you shop. And it is political wisdom—not paranoia—to assume that the food you buy from the food industrial complex may be poisoning you, while maximizing corporate profits. Still, it's difficult to fight General Foods. But eaters are trying. Societies—like the Ecological Food Society in New York—are springing up, buying and distributing organic products free of pollution and synthetic additives on a national level. Sales of one of the nation's largest organic food distributors—Kahan & Lessin Co.—have doubled since 1968. On a local level, community cooperatives and food conspiracies buy wholesale or at special prices from retailers, then deliver groceries to member families. Detroit's People's Food Co-op, which just started, is already building a large clientele of lower- and middle-class families who decided to chuck the supermarket's corporate style of eating. You don't have to be a radical or a freak to want good food.

You can start battling the corporation on your own. You can't avoid all additives and pollutants, but you can avoid paying for foods which do nothing good for your body—and could be slowly poisoning it.

• Don't eat foods with artificial colors ("I would certainly stay away from synthetic colors," Lederberg says).

• Don't eat bakery products, especially bread, made with bleached flour. Go to a good local bakery or make your own.

• Avoid dehydrated and other "convenience" foods like boxed mashed potatoes, dry packaged soups, and imitation Beef Stroganoff. The closest you'll come to real food is some vegetable and beef powder. The rest is synthetic.

• Don't eat packaged snacks or breakfast cereals.

• Don't eat imitation foods—from imitation orange juice to nondairy creamers to soy protein products. Soy foods are a tricky area. It's true, as General Foods and Worthington, the two biggest producers, point out, that soy products contain as much protein as real meat. But that's only part of the story. To taste like meat (or vegetables) the soy isolates must be smothered and pumped with every synthetic additive known. And furthermore, Dr. Mayer warns, "When we replace natural foods with synthetic protein substitutes, we lose many trace minerals and vitamins. We don't know everything about this area, so we're in a transition period that has serious danger."

• Stay away from products which contain hydrogenated vegetable oil.

Eaters will have to make certain sacrifices: Eating real meats and poultry, and more fresh fruits and vegetables, means making dinner will take thirty minutes instead of fifteen.

But it's worth it. Look at the facts. The food industry insists that our food supply has never been better. "In some areas of the world, 40 percent of the children die before they are big enough to steal food from the table," moans a General Foods vice-president histrionically. But in their hearts, Americans know something is wrong here. Our infant mortality rate is fifth highest in the world; heart attacks and cancer are soaring. "Americans spend six times as much on health as they did thirty years ago and with no statistics to show for it," Mayer points out. "The average American spends much more on health than people in any other country in the world, and we're way down on the scale in health." The life expectancy of the average American male is 68–69; the average woman's, 72. In Sweden they have fewer additives in their food: and their life expectancy is six years higher.

When Norman Mailer ran for mayor of New York, he rejected a proposal to save water by filling toilet bowls with chemicals because, he said, Americans are becoming as alienated from their bodies as from the earth. "We should at least smell our own shit," he said. But even the waste we excrete isn't real anymore. It's all laboratory made.

The Contributors

RENATA ADLER, born in Milan, Italy, in 1938, was graduated from Bryn Mawr *summa cum laude* and subsequently studied at the Sorbonne and Harvard. A staff writer on *The New Yorker*, she served for a year plus as film critic of *The New York Times*. Her reviews there were collected as *A Year in the Dark* (1969), and her longer essays appeared as *Toward a Radical Middle* (1969).

JULIE BAUMGOLD, a contributing editor to *New York Magazine*, conducted its "Best Bets" column for several years. Her essays have also appeared in *Vogue* and other magazines.

STUART BYRON, born in New York in 1941, has written on movies and gay activism for *The New York Times*, *The Village Voice*, and elsewhere. Currently a free-lancer living in New York, he was for two years a staff reporter and reviewer on *Variety*.

FRANK CHIN, born in Berkeley, California, in 1940, is a consultant and lecturer on Chinese-America currently living in San Francisco. He has worked as a staff writer for the King Broadcasting Company in Seattle and recently wrote and co-produced a documentary film on New York's Chinatown.

JEFFEREY CHAN, born in El Cerrito, California, in 1942, a received an M.A. in creative writing from

San Francisco State College, where he is currently chairman of the Asian-American Studies Program.

CLAUDIA DREIFUS, born in New York in 1944, is a feminist, a freelance journalist and sometime labor-union organizer. Formerly a political reporter on the *East Village Other*, she has written a book, *Radical Lifestyles* (1971).

DAVID DURK has served on the police force of New York City for the past decade, currently holding the rank of sergeant. His essays on law enforcement have appeared in *The Atlantic, The New York Times Magazine* and in other periodicals, and he is currently finishing a book on the police.

NORA EPHRON, born in New York and raised in Los Angeles, was for several years a reporter on the *New York Post*. She is also the author of *Wallflower at the Orgy* (1970), a collection of essays previously published in several magazines.

MICHAEL GLENN was born in New York in 1938 and raised in Atlanta, Georgia. He earned his A.B. at Princeton, his M.A. in comparative literature at Harvard, and his M.D. at Columbia University's College of Physicians and Surgeons. A co-founder-editor of *The Radical Therapist*, he has contributed polemical essays to its pages; his creative fictions have appeared in the *Hudson Review* and *The Young American Writers* (1967).

ABBIE HOFFMAN, born near Boston in 1938, took his M.A. in psychology at Berkeley and worked in a hospital before joining Liberty House in New York and committing himself to free lance radical agitation. A prolific writer and lecturer, he has published many essays; among his extended works are *Revolution for the Hell of It* (1968), and *Steal This Book* (1971).

JOHANNA KAPLAN lives in New York and teaches mentally disturbed children at a school associated with

Mt. Sinai Hospital. Her stories and essays have appeared in *Harper's* and *Commentary*.

CRAIG KARPEL, born in Midland, Texas in 1944, was graduated from Columbia College where he majored in medieval European history. A contributing editor to *Esquire,* he has written for *Ramparts, Playboy* and the *Whole Earth Catalog*. He and his wife Alison currently live in Pittsfield, Massachussetts.

STEPHEN KURTZ, born in 1941, studied philosophy at C.C.N.Y., Oxford, and Columbia and subsequently worked in the architecture departments of the Museum of Modern Art and a publishing house. A contributor to art and architecture magazines, he is currently completing a book on recent architecture.

RICHARD PARKER, born in 1946, studied at Dartmouth and Magdalen College, Oxford. Formerly a member of SDS and a junior fellow at the Center for the Study of Democratic Institutions, he now works for an underground newspaper in Santa Barbara. His first book, *The Myth of the Middle Class,* will appear soon.

RICHARD REINGOLD, who studied at Columbia University's School of Journalism, has contributed to *New York* and other magazines.

RON ROSENBAUM, born in New York in 1946, studied and taught at Yale University before joining the staff of the *Village Voice*. His work has also appeared in *Esquire* and *The New York Times Book Review*.

BARRY SCHWARTZ, born in Brooklyn in 1942, is associate director of the center for the Study of Social Change and assistant professor at New York City Community College. The co-editor of several anthologies, as well as a series of texts, he co-authored *Psychedelic Art* (1968) and recently finished another book on humanism in twentieth century art.

RAY SMITH, born in 1941 in Cape Breton, Canada, spent his youth in Halifax and was graduated from Dalhousie University. His short stories have appeared in several magazines and anthologies; some were published as a book entitled *Cape Breton Is the Thought Control Center of Canada* (1968).

PAUL THEROUX, born in Massachusetts in 1941, has taught in Italy, Uganda, Malawi and Singapore. A regular contributor to *The Christian Science Monitor* since 1964, he has also written poems, stories and four novels, including *Fong Among the Indians* (1968) and *Jungle Loves* (1971).

WILLIAM IRWIN THOMPSON was born in Chicago in 1938, grew up in Los Angeles and attended Pomona College, later taking his doctorate in English at Cornell. Presently an associate professor of the humanities at York University in Toronto, he has written two books: *The Imagination of an Insurrection: Dublin, Easter, 1916,* (1967) and *At the Edge of History* (1971).

NAOMI WEISSTEIN teaches psychology at Loyola University in Chicago. Formerly active in both CORE and SDS, she has recently been trying to organize an all-women rock band.

SUSAN WOOD, a photographer currently residing in Manhattan, has also written for numerous magazines, including *Nova* in London and *New York* in the States.

DANIEL ZWERDLING, born in Washington, D. C. in 1949, is a staff writer for *The New Republic*. His essays have appeared in *Ramparts, The Guardian, Today's Education,* as well as in several anthologies, and he has done commentaries on consumer issues for the Canadian Broadcasting Corporation.

RICHARD KOSTELANETZ, born in New York City in 1940, has published poetry, fiction and critical essays in magazines around the world. His books include *The Theatre of Mixed Means* (1968), *Master Minds* (1969), and *Visual Language* (1970). Among the anthologies he has compiled are *Beyond Left & Right* (1968), *Possibilities of Poetry* (1970), *Imaged Words & Worded Images* (1970), *John Cage* (1970), and *Social Speculations* (1971). He was also co-author and editor of *The New American Arts* (1965).

Debunking Now—an Afterword

> With the rise of Theodore Roosevelt, the young journalist gave himself wholeheartedly to the new movement for exposure and reform. These great days kept him busy from morning to night. He bloomed: his powers were free and absolute. An eager public accorded him a hearing, praise and honor, and money. He redoubled his efforts, writing the facts of contemporary life in the style that journalism had developed for him: a clear, bold, straightforward style, concerning itself with facts and figures. . . . The "muckraker," for so he soon came to be called, dealt with facts and not with theory.
>
> —*Louis Filler, Crusaders for American Liberalism, 1939*

It is a cutting paradox that behind the unprecedentedly huge deceits and corruption of our time there should be a resurgence of honesty, both individual and collective moralism seeming to take their growing energies from the mounting evils of society. The inexcusable destruction and duplicity of the Vietnam war, for instance, have pro-

From *The Humanist* (July–August, 1972). Copyright © 1972 by *The Humanist*. By permission of the author and publisher.

duced the most relentless exposure of such atrocious waste that this country has ever seen: and it appears that no dirty stone will remain unturned in this ritualistic expiation. Criticism of the war, which at first represented just a sophisticated minority, has since begun to radicalize, perhaps permanently, an emerging generation, as well as eventually gain the attention and support of most Americans. It is also indicative that, though the ante of corruption can be far greater today, urban politicians, for instance, are no longer so predictably dishonest, while those inclined to malfeasance, by all counts a minority, are usually discredited and often sent to jail. It is also clear, moreover, that the scrupulous critic has gained an honored place in American culture. Ralph Nader's detailed and comprehensive criticism of corporate deficiency has made him a genuine national hero, whose name is even mentioned for the presidency, so eagerly do Americans admire (if not exploit) their incorruptible activists. Furthermore, more people—especially young people—are energetically involved in more high-minded enterprise than ever before in the U.S., or in any other contemporary culture. As such popular critical responses would have been inconceivable a decade ago, these developments indicate, by most standards we know, a kind of national advance in moral awareness.

Through a culture runs a dialectical tension between criticism and reality, and how this dynamic relation is temporarily balanced determines a particular society's current moral tone. In contemporary America, such conflict goes radically unresolved, as criticism and deceit seem to thrive apace and apart. Along with progress in muckraking comes much more muck to rake. This explains not only the persistence of the contradictions noted above, but also why people who are dishonest in some dimensions of their lives can often be highly moralistic in others, or why, to give a specific example, the increasing duplicity of the rock music business was as inevitable as its exposure. It follows that, just as today's dishonesty capitalizes upon the U.S.'s unparalleled economic affluence, so does the new moralism also depend upon it, by allowing greater numbers of uncompromised activists the raw base of economic security.

Unresolved paradoxes of this sort are scarcely new in America, which has always ranked among the most idealistic and the most defiled of nations—where developments seem to develop to unprecedented contemporary degrees. Behind the abundance of both ideals and exploitation has been a kind of capitalistic energy. It seems precisely because the U.S. is such an avowedly high-minded culture, hypocrisies notwithstanding, that the exposure of deceit is itself so highly respected. It follows that, in spite of continuing corporate impropriety and the like, there has been a persistent, distinguished, and well-supported muckraking tradition in the United States, including not only such turn of the century progressives as Lincoln Steffens, Jacob Riis, and Ida Tarbell, but in more recent times C. Wright Mills, Fred J. Cook, Jack Anderson, and James Ridgeway, along with Ralph Nader and Robert Sherrill.

It seems that muckraking is particularly indigenous to liberal societies precisely because it depends upon the perception of disparity between a culture's avowed aspirations and compromised behavior; debunking thus represents liberalism's response to (and war with) the maladies of capitalism. Like other Anglo-Saxon societies, we expect honesty of public officials, say, and thus we support exposure of their venalities. Only in a liberal society, as distinct from an authoritarian or totalitarian one, does the exposure of outrageous deceit finally inspire not just imprisonment but equally outraged public protest.

Philosophically, the debunker's outlook echoes a liberal tradition that dates back at least as far as Jeremy Bentham's proposals for revealing how "eulogistic coverings" mask less principled purposes; it is debunking's profoundest truth that things are never quite what they seem. This connection with philosophic liberalism also explains why the best such writing is neither ideological nor even ethically innovative. It depends instead upon familiar, widely-acknowledged "liberal" values; for the muckraker in practice represents the majority of his readers and he presumes that they would be as outraged as he is if they knew the truths which he is about to divulge. Though inevitably self-appointed, the debunker is ultimately a populist; only widespread, almost popular, support can keep him employed.

Among the unending missions of all social criticism is the preservation of the means prerequisite to its ends. Since debunking necessarily depends upon a press free enough to publish a writer's disclosure without fear of reprisal and to distribute such publications unhindered, muckrakers often expose the perversions of these liberal ideals as well as clogs and corruptions in the channels of communication. It follows that much debunking emphasizes intellectual hygiene, or cleansing the mind of not just irrationalities and false beliefs but those untruths whose impact is deleterious. The human cost of false stereotypes, for instance, is generally more than merely intellectual, since these untruths are usually popularized by the powerful class as leverage for discounting, or discriminating against, the powerless—men of women, white of black, old of young, etc. For more reasons than one, to be sure, is tough-mindedness essential in these ruinous times.

Though debunking seems intrinsic in liberal culture, it also represents a radical activity within that society—if not that kind of "radical action" that is particularly suitable to the writer (who is usually unfit temperamentally for more social forms of activism). It is largely by revealing situations that can no longer be tolerated that such disclosures suggest that action can—if not *must* and probably *will*—be taken. For that reason as well does debunking customarily depend upon those humanitarian values commonly held in a liberal society—integrity, humane consideration, openness, empiricism, freedom, opportunity, truth, etc.—in addition to assuming that every revelation of their opposite will strike readers as morally objectionable. In a society that respects such ideals, and at least protests their compromise, muckraking can be extremely influential; for precisely by exposing disparity—by "telling it like it is"—does debunking both presume and encourage not only the likelihood of pragamatic, piecemeal reform but also the survival of liberal civilization.

Such writing is rarely identical with propaganda, which represents a genre of press-agentry, even if done on behalf of "radical" causes; for partisan polemic usually undermines its own hard-headed revelations by sentimentalizing the writer's position and/or sounding too many false notes. The unfortunate truth is that partisans usually deceive on behalf of their own cause or organization, no matter how much reality they reveal about the others'. Genuine debunking, in contrast, is totally skeptical in its attitude and incorruptibly individualistic in its perspective, favoring neither "sides" not ideologies; for the muckraker bases his critique not upon a constituency but upon himself—his own perceptions and articulated values. Partisan polemic therefore remains as generally unconvincing as ideology-flexing, unless the reader is already intellectually predisposed; both submerge any interest in detailed criticism beneath a writer's presentation of derogatory invectives and/or pet slogans. Precisely because the platitudinous abstractions of ideologues persuade only the converted (and are sometimes published by broad-minded magazines that would fear true muckraking), they are generally harmless in practice. The process of exposing iniquities in the system is more likely to bring change than exposing "the system" without reference to iniquitous specifics.

Critical writing becomes truly *radical* when it severely demolishes its intended targets and/or induces actual change in people's minds and behavior, whether that reform be throwing a politician out of office, discouraging the purchase of certain goods or services, or discarding false or innocent ideas. In such radicalism is not only a role natural to truth-telling reporters but also a potential power peculiar to their trade. The example of Ralph Nader shows that the impact of such popularly-invested personal authority can sometimes be enormous, particularly on the crucial task of eliminating iniquitous practices; for few nonpropertied individuals in the U.S. can command such national clout. There is no doubt that just as Upton Sinclair was socially more powerful as a writer than as a candidate for California's governorship, so Ralph Nader as a presidential aspirant would inevitably sacrifice his real power (and perhaps much of his credibility as well) for the pottage of position and authority. The truth not to be forgotten is that the writer's radicalism never functions more effectively or inspires more fear than when he writes radically.

There are good reasons for regarding such debunking as a literary art that, though it deals with and takes inspirations from society, nonetheless follows its autonomous artistic traditions, structural conventions, and esthetic standards. In this art, elegant and witty prose is obviously superior to witless style, just as effective expository structure is more laudable than ineffective; but values of this kind are, like the avoidance of pious sentiment and cliché, familiar to and derived from, all writing. Fine debunking generally displays a polemical energy bordering on the obsessive and yet a scrupulous emphasis upon verifiable facts which are often quoted to fanatical excess. As investigative reportage, it is, at minimum, informative; but by marching all the available evidence to a ritualistic conclusion good debunking tends to massacre its target. As H. L. Mencken observed, "Readers and connoisseurs of criticism delight in brutality and esteem a critic in proportion as he is lethal."

Beyond that, let me suggest that present-day first-rate muckraking tends to be more passionate and determined than its precursors; it temperamentally descends not, like so much renewed liberalism, from John F. Kennedy's influence, but from his brother Robert's energetic example. It is often more personal than comparable earlier writing, as it may sometimes disclose the author's own involvement in a situation and/or his earlier belief in certain false myths. Such personal revelations, even if self-embarrassing, establish a sense of courage and honesty that in turn bestows the authority of authenticity upon the rest of the exposure (and expiation). The assumption is that a writer honest with himself will also be honest with his readers; yet few literary displays are more embarrassing than a patently self-deluded muckraker. Especially passionate debunking sometimes exorcises former infatuations. The critic Leslie A. Fiedler identifying "the difficult pleasure possible only to one recognizing a truth which involves a personal humiliation of the surrender of values long held."

An ideal intrinsic in art, unlike moralism, is the doing of what has not yet been done, so that innovation, whether in style or subject matter, is, by artistic values, critically commendable. Since most muckraking eschews stylistic and/or structural innovation for the sake of effective, unhindered communication, artistically ambitious debunkers must surpass their predecessors by dealing with what has not been exposed so thoroughly before, or perhaps not been noticed at all. Although it might be morally estimable, it is artistically easy and second-rate to expose *today* such familiar targets as racial prejudice, the Vietnam war, automotive manufacturers, the FBI, and even the CIA. "Those subjects," as we say, "have been done to death." In contrast, the great debunkers, like the great artists, acknowledge the tougher task of making the invisible visible and thus enable their readers to see anew. In such artistic obligations is also a *moral* imperative to scrutinize everything that, often to our detriment, has not been regarded so closely before. Such debunking is more challenging to both reader and writer, often instilling a further discomfort, which I would characterize as partially esthetic, that comes from the uneasy recognition that certain dimensions of experience have escaped our close examination. Though the electronic media occasionally flirt with debunking (and debunkers), the toughest, least compromised examinations still appear in print, which can offer dimensions of detail and honesty that would be unlikely, if not inconceivable, in the new media, which are rarely innovative, instead reiterating, usually by vivid illustration, what has already been divulged in print.

Precisely because certain ideals are nowadays taken far more seriously than before, especially by the young, whole classes of odious inequities that were previously ignored or rationalized (e.g., discrimination against homosexuals, duplicities in the literary scene), are now relentlessly exposed, and these developments explain in turn why much of this new high-style debunking should come from young (or rejuvenated) writers. The autonomy and courage of the "underground press" epitomize this renewed journalistic

motive, though the typically subliterate level of its prose
and thinking forbid sophisticated understanding; more revealing perhaps are the quality-minded rock papers, the
better ecology periodicals, and the new "journalism reviews" springing up in Chicago, New York, and elsewhere. Such writing is incomparably valuable, in more
ways than one; and if the original muckrakers in Louis
Filler's history "ushered in modern times," the new journalists help forge the critical paths into the postmodern
age.

RICHARD KOSTELANETZ